TWO OLD FOOLS DOWN UNDER

NEW YORK TIMES BESTSELLING AUTHOR

VICTORIA TWEAD

Ant Press
Large Print
Edition

LARGE PRINT EDITION

Copyright © 2019 by Victoria Twead

Published by AntPress.org

Paperback ISBN: 978-1-922476-12-8

Large Print edition ISBN: 978-1-922476-23-4

Hardback edition ISBN: 978-1-922476-35-7

Hardback Large Print edition ISBN: 978-1-922476-55-5

Also available in digital editions.

All rights reserved.

No part of this book may be reproduced in any form or by any electronic or mechanical means, including Artificial Intelligence "training", information storage and retrieval systems, without written permission from the author, except for the use of brief quotations in a book review.

If I have made mistakes in any of the recipes, please forgive me. I am no chef or mathematician. Similarly, please overlook any Spanish language errors; I still have much to learn.

This memoir reflects my recollections of experiences over a period of time. In order to preserve the anonymity of the wonderful people I write about, some names have been changed, including the name of the village. Certain individuals are composites and dialogue and events have been drawn from memory and, in some cases, compressed to facilitate a natural narrative. —VT

For Thea, who wears many hats: baker, guide, medic, ranger, weather forecaster, dog-sitter, etc.

And for Debbie Reynolds, my confidante, my guide to all things Australian, one of Lola's favourite aunties and a brave lady.

And to the memory of Linda Astle, a very special friend, much missed by her family and all who knew her. Readers may remember Linda. She was proclaimed the Pudding Queen in El Hoyo after winning the village fiesta Pudding Contest with her bread-and-butter pudding.

CONTENTS

The Old Fools Series	viii
FREE Photo Book	ix
1. DOWN UNDER	1
Aussie Breakfast Bowls	14
2. HOUSE HUNTING	16
Summer Vegetable Lasagne	29
3. PURCHASES	32
Strawberry Swirl Pavlovas	46
4. A FRENZY AND PHONE CALLS	48
Easy Salmon Mousse	60
5. LOLA AND COLD FEET	62
Gender Reveal Cake	72
6. MOVING	75
Teriyaki Steaks	89
7. TRADIES	91
Lobster and Summer Fruits Salad	103
8. NEW FRIENDS	105
White Chocolate and Macadamia Biscuits	118
9. PUPPY SCHOOL	120
Thea's German Cheesecake	131
10. GRASS	133
Silverbeet, Broccolini and Mozzarella Pizza	145
11. NEIGHBOURS	147

Baked Pumpkin Risotto	158
12. BATS	160
Fig and Walnut Breakfast Loaf	172
13. A BANANA AND BEETLES	174
Creamy Camembert Potatoes	187
14. CLONES AND A RUSSIAN	189
Speedy Beef Stroganoff	200
15. TERRY	202
Fast Food Minestrone	214
16. HOSTIBALS	216
ANZAC Biscuits	227
17. CATS AND DOGS	229
Home-made Dog Biscuits	241
18. MORE CATS AND DOGS	243
Strawberry Mice	256
19. WATER BALLET	258
Dead-Easy Damper	271
20. DEBBIE REYNOLDS	273
Debbie Reynold's Mum's Pavlova	284
21. A FRIGHT	286
Trout with Lemon Parsley Butter	298
22. BREATHLESS	300
Spinach and Feta Quiche	312
23. BED NUMBER FIVE	314
German Butter Cake (Butterkuchen)	325
24. ROLLERCOASTER	328
Honey-Glazed Spare Ribs	340
25. MONSTERS BENEATH	342
Slow Cooker Chocolate Fudge	354

26. BAD STUFF	356
Creamy Curried Snags	365
27. DIFFICULT DAYS	367
Aussie Ham and Cheese Pull-Aparts	379
28. WORMS	381
Cheating Apple Dump Dessert	394
29. SUMMER DAYS	396
Lemon Myrtle Cake	409
30. OXYGEN	411
Vegemite Pasta	423
EPILOGUE	425
A request…	435
So what happened next?	437
The Old Fools series	440
The Sixpenny Cross series	444
More books by Victoria Twead…	446
About the Author	449
Contacts and Links	450
Acknowledgements	453
More Ant Press Books	455
Publish with Ant Press	459

THE OLD FOOLS SERIES
AVAILABLE IN PAPERBACK, HARDCOVER AND EBOOK EDITIONS

Two Old Fools Down Under is the sixth book in the *Old Fools* series by New York Times and Wall Street Journal bestselling author, Victoria Twead.

- Chickens, Mules and Two Old Fools
- Two Old Fools ~ Olé!
- Two Old Fools on a Camel
- Two Old Fools in Spain Again
- Two Old Fools in Turmoil
- Two Old Fools Down Under
- Two Old Fools, Fair Dinkum

Prequels

- One Young Fool in Dorset
- One Young Fool in South Africa

Latest Release:

Dear Fran, Love Dulcie: Life and Death in the Hills and Hollows of Bygone Australia

FREE PHOTO BOOK
TO BROWSE OR DOWNLOAD

For photographs and additional unpublished material to accompany this book, browse or download the

FREE PHOTO BOOK

from

www.victoriatwead.com / free-stuff

1
DOWN UNDER

I've always wanted a dog. I've had cats, all big personalities and all much missed. I remember Fortnum and her brother, Mason, who grew up with the children. Fortnum was a beautiful, delicate tabby with the heart of a lion, unlike her brother, Mason. He was huge, but cowered behind his little sister as she fought all the battles with the neighbouring feline community.

And there was Chox, the Siamese mix who enchanted us in Spain and ended up living in Germany.

There were always excellent reasons for us *not* to have a dog: we were working and out of the house all day. Or travelling too much and unable to give a dog the time or stability it deserved.

So I made myself a promise. One day, when the time was *exactly* right, we'd have a dog.

It was September 2015, and I had just landed in Australia clutching my precious, newly-granted Permanent Residence visa.

We no longer needed to travel. Our year working in Bahrain had cured my itchy feet and Joe was probably not well enough to explore the far-flung corners of the earth.

We'd stopped looking for greener pastures because we'd found them. Home is where the family is. Australia was where the family was and Australia was where we would put down our roots.

The possibility of owning a dog was suddenly within my reach for the first time in my life.

"You won't rush out and get a dog the moment you land in Australia, will you?" Joe had asked, watching me carefully.

"No! Of course not! I'm going to be far too busy catching up with little Indy, and house-hunting, to think about getting a dog."

But I lied.

"Good. When I've finished my treatment in the UK, and we've got a place of our own to live, then there'll be plenty of time to discuss whether we want a dog or not."

Back in Spain, Joe and I had discussed what type of home might suit us best in Australia. At one point in the past, Karly and Cam had considered building a granny flat for us, but it hadn't been feasible.

"I'll leave it totally up to you," said Joe. "Something not too big, something easy to look after, low maintenance. A place that doesn't need any work done at all."

I had agreed, but I was in for a shock. House prices in Sydney were amongst the highest in the world. Our budget would barely buy a flat, or unit as they are called in Australia, let alone a house.

"I had no idea they were so expensive!" I said to my daughter. "I think I'm going to have to think again. Perhaps a retirement village might be the answer? Some of them look really nice. They have nice grounds, swimming pools, gyms, medical facilities. You can even have pets in some of them."

"A wrinkly-ville? Are you quite sure?" A 'wrinkly-ville' was Karly's rather disparaging description of a retirement village. She was dubious. "I don't think you're old enough to be happy in one of those. Not yet."

"Well, I think it's worth considering. I'd enjoy having big gardens."

"Shared with all the other residents."

"And some of these places are close to a beach. And there are some not too far from you. If it's comfortable and affordable, I should at least look. I think it might suit Joe very well, and there'd always be doctors available."

"Okay, we'll look."

There was so much to think about.

Indy was delightful. Three years old and full of mischief and imagination. Her favourite game was Princesses and she chose to wear tiaras on most days. Not only did *she* wear bejewelled crowns, but Princess Nanny was expected to wear them, too. In addition, Indy had sheets of multicoloured plastic sticky-back jewels.

"Di' monds," she said as she pressed huge sparkling 'jewels' onto my earlobes. "I make you a little bit quite pretty."

Sometimes I would completely forget about my tiara and generously-sized earrings when I answered the door.

"Sign here, please," said the delivery man, looking at me strangely.

Only much later, when I caught sight of myself in a mirror, did I remember my finery.

Often we'd play 'mermaids' and swim together across the dining room floorboards. Or 'shops' in the side garden where my son-in-law, Cam, had set up a Wendy house, called a cubby house in Australia. That little side garden was full of interest with its chicken coop, Balinese hut, cubby house and trampoline.

Adjoining the chicken garden was my den. If I needed peace, I could retreat to this, my writers' lair, which had been created especially for me. I had a desk, Internet access, a TV, a kettle for coffee, a sofa, and a cupboard where I kept a few toys for visits from Indy.

It was here, sometimes accompanied by Indy's tabby cat, Bandsaw, that I conducted all my research into retirement villages and houses for sale. In the evenings, I would Skype with Joe, or write, while bugs the size of small family cars threw themselves at my window.

During the day my lair was cool and I could gaze out of the window at the blue sky. It was springtime and the air was full of birdsong. Not the polite, tuneful tweeting we expect from British wild birds, but the raucous shrieks of cockatoos and the repeated snaps of whiplash birds.

The Happy Birthday bird sometimes sang his song, although nobody ever believed me when I mentioned it. Now that I know a little more about Australia and its wildlife, I'm guessing it might have been a magpie. Magpies sing beautifully and can be excellent mimics. They also live for many years, which would explain why I heard this particular bird repeatedly over several years. I'd first heard it on previous visits from Spain, and it was still performing the same birthday song.

Not so melodic was the sound of next door's dog. He was an enormous basset hound, usually silent, but given to occasional bouts of miserable howling. I wondered what was making him so unhappy.

"So how is the house-hunting going?" asked Joe during one of our online sessions. "Any possibilities yet?"

"Well, actually, I'm quite excited. We've got an appointment in the morning at a wrinkly-ville that's only about ten minutes away from here. It looks fabulous. Very leafy, lots of trees, and it's built round a lake."

"Hmmm. I'm still not convinced that we'd be happy in a retirement home. Mini-bus outings and weaving baskets in craft clubs are not exactly my scene."

I tried to imagine Joe basket-weaving and failed.

"Oh, I'm sure they're not really like that. I'll bring back a full report after the visit tomorrow. Has the hospital given you a start date for your radiotherapy?"

Joe already had the tiny gold beads (called fiducial markers) inserted in preparation for his radiation therapy. They are inserted painlessly and provide greater accuracy for targeting the cancer whilst sparing healthy tissue. We hoped that this course would successfully eliminate his prostate cancer.

"Ah, yes. I have to endure twenty sessions spread over four weeks. It's all going to happen in December."

"So it'll all be finished by Christmas?"

"Yes, that's the plan."

"That's good news! How's your breathing?"

"Not great. I get very out of breath at the slightest thing. I have an appointment at the medical centre this week."

We'd been given the dreadful news that Joe had COPD, or Chronic Obstructive Pulmonary Disease, and we knew there was no cure. However, it could be managed.

"Perhaps they'll give you stronger inhalers."

"Maybe. It's just so cold here. I'm not used to it after Spain."

"Well, you'll soon be out here in the sunshine and moaning about the heat. Right, I must go. Speak again tomorrow."

Finding somewhere to live was a matter of urgency. Of course, we could both stay with Karly and Cam as long as we needed, but I wanted to have found somewhere to live before Joe arrived. He needed a tranquil environment. Sharing a house with a young family, which included an active toddler, a large dog, a cat and a baby on the way was not ideal. Neither did I want us to outstay our welcome.

I had three months to find us a home.

And the clock was ticking.

As I hadn't bought a car yet, Karly was chauffeuring me around. Indy was at her paternal grandmother's house, so Karly and I set off alone. I was excited. Maybe finding somewhere to live would be easy.

I'd read the particulars of the retirement village we were visiting from cover to cover, and it seemed ideal. There was usually a waiting list for new residents but they had a vacancy pending. Whenever a home became empty, the policy was to strip it out entirely, paint it throughout, and refit it with new flooring and appliances.

This village wasn't near any beach, which was a pity, but as we turned in, we admired the homes shaded by pine trees. A pretty fountain played in the centre of a small lake. At Reception, we were met by Margo, who shook our hands enthusiastically.

"Welcome!" she said. "I'll give you a tour, and I can show you the unit. It's got workmen in it at the moment, but it'll give you an idea of what it's like."

"Perfect!"

"This way! I'll show you the clubhouse and dining hall first. If you do join us, you may like to eat in the dining hall occasionally."

She clicked off in her high heels with Karly by her side. I trailed behind a little, absorbing the ambience, trying to imagine living there. Would we fit in? Would Joe like it?

"And here's the gym! Hello, Stan!"

The gym was well-equipped but deserted, apart from an ancient chap wearing shorts and T-shirt perched on an exercise bike. He stared straight ahead with glazed eyes, veins standing out on his forehead. His lips were drawn back revealing clenched teeth, and his knuckles were white as he gripped the handlebars. Sweat poured from him as his skinny white legs pumped relentlessly.

"How's it going, Stan?" cried our guide, but Stan didn't even glance our way.

"I'll show you our pool," said Margo gaily, not at all troubled by Stan's lack of response. "It's hugely popular with our residents. Bye, Stan! Catch up with you later!"

But Stan ignored her cheery wave. Whether he was hard of hearing or deep in some kind of sporting coma, I couldn't say.

The pool was nice. Two ladies stood at one end, chattering. They didn't look very wet.

"Muriel, Evie!" hailed Margo. "How are you?"

They waved back then continued their discussion.

"We have weekly aqua-aerobics classes," said Margo.

I tried to imagine Joe jogging and bouncing alongside a bunch of others but doubted that would ever happen.

"And we have loads of other activities! We have trips to places of interest and clubs. Do you like crafts? We have a thriving scrapbooking club and a make-your-own Christmas decorations club!"

Oh dear.

I might enjoy marching to music in the swimming pool, and even fashioning a festive Christmas bauble or two, but Joe would regard it all with horror. I consoled myself with the knowledge that none of these activities was compulsory. If Joe didn't want to join in, he wouldn't have to. He could simply pop out to the clubhouse and take part in the occasional Happy Hour if he felt like it.

"And here's the library," crowed Margo, pushing open some swing doors. "We have thousands of books and the library is always buzzing."

I could see the books but there wasn't a soul in the library. Definitely no buzzing. Just a rattling snore rising from one of the armchairs in the far corner.

"Oh, I think that may be Lily," said our guide in hushed tones. "We won't disturb her. I'll take you to see the houses and the vacant property instead."

Many of Sydney's suburbs are hilly and this retirement village was no exception. The little streets were nicely laid out, but steep. Joe would struggle. Karly and Margo chatted and I did my best to keep up.

"Do you have much of a problem with big spiders?" asked Karly. "I imagine these big trees would attract them." Karly and I shared a spider phobia.

"No, never heard anybody complain about spiders," said Margo, shaking her head. "I probably shouldn't tell you this, but we do see quite a few pythons."

Karly and I stared at her. Pythons were not part of our lives in England. Or in Spain for that matter.

"Ah, here we are," said Margo. "Number 75. Just as I thought, the tradies are busy working on it." In Australia, tradesmen are often referred to as 'tradies'.

She knocked on the door but the power tools within drowned out the sound and nobody answered.

"Never mind! I don't have the key but we can go around the back and through the garden gate. This house is particularly nice because the back faces onto the lake. Follow me!"

The lake looked cool and peaceful. Tall trees and the sky above were reflected on the surface which was undisturbed except by the fountain in the middle, and two black coots paddling furiously away from us. Dragonflies flitted and doves cooed in pine trees. A pretty walking track encircled the lake and inviting wooden benches stood at intervals.

"This is lovely!" I said to Karly.

A movement caught my attention and I stared, enchanted. Basking on the bank in the sunshine was a beautiful water dragon. It was a large one, perhaps about a metre (three feet) nose to tail, so probably a male. He regarded us haughtily, his proud nose in the air. Then there was a plop, and the dragon vanished, leaving just a ripple as the only clue to where he had dived.

Although Australian water dragons are shy in the wild, they can become used to constant human presence in their habitat. It's common to see water dragons in city parks where they have become accustomed to sharing the grounds with people. However, if necessary, they are fast runners and strong climbers, able to clamber up tree trunks in seconds. If alarmed, they will usually hide in thick vegetation, or they may scale a tree and drop from an overhanging branch into water. There they can sit on the bed of shallow creeks or lakes for well over an hour, hiding from enemies.

Joe would love this! I thought. We share a passion for wildlife and Joe has always been fascinated by reptiles.

And I could walk our future dog around the lake, I thought. I hoped the house itself wouldn't disappoint.

"Coo-ee!" called Margo. "Over here! We can get into the house via the patio doors."

She was beckoning to us, walking backwards up the narrow garden path towards the big sliding glass doors, which stood open.

"This way!"

We turned and headed towards her. Karly was ahead of me and had almost reached Margo when something caught my attention. Something wasn't right.

"Stop!" I shouted. "Don't move!"

AUSSIE BREAKFAST BOWLS

A fabulous, nutritious way to start the day. Garnish with avocado slices and cherry tomatoes for extra colour and flavour.

Ingredients (serves 4)

4 large bread rolls

4 tablespoons melted butter

4 rashers cooked bacon, each rasher cut in half

4 small handfuls baby spinach leaves

4 cherry tomatoes, finely sliced

1 cup grated tasty cheese

4 eggs

Salt and pepper

Avocado slices and cherry tomatoes for garnish

Method

Cut about 2-3 cm (1 inch) off the top off each of the bread rolls and remove and discard bread filling.

Place one tablespoon of melted butter into each of the bread rolls.

Place two bacon pieces into each bread roll.

Place a small handful of baby spinach leaves into each bread roll.

Share the cherry tomato slices between each of the bread rolls.

Share the cup of grated cheese between each of the bread rolls.

Break an egg into each of the bread rolls.

Carefully place loaves/rolls onto a baking tray lined with aluminium foil and place in a 180°C (350°F) oven for 15-20 minutes, until the egg is cooked to your liking.

Serve each roll on a plate and top with salt and pepper.

Garnish with avocado slices and cherry tomatoes.

From newideafood.com.au

2
HOUSE HUNTING

Margo stumbled back in surprise. I pointed at the ground by her feet and her hand flew to her mouth. Her eyes grew huge.

A huge diamond python, as thick as a man's arm, was draped across the path.

"Ohmigosh, ohmigosh," squeaked Karly, sidestepping neatly.

"I can't believe it! I stepped over it," whispered Margo, her eyes still the size of two full moons. "I nearly trod on it!"

The python wasn't bothered. Perfectly camouflaged, he was warming himself on the pavers and not in the mood to move.

"Hey!" called a workman, appearing at the patio door. He must have seen us approaching. "Is there a problem?"

He was a large man, wearing the obligatory Aussie tradie uniform comprising work boots, shorts and neon T-shirt. A tool belt was slung around his hips. His burly mate appeared beside him, ear defenders still in place, a power tool in his hand. The pair of them began to walk down the path towards us, unaware of the reptilian obstacle.

Margo's voice had returned.

"Watch out, there's a snake there!" she warned, pointing to the python. "Could you please remove…"

But she never finished the sentence. Like magic, the pair turned on their heels and vanished back into the house. The glass doors closed behind them with a decisive click.

"Well!" exclaimed Margo, exasperated.

"That wasn't very gallant," said Karly.

"It's just a diamond python," shouted Margo at the blank glass doors. "It's harmless!"

No reply from within.

Diamond pythons are common in Sydney. They are no threat to humans and exist by hunting lizards, rats, mice, and the occasional possum if they can catch it. They usually live in the bush but also take up residence in the roof spaces of private houses.

Understandably, many people are not keen to have snakes in their roofs, but perhaps they should welcome their lodgers. The pythons will happily eliminate any unwanted rodent pests, and once the food supply is exhausted, the snakes will move on. They provide an excellent free service.

The sunlight caught our snake's beautiful yellow and black scales, making them shimmer. He rippled ever so slightly, stirring from his slumber.

Margo clacked up the path to the patio doors and peered in through cupped hands.

"Honestly!" she said to us over her shoulder. "They've locked themselves in!"

She rapped sharply on the glass with her knuckles.

Nothing. She tried again.

"Hey! Guys! Give me one of your brooms or something so I can chase it away!"

There was a pause, and then the doors slid apart just wide enough to allow a broom to be passed out. I saw the workman's tattooed fist, but not its owner, and the doors snapped together again the instant Margo accepted the broom.

Margo was made of sterner stuff.

"Off you go, Mr Python," she said, preparing to sweep him away.

The python reared his head slightly to assess the situation. Then, in one sinuous, fluid movement, melted away into the undergrowth. He was gone.

HOUSE HUNTING

"Wow!" I said.

"Gosh!" said Karly.

"Oh dear, I expect all this wildlife has put you off considering Fernview Village," said Margo.

"On the contrary!" I exclaimed. "I think it's wonderful to be so close to nature and watch water dragons and waterfowl on the lake. And the odd python is very welcome, too. Joe would love it."

"Oh good. Let's go inside and I'll show you around the house."

The tradies must have seen Margot deal with our uninvited reptilian visitor because the patio doors were now miraculously unlocked and the pair were working extra busily. I noticed they looked a little sheepish and made no eye contact with any of us.

Stepping inside, I was disappointed.

Obviously it was being refurbished and not looking its best, but I was struck by the size. The place was tiny. Although it had two bedrooms, the entire home was smaller than our roof terrace in Spain. Not big enough to swing a koala.

"No good, then?" asked Karly as we drove home.

"No. It was just too small. We would be really cramped."

"Well, that's the trouble with property in Sydney. Land is so expensive."

"Yes, I'm beginning to understand that now."

We collected Princess Indy and headed home. Indy was at that age when she loved to sing. As we drove, we all belted out her current favourite:

> Five cheeky monkeys a-sitting in the tree
> Teasing the crocodile,
> "You can't catch me!"
> Along came the crocodile, quiet as can be
> And snapped one monkey out of that tree.

Back home, Cam had finished his working day. We retreated to the chicken garden with cool drinks to discuss the day's events and watch Princess Indy playing in the sandpit.

"Never mind," I said, "there are plenty more places to see. I like the look of that one near the beach. We have an appointment…"

But my voice was drowned out by the mournful howling of next door's basset hound. Further conversation was impossible.

We looked at each other and rolled our eyes.

Suddenly, a head popped up over the fence, immediately above us. A man with huge, sweeping moustaches was peering down at us. The fence was extremely high at that point and I assumed he was standing on a ladder. I'm not sure who was the most surprised.

"Oh!" squeaked Karly, nearly spilling her drink.

"Oh!" said Moustache Man. "Sorry! I wasn't spying on you, honestly. I was just wondering what was making my dog howl like that."

"We were wondering the same thing," said Cam.

"Well, I think it's a cat," said our neighbour.

"Really?"

"Yes, I've seen one a few times. It seems to enjoy teasing my dog."

"Oh dear. How?"

"It sits on that branch up there," he said, pointing, "then it walks along the fence just out of reach. It drives my dog crazy."

"Oh dear. What sort of cat?"

"A tabby one."

"Oh."

"Anyway, the cat seems to enjoy it more than the dog. Sorry to have bothered you."

And the head vanished as suddenly as it had appeared.

We looked at each other guiltily, trying not to laugh. Next time we sang Indy's song, the words had changed:

One cheeky Bandsaw a-sitting in the tree
Teasing the basset hound,
"You can't catch me!"
Along came Moustaches, quiet as can be
And snapped naughty Bandsaw out of that tree.

Those neighbours sold their house and moved away soon after. We can only hope that the cats in their new neighbourhood are a little more charitable than Bandsaw.

We visited many more retirement villages during the weeks that followed. Looking back on them now, they kind of merge into each other in a blur. Most were pleasant, but I couldn't really imagine us living in any of them.

I remember one in particular, not because of the village itself, but because of Karly's latest health craze. She'd just discovered smart water bottles. I had no idea what these were until she explained that they automatically tracked one's water intake and reminded one when a drink was recommended. I believe sensors monitor the water level, and the weight of the bottle, and the information is relayed to a phone app that activates an alarm.

My daughter is a fitness freak and quick to

embrace new health discoveries. Somehow I was also persuaded that life could not possibly be complete without my very own smart water bottle. So that day we set off, each armed with our smart bottles, Indy in tow.

Beep, beep.

"Drink, Mummy. Drink, Princess Nanny."

Obediently swigging water whenever our apps (and Indy) ordered us to, we headed for the retirement village. Unfortunately, we took a wrong turning somewhere and the water was beginning to have an effect.

"Where's the guest parking?" asked Karly.

"I don't know. Hope it's close. I really need the loo."

"Me too."

"Me too! I a little bit quite need a wee," announced Indy who was fascinated by anything to do with lavatories, particularly public ones.

We parked quickly and hurried into Reception. A well-dressed lady stepped forward to greet us.

"Good afternoon and welcome to Forest Glen! Allow me to introduce myself. I'm Sandra, and I imagine you are Mrs Twead." She shook my hand. "And you must be her daughter?" she said, turning to Karly.

"Yes!" said Karly, looking flushed and hopping up and down.

I'm sure I was wearing the same anxious expression and twitching just as much.

"Ah," said Sandra. "You look flushed. Is it hot outside? Can I get you a glass of water before the tour?"

"No, thank you!" we said in unison.

"Could we possibly use your bathroom?" asked Karly.

Beep, beep.

"Drink, Mummy. Drink, Princess Nanny," ordered Indy.

Poor Sandra was looking uncomfortable. These twitchy viewers were clearly not behaving like her usual potential buyers. However, she directed us to the bathroom and we emerged much relieved and ready for the tour.

We boarded a golf buggy with Sandra chauffeuring.

"We are just passing Forest Glen's own nine-hole golf course," she said, warming to her task. "And over there is the clubhouse where…"

Beep, beep.

"Drink, Mummy. Drink, Princess Nanny," Indy commanded.

"I'm so sorry. We should explain," I said, seeing the poor lady's baffled expression. "We have new smart water bottles that tell us when we should hydrate."

"Actually, we're not used to drinking quite so much water," Karly added apologetically.

"Ah!" said Sandra, now understanding the situation and becoming the perfect guide. "Shall we pop into the clubhouse? There's a nice bathroom in there."

Beep, beep.

"Drink, Mummy! Drink, Princess Nanny!"

The remainder of the tour was punctuated by beeps and bathroom stops.

Forest Glen Village was nice, I think. Although it boasted plenty of toilets, and Sandra was exceptionally attentive, the villas were tiny and I didn't feel it was for us.

On another occasion, we'd just completed a guided tour around a village that had also seemed promising. Our guide had stopped to show us their program of events, talking us through the activities on offer. The knitting clubs and craft sessions were becoming familiar now.

"And on the first Tuesday of every month, we have a get-together. We barbecue beef burgers, or serve a curry, or Thai food, and drinks are half price at the bar."

"Gosh, that sounds fun," exclaimed an elderly lady who had joined our little group and was listening avidly. She was rather eccentrically dressed in a floaty dress and lace cardigan. Her feet were clad in white ankle socks and sandals.

She had a friendly smile. I assumed she was also considering moving into this retirement village.

Our guide returned her smile and continued.

"On those Tuesdays, we sometimes organise a ten-pin bowling event or a quiz night."

"Oh, how super!" enthused our new companion. "I love ten-pin bowling!"

Our guide didn't comment but carried on listing future events.

"Next week we're going to order in fish and chips and have a darts night," she said, pointing at dates on the calendar.

"Darts? How lovely!" thrilled the lady. "I've *always* wanted to play darts. Can I come?"

Our guide sighed and patted her arm.

"Edna, dear, you've been coming to our Tuesday get-togethers since 2004."

"Have I?"

"Yes, dear. Now, would you like to sit in the shade and I'll organise a nice cuppa for you?"

With a cheery wave, Edna allowed herself to be led away. Our guided tour was over.

"The thing is," said Karly, as we drove home. "I don't think you're ready for a retirement home. The average age of the residents seems to be in the eighties, and you're only sixty."

This wasn't a new refrain from my daughter, and I was beginning to agree. The age factor was definitely a worry, not eased by the knowledge that Sydney accommodation was expensive and would be much smaller than Joe and I were used to.

"Cam suggested that we drive up the coast this weekend. Out of Sydney, but not too far away. We could look around, maybe visit some open houses. That way, you could see what you *could* get for your money."

"Not retirement villages?"

"No. Not retirement villages."

When I discussed it with Joe, he agreed that it was a good plan.

"I know some of the villages are really nice places," he said, "but I'm not sure we're ready for a wrinkly-ville yet. I think we like our privacy and independence too much."

I agreed and in the quiet of my den, I researched possibilities using Google maps. Luckily, my family lived in the northern suburbs of Sydney. It would be a simple matter to join the motorway and head north to the area known as the Central Coast.

Could this be the answer? Could I find a property here that gave us what we wanted? House prices looked attractive, much lower than those in Sydney and its suburbs. I began to feel quite excited.

No, we wouldn't be very close to the family, and city attractions would be less accessible. But there were huge compensations. Heaps of pristine beaches stretching for kilometres, including dog beaches, I noted. Forests, open grassland, lakes, dense bushland, national parks. The Central Coast seemed to have it all.

Then I saw a couple of sentences that made my heart race.

The Central Coast offers dozens of lookout points where watchers can view the humpback whale migration twice a year. Humpbacks swim north to breed in the winter, then return with their newborn calves later in the year.

Yes, for wildlife enthusiasts like Joe and me, the Central Coast had a lot to offer.

"That sounds amazing," said Joe. "But look carefully. We definitely don't want to take on a renovation job. I think we've had quite enough of those! I don't think I could cope with another."

"I agree! I'm going to look for a house which doesn't need *anything* doing to it."

"And we don't want a swimming pool. They require far too much maintenance."

"Absolutely."

"And take your time. Don't make up your mind too quickly. The right place will come along."

"I know. Don't worry. We're only going to look, anyway."

SUMMER VEGETABLE LASAGNE

Australia has every climate and it's possible to source most ingredients, from tropical fruit to Brussels sprouts without importing from abroad. Even cheeses like ricotta and parmesan, or baby zucchini with flowers attached, are produced in Australia. Recipe from Delicious.com.au

Ingredients

500g (17oz) ricotta

2 cups (160g) finely grated parmesan

200g (7oz) frozen peas

½ bunch basil, leaves torn

Finely grated zest and juice of 1 lemon

1 tsp dried chilli flakes

¾ cup (120g) roasted almonds, chopped

½ cup (750g) butternut pumpkin (butternut squash), seeds removed, halved, peeled

2 tbs extra virgin olive oil

2 tbs honey

4 yellow squash

4 baby zucchinis (courgettes) with flowers attached

1 tbs apple cider vinegar

Method

Preheat oven to 200°C (390°F)

Place ricotta, parmesan, peas, basil, lemon zest and chilli flakes in a food processor and whiz until roughly combined.

Transfer to a bowl and stir through ½ cup (80g) almonds.

Season. Cover and chill until ready to use.

Thinly slice pumpkin into 5mm-thick slices. Combine 1 tbs each oil and honey in a bowl.

Microwave the pumpkin in a heatproof bowl on high for 3 minutes. (Alternatively, steam pumpkin for 1 minute.)

Brush with honey mixture, then place one-quarter of pumpkin in a single layer in a 22cm (8 inches) baking dish and spread with one-third of the ricotta mixture.

Repeat process two more times, finishing with a layer of pumpkin.

Bake for 35 minutes or until pumpkin top is golden and caramelised. Cool slightly.

Meanwhile, thinly slice squash.

Cut zucchini into thin rounds and gently remove petals.

Combine vinegar, lemon juice and remaining 1 tbs each oil and honey in a small bowl. Set aside.

Top lasagne with squash, zucchini rounds and flowers, and remaining ¼ cup (40g) almonds.

Drizzle with the honey dressing to serve.

3

PURCHASES

The weekend couldn't come quickly enough. Cam drove, Karly was in charge of navigation, using estate agents' apps to guide us to houses for sale, and Indy and I sat in the back. We played a game that I hoped she had grown out of but it remained a firm favourite. She had a toy CD player and every time she pressed the Start button, a nursery rhyme played.

"Dance, Princess Nanny!" she cried.

I would jig and pretend to dance until she pressed the Stop button, whereupon I froze. It was like a solitary game of musical statues and it amused Indy endlessly. Me, after the first five minutes, not so much.

When she finally dozed off to the hum of the car's engine, I could concentrate on the passing scenery. The motorway passed over the giant Hawkesbury River and cut through towering rock for many miles. After an hour, we turned off and began our property quest.

I liked what I saw. We'd left the Sydney traffic behind and the roads were wide. There were plenty of trees and untouched bushland. Many districts had inviting-looking beaches. People looked relaxed, tanned and unhurried. Many didn't even bother with footwear as they strolled along ample sidewalks.

"Sea-girls!" cried Indy as gulls wheeled overhead.

As with any region, there were salubrious areas and others less so. Some houses were in smart streets, while other, cheaper houses, appeared scruffy and neglected.

It was helpful that my son-in-law was a builder. He could offer advice, and we rejected some properties for reasons I may not have noticed had I been alone.

The business of house-buying is very different in Australia, compared with England and Spain, where the buyer arranges a private viewing through an estate agent. Cam explained to me how it worked.

"In Australia, we hold 'open homes'," he said. "The sellers will arrange times with the real estate agent for property-hunters to have a look around.

It's usually for just an hour, or even half an hour."

"So there are lots of viewers all walking around at the same time?"

"Yes. Sometimes people will make an offer after the viewing, and if one is accepted, the sellers take it off the market."

"I can see it's a good, informal method of viewing," I said, "but if houses are only open for half an hour, could potential buyers miss seeing properties if the times coincide?"

"Yes, but houses often have a couple of open days or more. And you could request a private viewing if you really wanted."

"Oh, I see."

"Often a house goes to auction if a seller thinks it'll reach a higher price if potential buyers bid against each other. Homeowners usually set a reserve price, and if bidding doesn't reach this price, they aren't forced to sell the house."

"How about this one?" interrupted Karly, passing me her phone.

"Looks nice!"

It was a wooden, chalet-type, but we dismissed it after a quick viewing. Apart from being tiny, it could only be reached by a shared drive, and many of its timbers were rotten.

"No, thank you," I said, staring into dark

corners where half-dead cockroaches lay on their backs waving their legs.

"This one?"

"No, it's on a main road."

"How about this one?"

"No, too close to the railway."

One was very nice, but I felt the vast, manicured garden would need too much work. Another was too crowded in by its neighbours.

The last house on our list was in a cul-de-sac. It was a typically Aussie, unpretentious, brick-built, single-level house and I liked the look of it immediately.

"The photos look amazing," said Karly, looking at her phone.

The estate agent was waiting to welcome us on the doorstep, and we could see other viewing parties milling around inside.

I don't know what it was about that house, but I felt right at home as soon as we walked in. Perhaps if I'd looked more closely, or if I hadn't left my glasses at home, I might have thought differently. But there was a smile on my face because I could actually visualise Joe and I living in this house. It had three bedrooms (perfect) and wasn't too big or too small.

"You really like this one, don't you?" asked Karly, watching me.

"I do!"

The kitchen was very cramped, and the bathroom badly in need of a makeover, but Cam swept those problems aside.

"Easy to refurbish those," he said, "and you'd still have money left over in your budget."

And when I saw the pool I was in love.

It wasn't the regular rectangular blue-painted pool, the type that is often formed by a prefabricated fibre-glass liner or tiles. No, this was a sparkling oasis pool edged with giant boulders and palm trees. It was extravagantly exotic and unusual, and I wanted to jump straight in.

"Well?" asked Karly as we got back into the car. "You haven't said anything for ages."

We clipped on our seat-belts and set off.

"Dance, Princess Nanny," said Indy, but my head was too full of thoughts and ideas.

"I'm going to put in an offer," I said.

That evening, I talked with Joe.

"You did what?" he asked.

"I put in an offer."

"Vicky, have you gone crazy? Whatever made you do such a thing? Is the house perfect?"

"No, not really, but you should see the pool."

"Pool? Pool? We agreed we didn't want a swimming pool!"

"I know, but this one is different. It's fringed with palm trees and…"

"How many bedrooms?"

"Three."

"Okay. Bathrooms?"

"Only one, but Cam explained that's the brilliant thing about Aussie houses! They're not built like British houses. All the interior walls are just plasterboard. Nothing structural or load-bearing. They can all be demolished, and the whole house can be reconfigured to suit ourselves."

"Wait a minute," said Joe from the other side of the world. "Are you saying we are taking on another huge renovation job?"

"Well…"

"We agreed! No pool! No renovations!"

"Anyway, my offer was rejected."

"Well, hallelujah! Thank goodness for that!"

"So I put in a higher offer."

By the end of September, I had bought a car. It was terrific to be mobile and I felt much more independent. It had a reversing camera, it switched on its own lights at dusk, and the windscreen wipers automatically leapt into life when it rained. I was delighted with these and all manner of mod cons I didn't know even existed when we lived in Spain. I named our car Bruce and was grateful to his satnav voice for nagging me if I exceeded the speed limit.

Bruce was roomy, which I secretly thought might be useful for our future dog.

Karly's pregnancy was progressing well, and I felt I could be useful by watching Indy while Karly and Cam made preparations for the new baby. Indy still had no idea about the new addition to the family.

After hospital scans assured them that things were proceeding exactly as they should, Cam and Karly decided the time had come.

"Indy, we've got something very important to tell you."

Indy's blue eyes couldn't have been wider.

"Some very exciting news."

Indy put her head on one side, listening intently.

"Indy, you are going to be a... BIG SISTER!"

Indy's mouth dropped open as her three-year-old brain tried to process this information.

"Mummy has a baby in her tummy and when it comes out, you'll be a big sister!"

"A baby?"

"Yes, a really tiny one."

"A little bit quite tiny one?"

"Yes! You can help look after it."

"I can help!"

"Yes, you can help, and when the baby grows, you can play with it."

"Tomorrow?"

"No, not tomorrow. Not for a long time because it has to do some more growing. When it's ready, Mummy will go to the hospital, and they'll help it come out of Mummy's tummy."

"Yes! And when I was a baby I used to go waaaah!"

"That's right, and our new baby will go waaaah, too."

"And I can play with it."

"Yes, you can. Would you like a little sister or a little brother?"

"Sister. We can play Princesses."

"And what name shall we choose for our new baby?"

"Um, Dragon."

My second offer for the house was also refused. With Cam and Karly's help, I made my last offer. I instructed the estate agent to tell the sellers that I would not be attending an auction, if they chose to hold one and that this was my final offer. If they accepted, I wanted the big mirror in the dining area included in the sale.

Twenty-four hours later I had a response. The sellers accepted my offer and called off the upcoming auction.

The house was ours.

"You're going to love it, honestly!"

"Are you sure?"

"Absolutely sure. It's got great potential."

"Great potential?" echoed Joe. "Great potential? But we weren't looking for a house with great potential!"

"Oh, and did I tell you about Splinterbone Crag? Seriously, it's a cliff literally less than a five-minute drive away. Apparently, it's a fabulous place to watch the whale migration! I can't wait!"

"Yes, but…"

"And there are *so* many gorgeous beaches!" I didn't add that many of them welcomed dogs. "We could go to a different one every day of the week, all within a fifteen minutes drive away."

"Vicky, I…"

"And three good shopping centres within easy reach. Oh, and a chemist, veg shop, butcher, and supermarket all within walking distance."

I heard Joe exhale and sensed he had given up, but I hurried on, just in case he hadn't.

PURCHASES

"Have you been to the medical centre? Any news? Did they give you a new puffer?"

"Yes, the nurse gave me a new inhaler. It seems to help a little bit."

"That's good. Oh, and I forgot to tell you. I got an email today, and you'll never guess in a million years who it was from!"

There was a long pause, then, "So are you going to tell me?"

"I'll give you a clue. Somebody in Spain. Somebody from the village."

"Gosh! I can't think of anybody who would sit down and write us an email. I give up. Who?"

"One of the Ufarte twins!"

"Really? Which one?"

"Catalina."

"Which one's that?"

"I'm not sure, I never could tell them apart."

"Why did she write?"

"Listen, I must go, Karly's calling me. I'll forward the email."

After dinner, it was time for Indy's bath, and then her bedtime. She was no trouble at all to put to bed. After her story, she'd want to play Princesses, so we told her she could be Sleeping Beauty. She must pretend to be asleep under a spell, waiting for a handsome prince to arrive. She closed her eyes and we kissed her goodnight.

She was fast asleep within minutes. It worked every time.

Later, I read the email through again.

Hola tía Vicky y tío Joe,

I hop you are well. I am well and my sister and family is completely wells. My teacher at school she say all the class will take english penpalls. please can you be my english penpall. The grades of my sister is good and I like to be good too.

How are you like Australia? Are there much kangaroos near your house? My mother she say *tío* Joe is sick. I am sorry *tío* Joe is sick.

If you can be my english penpall i am very happy,

Felicitations, Catalina xx

I could picture the Ufarte twins labouring over their homework at the kitchen table while Mama Ufarte stirred a saucepan behind them. It was late September so the weather would still be mild in the village of El Hoyo. Perhaps, later, the family would sit outside. There would be the smell of over-ripe grapes in the air from nearby vines, as unpicked fruit began to ferment. When the sky darkened, the hum of wasps would subside, and Papa Ufarte would sit on the doorstep, picking out chords on his guitar.

PURCHASES

I sighed. Was it only a month since we had left Spain?

So much had happened already. I now had a car that talked to me and knew when it was getting dark. I'd bought a house with a swimming pool in a district I'd never even heard of before. In a couple of months, I'd be moving up the coast. And we were expecting another grandchild.

Hopefully, Joe would be joining me soon.

Catalina's email had reminded me of what we'd left behind, but I didn't feel homesick. I had too much to look forward to.

I wrote back to Catalina telling her that I'd be absolutely delighted to be her penpal and sent my best regards to her parents and family. I couldn't resist also asking her a few questions about the village. Joe would probably say I was being a nosy parker, but I prefer to think that I was just exercising the linguistic skills of Ufarte Twin #1 (or was it #2?).

When we left Spain, we'd brought very little with us, deciding that we didn't know where we'd be living or whether our old furniture would fit. The cost, too, of shipping from Spain to Australia would have been enormous.

It was a little bit like getting married in the old

days. I began collecting stuff for our future home and soon the goods began to pile up in my lair. Karly and Cam had a bed they could lend me, but I had no sheets, pillows or bed linen of any kind.

During these shopping trips, I learned unexpected language differences, particularly in the field of bed linen.

"Can you tell me where your linen department is, please?" I asked once.

"Um, linen? What are you looking for, exactly?" asked the shop assistant, tilting her head to one side and raising one painted eyebrow.

"Well, a duvet, actually."

"Duvet?" Blank look.

"Yes, for the bed… Like a quilt, you know?"

"Oh! You mean a doona!"

"Do I?"

"Yes, I'm sure you do."

"And where would I find one?"

"In Manchester."

Now it was my turn to look completely baffled. Manchester, England seemed an unreasonably long journey to make in order to buy a duvet.

"Manchester?"

"At the back of the store, on your right."

The lady was right, of course. Under a big MANCHESTER sign were plenty of pillows, sheets, quilts and bedcovers to choose from.

PURCHASES

And doonas.

I am told that during the 18th and 19th centuries, Australian settlers had little success growing cotton crops. This meant that linen had to be imported. Much of it came from the northern cities of England, and wooden boxes and crates packed with cotton goods were stamped *Manchester*. The word stuck and came to mean table linen and bedding. Nowhere else in the world is that word used to describe cotton merchandise.

Soon I became the proud owner of a new set of saucepans, some wine glasses, a knife set, and all manner of kitchen utensils. Imagine starting from scratch at the age of sixty. It was great fun and thanks to stores like Kmart, it wasn't expensive.

I soon had an intimate knowledge of all the local shops. But there was one shop that I frequently walked past, but never entered. My head would turn, and my footsteps slowed to a stop as I stared in.

And what was displayed in the window of this particular shop which drew me like a magnet?

Puppies.

It was a pet shop.

STRAWBERRY SWIRL PAVLOVAS

Australians adore pavlovas, and family celebrations are rarely without one. This is a wonderfully easy variation from www.taste.com.au

Ingredients (makes 8)

250g (9oz) fresh strawberries, hulled, quartered

2 tablespoons caster sugar

150ml (5 floz) thickened cream

150g (5oz) mascarpone

1 teaspoon vanilla bean paste

8 meringue nests

Strawberries, extra, to decorate

Mint leaves, extra, to decorate

Method

Place quartered strawberries in a bowl. Sprinkle with 1 tablespoon caster sugar. Set aside for 30 mins or until they begin to release their juices.

Place strawberries in a food processor and process until coarsely chopped.

Place cream, mascarpone, vanilla bean paste and remaining sugar in a bowl. Use an electric beater to whip until soft peaks form.

Gently fold in the strawberries, being careful not to over-mix.

Arrange meringue nests on a serving platter.

Divide strawberry cream among the meringues and top with fresh strawberries and mint leaves.

4

A FRENZY AND PHONE CALLS

I was on the verge of moving into our forever home, and I felt that dog ownership was almost within my grasp.

I'd reluctantly dismissed the idea of adopting a rescue dog. This would be my first dog and I didn't feel confident enough to take on a dog with unknown traits or background.

Australian dog rescue centres are crammed with large breeds, most being staffie or pitbull crosses. I'd heard they can be excellent with small children but are not always good with other dogs. I didn't feel experienced enough to offer one a home.

I carried out a lot of research and already had an idea of the dog I wanted someday. I narrowed the type and traits down and created a wish list:

A FRENZY AND PHONE CALLS

- A dog that didn't moult would be excellent because of Joe's breathing problems and Indy's asthma.
- A reasonably small dog would be ideal because our new home wasn't very big.
- A breed that is known to be good with children, adults and other dogs would be perfect.
- A dog that enjoys walks and is easy to train would be nice.

It was a lot to ask.

The pet shop was scrupulously clean and always busy. Sometimes there were baby rabbits or guinea pigs in the window. Occasionally there were kittens or puppies, delightful little bundles that soon found homes.

Well, it wouldn't do any harm just to go in and wander around, would it?

I walked in, admiring the tanks of exotic fish and bright green stick insects.

A notice caught my eye.

We prefer not to display puppies for long because they can become distressed. However, if you are looking for a puppy, we may be able to help. We obtain our puppies from a handful of trusted breeders and never deal with puppy farms. If you would like more information, please ask.

"Can I help at all?" asked a voice beside me. "Were you interested in getting a puppy?"

"Oh! Um, not really, I was just looking… I mean, I would like a puppy, but I'm not ready to have one yet."

"What breed were you thinking of?"

"Well, we have asthma and breathing problems in the family so…"

"Ah, a poodle might suit you. They don't shed at all."

I couldn't quite picture Joe sharing a home with a poodle. I'm not sure why.

"I'd like a breed that is known to be good with children. I have a three-year-old granddaughter and another grandchild on the way."

The assistant nodded wisely.

"It would be my first dog, so a breed that is easy to train? And not too big and loves walks." I was thinking of how owning a dog might also benefit our health. Going out for daily walks would be good for both Joe and me.

"I think I know the perfect puppy breed for you," said the assistant brightly. "I think either a cavoodle or a spoodle would suit you perfectly."

"A what?"

"A cavoodle is a poodle crossed with a cavalier spaniel. Cavalier spaniels are very loving dogs. They were bred to be lap dogs for royalty."

I adore cavalier King Charles spaniels, but I

think they get a rough deal. The way they have been bred to make their eyes bulge means they are prone to eye problems and even epilepsy in later life. I feel the same about dogs who have been bred with short snouts. It might make them look super-cute, but it doesn't seem fair to breed dogs with deformities that can make them struggle to breathe.

"What's a spoodle?" I asked.

"You're English, aren't you? I believe they're called cockerpoos in England. Half poodle and half cocker spaniel. A very intelligent breed. They don't shed and are always ready for a walk."

She pulled out a picture from a drawer, and I was smitten.

"Funnily enough," she said, "we are expecting a litter of spoodles in about a month. Shall I take your phone number and contact you when they're ready?"

"So how's it going?"

"Fine. All the house paperwork is going through smoothly. It looks like the final exchange and moving date is going to be November 6th. I'm going up to see it again, a week before moving day, to walk around and check that everything is okay. That's the way they do it here. I can't wait, it's all so exciting!"

"And you've been collecting stuff for the house?"

"Yup. Cam is going to lend us a bed, and I've been gathering bits and pieces. I'm taking the sofa that's in my lair, and the desk. As soon as I move in, I'm going to look for tradies to get stuff done as quickly as possible. It would be terrific if work can begin before you arrive."

"Do you think there's much work to be done?"

"A little bit. Not too much, though."

As I type these words, I can't believe how naïve I was. Perhaps it was just as well that I didn't know what the future held.

"Gosh, I wish I was there to help you, Vicky."

"Concentrate on your health, Joe. That's the most important thing. Don't worry. I'll manage perfectly."

"Well, at least you didn't rush out and get a dog. I was afraid you were going to. If you had it would have made things even harder."

"Er, yes."

Moving day drew closer. I now had the plans of the house and spent hours poring over them, considering the best way to use the space

A FRENZY AND PHONE CALLS

available. I felt the two most significant drawbacks were the single bathroom and the tiny kitchen which was almost a kitchenette. Maybe we could build an extension, or knock a few walls down and reconfigure the layout.

"Have you seen the widescreen smart TVs they're offering at Aldi on Saturday?" asked Karly, interrupting my thoughts.

There was no doubt about it. The TVs were a bargain. We would need a TV, so perhaps I should buy one. But Aldi isn't an ordinary store. Their special deals change every week and bargains quickly sell out.

"We'll have to be there, ready and waiting, queueing before the shop opens," said Karly. "Deals like this get snapped up immediately. In fact, I suggest you and I go to our Aldi store, and Cam can go to one in a different district."

That Saturday, Karly, Indy and I sped towards the local mall, while Cam went to another.

We parked and joined the queue that was already forming at the store's entrance. We were third in line, so I felt we were safe. As the minutes ticked by, more people gathered, and by the time the manager approached to unlock the glass doors, quite a crowd had assembled.

As he jiggled his key into the lock, I felt the atmosphere change. The doors slid apart and the manager hastily stepped back as a horde of shoppers surged into the store, polite queue forgotten.

"Quick!" yelled Karly. "Make for the centre aisle!"

But the stampede was too much for me, and I was tossed aside as it raged through the store. Everybody wanted a widescreen smart TV.

"Excuse me!" my valiant daughter cried, knuckles white on the trolley, elbows at right angles as she forged ahead.

"Skooze meee!" echoed Indy, standing in the prow of the shopping trolley, like Rose in the film *Titanic*, her hair flowing behind.

I arrived at the flatscreen TV display just after my daughter and granddaughter did. Where a mountain of TV boxes had once existed, now only one remained, and a man was already reaching for it. I shouted the first thing that came into my head.

"Look out! Pregnant lady!"

It was just enough to make the man hesitate for a second, allowing Karly to grab the heavy box.

"My mummy has a baby in her tummy and it's called Dragon," Indy informed the man, as we attempted to manhandle it onto the trolley.

He rolled his eyes and walked away, defeated.

The box was enormous and wouldn't fit in the trolley, so progress was slow to the checkout.

A FRENZY AND PHONE CALLS

"My mummy has a baby in her tummy," Indy told everybody in the queue.

The fellow customers who could see over their widescreen TV boxes smiled at her.

"My mummy's baby is called Dragon," Indy told the checkout girl.

Somehow we managed to wrestle the TV out without crippling too many people, and reached the car. Our next problem was getting it into the vehicle. It soon became apparent that it was never going to fit.

As we took a breath to plan our next move, our phones rang simultaneously.

I didn't recognise the number that flicked up on mine, so ignored it. Meanwhile, Cam was ringing Karly.

"Sorry," he said, "I got there before they opened, but I couldn't reach the TVs in time. Seriously, it was crazy! As soon as the doors opened, it was like a feeding frenzy."

"I know, it was the same here! I managed to grab the last one but we can't get it into the car. We've tried all sorts of ways and it just won't fit."

"Okay, on my way."

As we waited for Cam to arrive in his ute, I checked who had phoned me. Whoever it was had left me a message. I held the phone up to my ear and listened.

"Hello, this is June from the pet shop. Our spoodle breeder has just informed us that the litter will be ready next week. Can you please ring back and confirm that you still want a golden female? If it's too early for you, we can put you down for one from the next litter, early in the new year."

My heart raced. Next week?

I wasn't moving into our house for another two weeks. It would make no sense to get a puppy yet. Besides, it would be very unfair to ask Karly and Cam if I could bring a new puppy into their home. And what would LJ, their huge husky/staffie mix, think of a puppy in his domain? Would he harm it? And what would Bandsaw, the cat, make of a pup?

And Joe?

I knew exactly what his advice would be...

I struggled with these thoughts but, for the moment, kept them to myself.

Cam arrived and lifted the TV onto his ute as though it was a feather. He strapped it securely and we followed him home.

"You're quiet," observed Karly.

"Um, yes. I just listened to a message from the pet shop. The spoodle puppy is ready to collect next week. I just wondered if you'd mind me bringing her back to your house for the two weeks before I move."

A FRENZY AND PHONE CALLS

Karly hardly hesitated.

"I can't see a problem with that. We'll have to check with Cam, of course."

"Okay with me," said Cam later, smiling.

I could have hugged them. Instead, I rushed away and called the pet shop.

I'd already spent a lot of time researching how to look after and train a puppy. Now that the big day was just a week away, my research intensified. I have a lot of respect for the RSPCA and appreciated any advice they gave. Crate training soon came to my notice.

Although many Australians have never heard of it, crate training is popular in the UK and the US. I decided it was the way to go and it was probably the best decision I could have made.

I made lots of doggy purchases but the most important item was a crate. I made sure it was large enough to allow for my puppy to grow. The RSPCA site clearly explained how a crate is intended to provide a haven for a dog. By nature, dogs feel secure in small, enclosed spaces. A mother dog will hide her pups in a hole or den while she goes hunting. The pups will feel safe in the den and sleep until she returns.

Apparently, if carried out properly, crate

training would help my new pup to become toilet trained. It would also give it security if I had to go out and provide a retreat where it could escape for peace and quiet.

It all made sense to me and sounded quite easy. I couldn't wait to get started.

Joe and I had chatted for a while about the move, but I didn't broach the other subject occupying my mind.

"So, how's it all going?" he asked. "All set for the move?"

"I think so. The TV we got was a bargain. And I bought a big crate today, too."

"Crate?"

"Um, a crate for packing."

"What, a wooden one?"

I'm hopeless at telling lies. I tie myself up in knots and always get caught out in the end. So I took a deep breath.

"Well, no. It's a big, plastic one. And it's not for packing."

"What's it for, then?"

So I told him about the puppy.

There was a long pause. I waited, holding my breath.

A FRENZY AND PHONE CALLS

"A what? A cockerpoo? What on earth is that? A cross between a cockatoo and a...poo?"

But at least Joe was only questioning the breed. He wasn't putting his foot down and demanding that I cancel the collection of the pup.

"You're not furious?"

"No, what would be the point? I absolutely knew you were going to get a puppy. I'm just surprised it took you so long."

It seems Joe knows me better than I know myself.

I had a crate. I had food and water bowls. I had a frisbee, balls and dog toys, including a plush platypus with soft eggs in its pouch. I had dog treats and dog chews. I had puppy training pads. I had puppy shampoo and special ear-cleaning liquid.

I had everything except a dog.

And that was about to change.

On Monday morning my phone rang again and this time I recognised the number.

"Hi, June here again. Just to let you know your puppy has arrived and you can pick her up as soon as you're ready."

EASY SALMON MOUSSE

Serve on crackers, little toasts, or even cucumber slices. Super-easy to make in advance and can be stored in an airtight container in the fridge.

Ingredients

1 large pack of Philadelphia cream cheese

250g or 8oz sour cream

1 stick celery

2 spring onions, finely chopped

Ground pepper

2 x 220g tins or 8oz tinned red salmon

Juice of 1 lemon

¾ tablespoon gelatine, softened

Method

Beat cheese and cream together until fluffy. Add finely chopped vegetables.

Fold in salmon and lemon juice.

Blend in gelatine.

Pour into mould and refrigerate overnight.

5

LOLA AND COLD FEET

June, the manager of the pet shop, recognised me as soon as I arrived and showed me into the office.

"I expect you'd like to see her before we embark on the paperwork," she said.

On the floor, lined with newspaper, was a wooden playpen. Even before I saw the tiny puppies, I heard squeaks.

"There are three in the litter," she said, "all girls. The two brown and white ones, fast asleep in the far corner, are already sold, too. Yours is the gold one trying to escape."

My puppy was the one that was squeaking, standing on her stubby little hind legs, trying to scrabble up the bars of the playpen.

"Oh my, she's just *gorgeous*..." I said and felt my eyes misting over.

"Any idea what you're going to call her?" asked June.

I had thought of all manner of names over the past month. I'd made long lists of possibilities, then shortlists, staring at them for ages but not really liking any.

Never mind, I had thought, *I'll wait until I actually meet the puppy. Maybe a name will occur to me then.*

"No, I haven't decided yet."

And then, as I gazed at this beautiful young creature, it came to me like a bolt of lightning. The perfect name.

This puppy was breathtakingly beautiful, and golden, and naughty. I knew somebody else with those identical qualities. Lola Ufarte. Our wayward young neighbour in the Spanish mountain village we had left behind. Now this little pup would always remind me of Spain and the wonderful years we spent in El Hoyo.

"Actually, I think I will name her Lola," I said.

"Good name," said June, and we began the lengthy paperwork.

After I'd signed numerous papers and was given others to take with me, including records of her microchip number and an appointment for a puppy check with the local vet, I left, cradling Lola against my chest. She was soaking wet, having just waded through the puppies' water bowl.

"She's tiny!" said Karly when we got home.

Of course Indy wanted to play with her but we explained that Lola needed a few days to settle in first. LJ sniffed her all over and appeared to decide she wasn't worth wasting his time. Bandsaw growled, her tabby fur standing on end, but she seemed to know that Lola was too young and silly to be any threat.

I'd been warned that taking on a puppy was similar to caring for a newborn baby. I hadn't really believed that but soon discovered it was true. Puppies are extremely hard work.

For the first two days Lola cried a lot, which broke my heart. She only stopped when I cuddled her. I got nothing done and worried that I might be spoiling her. But slowly she began to adjust and settle.

The vet pronounced her bouncing with health, and I started her crate training, another challenge.

I began by making the crate an attractive place by putting in soft bedding, a cuddly toy, and an occasional treat. I didn't close the door and she entered the crate by herself when she was tired. After a few days, I could play with her, feed her, take her outside to relieve herself, then pop her in the crate to sleep. As her crate time increased, I was able to get some writing done and was even able to shoot off to the shops.

Now, as I look at her first collar, I find it hard to believe she was ever so small. She had hardly any neck, just rolls of fat. Her tail and legs were mere stubs and her coat was short and dark gold. But every day she grew.

We spent nearly all our time together. At night, Lola slept in her crate in my lair. I knew that allowing her to sleep on my bed, or even in my bedroom, would be a mistake because Joe would never approve. But I set my alarm to take her to the toilet twice during the night. She stumbled out of the crate, went outside, then snuggled back down without a murmur. Her training was going pretty well.

A week before the day of the move, I left Lola behind and drove up the coast to take a final look at the house and make sure all was in order. I met the estate agent outside, and he unlocked the front door.

"The present owners are out at the moment," he said, but his eyes didn't quite meet mine.

I knew they were young men and was

prepared to make allowances. Even so, I was shocked at the scene that met my eyes.

Junk was piled in the living room, waist-high. Black garbage bags spewed clothes over a jumble of fishing rods and tackle. Cardboard boxes barely contained the audio equipment and vinyl records stuffed into them.

It was clear that the house had been cleverly, probably professionally, styled the day of the sale. Now that the tasteful furniture and extravagant vases of flowers had disappeared, things looked very different.

Chipped floor tiles were no longer hidden. Window blinds, tied up and out of sight for the viewing, now hung broken. Loose cables spilled out from untidy holes in the walls. There was an underlying smell of cigarette smoke and animal urine, and I noticed that most of the interior doors were gouged, as though by claws. And how had I missed the disgusting stained and threadbare bedroom carpets?

Outside there were piles of dog faeces, buzzing with flies. And it seemed I had overlooked the window frames that had been crudely spray-painted without first masking the surrounding brickwork. The pool water was green, with leaves and debris floating in dirty islands. In the few short weeks since I'd seen the house, masses of weeds had sprung through the cracks of the brick paths.

There were even shocks in store for me in the garage. Somebody had fed hose pipes, to supply water through the hatch into the loft, and had set up lights in the cramped roof space. Even I could see that something very odd had been going on here.

"Everything okay?" asked the estate agent after I'd finished my inspection. "Seen enough?"

No, everything *wasn't* okay, and yes, I *had* seen enough. But I was too shocked to voice my emotions. I'd been an idiot. I shouldn't have rushed into it. I knew it was too late, so I nodded dumbly and crept back into the sanctuary of my car.

I cried all the way back to Sydney.

I couldn't bring myself to tell Joe just how ghastly the house was. After all, he had enough on his plate with his health. He'd trusted me to find us the right home, and I'd let him down.

At first, I said nothing to Karly and Cam. Then I finally admitted that I was convinced I had made a terrible mistake.

"The house is awful. I've been an idiot. I can't

believe I was so stupid to rush into such a ridiculous purchase."

"Now just a minute," said Cam, always able to think clearly in a crisis. "You had a budget, didn't you?"

"Yes."

"Well, according to my calculations, you got the house pretty cheap. If you spend the rest of the budget fixing it up, you'll end up with a beautiful house."

"Exactly the way you want it," agreed Karly.

"But you should have seen it! It was disgusting! I can't expect Joe to move into that!"

"We'll bring loads of cleaning stuff on the day of the move. We'll make it habitable, and you can start bringing in tradies to sort it out as quickly as possible. You can get a lot done before he gets here."

"Do you really think so?"

"Definitely!" they chorused.

"There is nothing about that house that can't be easily fixed," said Cam. "Honestly, as we discussed before, Aussie homes are shells. You can knock down walls or change things as much as you want. When the house is finished, it'll be worth a lot of money. It'll be like brand new and built to your personal specifications."

"You like the area, don't you?" asked Karly.

"Yes! I love it."

"Well, there you are then. No problems."

The more I thought about it, the more I realised they were right.

My spirits lifted.

Lola's crate training progressed quite well, although the toilet training was a bit more miss than hit. After she had napped, or finished playing, I took her outside and praised her when she performed. However, there were still plenty of times when I'd find puddles on the wood floor. But she never soiled her crate. I tried as much as possible to keep to my lair in case she disgraced herself on a carpet in the house.

Indy often joined us while her mum was busy or preparing dinner. I had a special cupboard for Indy's toys, but Lola was her favourite playmate. Many a time I would laugh because Indy was inside the crate and Lola was on the outside, wagging her tail so fast it was just a blur.

"Would you mind looking after Indy for an hour or so? I want to bake the reveal cake for tonight," said Karly one day.

"Of course!"

Reveal cake? I'd never heard of a reveal cake and I'm pretty sure they didn't exist when I was giving birth to babies. When it was explained, I understood why we didn't have reveal cakes in our day.

I knew Karly and Cam had gone to the hospital for a scan and they had returned, hand in hand, bursting with excitement. They had immediately phoned to invite Cam's parents and grandmother to dinner that evening.

"Everything go okay at the hospital?" I asked, although I could tell by their expressions that all was well.

"Yup! Cam and I know whether Indy is going to have a baby brother or sister. The hospital told us today!"

"Really? Wow!" I squeaked. "What are you having?"

"Not telling! When we cut into the cake tonight, it'll be either blue or pink inside. That's a reveal cake!"

"I'm going to be a big sister," Indy told Lola. "My mummy's got a baby in her tummy and it's called Dragon."

Lola licked her and they played their favourite game together. Indy pretended to be a puppy and the pair of them romped. Then Indy crawled into the crate, closely followed by Lola. There they flopped down together, resting, before springing back into life and more games.

Dinner that night was a happy affair. Indy wore one of her favourite princess costumes and both grandmothers, and great grandmother were ordered to wear tiaras.

Karly is a fabulous cook but I don't remember what she served that evening. However, I do remember that most of us couldn't resist glancing furtively at the splendid cake on the sideboard.

GENDER REVEAL CAKE

Three layers of moist, delicious vanilla cake dyed with food colouring, and frosted with easy, creamy vanilla buttercream. From prettysweetsimple.com

Ingredients

Cake

3 cups (15oz) plain (all-purpose) flour

1 tablespoon baking powder

½ teaspoon salt

1 cup (8oz) unsalted butter, softened

¼ cup (2floz) canola or vegetable oil

2 cups (14oz) granulated sugar

4 large eggs

1 tablespoon pure vanilla extract

1¾ cups (14floz) whole milk

Vanilla Buttercream Frosting

1½ cups (12oz) unsalted butter, softened

⅛ teaspoon salt

5 cups (22oz) powdered (icing) sugar, sifted, plus more as needed

5 tablespoons (2½floz) heavy (thickened) cream

1 tablespoon pure vanilla extract

Method

Preheat oven to 350°F/180°C. Butter three 9-inch (22 cm) cake pans, and line the bottoms with parchment paper.

Cake: In a medium bowl, sift together flour, baking powder, and salt. Set aside.

In the bowl of an electric mixer fitted with the paddle attachment, beat butter, oil, and sugar on medium speed until light and fluffy, 3-4 minutes. Scrape down the sides and bottom of the bowl as needed.

Add eggs, one at a time, beating well after each addition.

Beat in vanilla extract. With the mixer on low speed, add the flour mixture in three additions alternating with the milk in two additions, beginning and ending with the flour mixture. Do not over-mix the batter. The less you mix, the lighter the cake will be.

Divide the batter as evenly as possible into three bowls. Add food colouring to each bowl until desired colour is reached. Add just a tiny drop at first because food colourings can be very concentrated.

Pour each bowl of batter into prepared pans.

Bake for 25-30 minutes until a toothpick inserted into the centre of the cakes comes out clean.

Allow cakes to cool for 15 minutes, then gently remove from pans and allow them to cool completely on a wire rack.

Frosting: In the bowl of an electric mixer fitted with the paddle or whisk attachment, beat butter and salt on medium speed until smooth and creamy, about 2 minutes.

Add 5 cups icing sugar, heavy cream, and vanilla. Beat on low speed for 30 seconds, then increase speed to high and beat for 2 minutes. Beat in more powdered sugar if frosting is too thin.

Assembly: If the cakes have risen too much, cut their rounded tops off with a knife to make them flat. Set one cake layer on a plate or cake stand. Evenly spread a thick layer of the frosting over the cake to the edge. Top with the second cake layer and spread a thick layer of the frosting. Finish with the third cake layer. Spread frosting over the top and sides of the cake.

Store cake in the fridge, but bring it to room temperature before serving.

The cake can be made a day in advance.

6

MOVING

At last it was time for dessert — time to cut the cake.

"I think Princess Indy should do the honours," said Karly, and we all agreed.

Cam carried the cake from the sideboard and placed it on the table in front of an empty chair. All eyes were on Indy as she climbed up and knelt on the chair. Her hands were too small to manage the cake slice but, with help from her mum, the cake was cut. We all held our breaths.

A few crumbs fell out and we gasped. The inside of the cake was pink.

"A girl!"

"A little sister!"

"Indy, you're going to have a baby sister!"

Indy, caught up in the excitement, stood on her chair.

"My mummy's got a baby in her tummy and she's called Dragon!" she shouted to the world. "And she's my sister!"

Days passed, and Lola and I continued to enjoy each other. I took her to play in the chicken garden where the hens towered over her. Nervous of them at first, she learned to ignore them.

One day she found her bark and life was never quite so peaceful again. She also discovered the joys of fetching a ball, a passion she has never lost.

I needed to buy a set of essential tools and Cam had suggested I should also buy bug bombs which would kill any insects in the empty house. Bunnings, a vast Australian chain of DIY stores, stocked everything I needed. Bunnings allowed dogs in their stores provided they are carried or ride in a trolley. So I took Lola with us.

"Where's the rest of it?" asked a burly assistant, peering down at her. "Is that all there is?"

Lola wagged her stubby little tail and earned herself a smile and a pat.

"My mummy's got a baby in her tummy and she's called Dragon," Indy told him.

"Not me," I said hurriedly, "her mum is over there."

It was a good thing that her parents weren't trying to keep the baby news a secret because Indy told everybody. She informed the postman, the girl at the bakery, the cleaner in the mall, the waitress, complete strangers on the street, and all the staff of Bunnings. She told the street cleaner and the man who read the meter. She even told the wallabies in the park.

"Hey, wobblies! Guys! My mummy has a baby in her tummy and her name's Dragon."

The wallabies stared at her for a moment, then hopped away.

At the beach, anybody who would listen was told, and even the seagulls were informed.

"Hey, sea-girls! Guys! My mummy has a baby in her tummy and her name's Dragon."

At that age, Indy had a particularly clear voice that rang out, and her announcements and questions often embarrassed her mother.

On one occasion, the pair were standing in a queue at a cafe counter, waiting to be served. A man passed by, wearing the typical neon tradie shirt that all tradies, including her builder daddy, wear.

"Is that my daddy?" she asked, her voice clear and shrill.

"No, Indy, that's not your daddy," said Karly smiling.

Another man appeared some distance away, also wearing a lime green tradie shirt, but otherwise looking nothing like Cam.

"Is that my daddy?" she asked loudly, pointing.

"No, Indy, of course not!"

A third man entered the cafe, and Indy sang out again.

"Is *that* one my daddy?"

Karly knew Indy was being silly and she was beginning to tire of being stared at by everybody in the cafe.

"Indy, you know perfectly well who your daddy is," she hissed.

A man in the queue in front of them half-turned.

"As long as *you* do, love," he said, grinning.

"Good luck for tomorrow," Joe had said. "How does it all work?"

"Well, my solicitor will phone me to say that the money has arrived with the vendor's solicitor, then I go to the house and collect the keys from the estate agent."

"Wish I was there to help."

"Don't worry. I'll be fine. I'm only driving up and collecting the keys and letting off the bug bombs I told you about. Then, on Saturday, I'll have Karly and Cam with me. I'll load up the car with as much as I can carry, and Lola of course, and they'll bring the ute with the bed, mattress and other stuff."

"It seems strange to think that just as I'm going to bed, you're doing all this stuff on the other side of the world."

"Relax. Sleep well, I'm sure it'll go smoothly."

Hola tía Vicky y tío Joe,
Thank you to be my english penpall. My teacher she say she will surprise if my english will become better. I am well and my sister and family is completely wells but Pollito my little brother he say he does not like school and learning english is stupid.
Here the weather is very cold but we do not have snow. I want have snow because it is fun to have snow.

My *tía* Lola has a big diamond ring from father Samuel and they will marrys next year. Mama says it will be a very little weeding civil down in the city not like the weeding of Sofía and Antonio in the village. I will buy a new dress and my sister will buy a new dress but my brothers they say they don't want to go to the weeding but my Mama she say they are not permitted to not go. I am sorry we are not dance flamenco in the weeding civil but my Mama she say we can dance flamenco in the village later.

My teacher she say there are very much kangaroos in Australia so why they not coming to your house?

Please sending me picture of koala near your house.

We do not very much see the lady and man they are living in your house. At Christmas we will come to the village and perhaps we will see them. I will say you.

We remember when *tío* Joe say that there are sabre-toth tiger in the woods by the village. Please tell *tío* Joe we know there are not sabre-toth tiger in the woods by the village but we tell my little brother Pollito there are sabre-toth tiger in the woods by the village.

Felicitations, Catalina xx

MOVING

Moving day dawned with clear summer skies. Just as I'd been instructed, the solicitor phoned to say everything was in place and the estate agent would meet me at the house to hand over the keys.

Lola and I arrived and the scene that greeted me filled me with dismay.

All manner of vehicles were parked in front of the house and on the grass. People milled around and piles of boxes, furniture, and black garbage bags were heaped on the drive. Two giant mastiffs were tethered to a ute. One napped while the other lifted his giant head and barked at anyone who came too close. He was so big, he could have inhaled Lola and not even noticed.

The vendors were nowhere near ready.

The estate agent sprung out of a parked car and stuck his head through my car window.

"I'm very sorry but my clients aren't quite ready to leave."

"I can see that."

"Perhaps you could come back in a couple of hours?"

It was very inconvenient because I couldn't use the time to take Lola for a walk or explore the beaches. She hadn't finished her course of puppy injections and wasn't allowed in public places yet. I would have to sit in the car and wait.

We discussed the problem and he offered to detonate my bug bombs when the vendors left. As we talked, I watched the vendors over his shoulder and made a mental note to buy gallons of disinfectant and bleach before Saturday. He gave me a set of keys and I was free to drive back to Sydney. Even though I was the owner of the house, I still couldn't enter.

On Saturday, I returned in convoy with Cam and Karly and a bizarre thing happened.

The street was quiet when we arrived but, as soon as I put the key in the lock of our door, numerous *other* front doors opened. Faces peeped out, heads appeared and then people strolled towards us with big grins on their faces. It was like a massive welcoming committee.

"We live opposite," said one couple. "Welcome! We are *so delighted* the old owners have gone, they were *dreadful*."

"We couldn't walk past the house because their terrible big dogs were always loose," said an older lady wearing a white hat. I detected a German accent. "You are very welcome to the street. My name is Thea, and this is Nixi."

I looked down and smiled. Nixi was a small, tubby Jack Russell, with a permanently smiling face. She wagged her tail then rolled over for tummy rubs.

"Perhaps we can walk together when my puppy, Lola, has had her injections," I said to Thea, smiling.

"We used to call it the duff-duff house," said another neighbour.

"Duff-duff?"

"Yes, on account of the music. The double-bass, *duff-duff*. Used to go on all through the night."

"The lads were quite nice when they weren't high," said my next-door neighbour. "But that wasn't very often."

"He had his girlfriend there, and her baby. They used to have terrible rows. Once he came running out in the middle of the night, shouting at the top of his voice. He got into his car, then rammed her car over and over again in the drive."

"There were people coming and going all hours of the day and night."

"We reckon they were dealers."

"Why else would they have cameras set up everywhere?"

"And lights in the roof space."

"And the dogs! They kept having litters of puppies and selling them. I heard dead puppies were found in the pool."

"Oh no!" I was aghast.

And so it went on. Yes, it was a kind of welcoming committee, but only because the neighbourhood was so heartily relieved that the troublesome former residents had finally moved away.

But it was nice to introduce ourselves and meet some of the neighbours, whatever the reason for them turning out *en masse*.

The house, as I expected, was filthy, but the bug bombs had done their business and dead cockroaches, spiders and insects littered the floor. We set to work with brooms and bleach. I disinfected every light switch and door handle and discovered that many were loose or didn't work.

Karly tackled the bathroom. She did her best, but the bath had cigarette burns along its edge, and the grime on the tiles was so ingrained that they wouldn't scrub clean.

Meanwhile, I set to work in the 'kitchen', which was yet another disaster area. The oven and hob did not work at all, but there was a microwave. Several drawers wouldn't open. Cupboard doors hung from a single hinge or had no handles. There was no fridge, or even space for one, and the tap in the sink dripped constantly.

Nevertheless, by the time Karly and Cam left that evening, the house was habitable. Just about.

Cam had kindly concentrated on one bedroom, the one with the least disgusting carpet. He'd put up the bed, ensuring I had somewhere to sleep. Lola was already fast asleep in her crate. Worn out, I prepared for bed.

It was my first night in our new house.

I pulled the cord to shut the wooden window blinds and, to my horror, they came crashing down. The room was filled with clouds of dust that settled on everything. Dead insects covered the windowsill, my clean bed, and the floor.

Coughing and sneezing, I cleaned up the mess and finally climbed into bed. When I switched off the bedside lamp, I discovered that my next-door neighbours had a fondness for multi-coloured flashing garden lights. Having no window shades, these illuminated my bedroom all night long. Even with my eyes closed, the flickering lights seemed to pierce my eyelids and nearly drove me crazy. That night I slept with my head under the pillow.

In the morning, I started making a list of jobs labelling them either VU, QU or just U. (Very Urgent, Quite Urgent or just Urgent.) The length of the list was terrifying. Then I sat down with my phone, and a copy of the Yellow Pages, and began work.

First, I called the local vet to make an appointment for Lola's next injections and enrol her in Puppy School. Not a moment too soon as she was getting naughtier by the day. Paper, cardboard, and even plastic were not safe from her shredding puppy teeth.

I was just beginning on a list of builders to call when I heard a car draw up outside, footsteps approached and my front door flew open.

I don't know who was the more surprised, me, Lola or the enormous bald man covered in tattoos who had just crashed into my house.

"Oh! Has the house changed hands?" my uninvited visitor shouted over Lola's welcoming yaps, as she tried to scrabble up his tattooed leg.

"Yes!"

The visitor looked shocked, and I could hardly blame him. The previous, nocturnal, drug-dealing occupants, with their colossal dogs couldn't be more different to me, an elderly lady with a cute, fluffy puppy.

"Sorry!" he said, eyes wide, and he backed away out of the house.

Unfortunately, Lola ran out with him. Thus began an embarrassing sequence of events: me calling Lola, she ignoring me, and all three of us running up and down the street like idiots. I finally grabbed her in an unladylike rugby tackle while Tattooed Man's mates in the rusty parked car watched in amusement.

Returning to the house, I edited my list. 'Locksmith - change locks' was moved from Urgent to Very Urgent. Who knew how many people had keys? I wanted no more unexpected visitors.

Now it was November and temperatures soared. Christmas decorations appeared in all the shopping malls and I was struggling to find builders. I had the same conversation with many.

"Sorry, since that hail storm in September, we're completely booked up for months. We couldn't even *look* at your job until maybe July next year."

July? I wanted the work started before Joe arrived in January.

But it was not to be.

In September, monstrous hailstones had hammered down, leaving 1,200 homes without power and hundreds of homes without roofs, including the local shopping centre. The ceiling had partially collapsed and everyone had to be evacuated. The event made national news and aerial views showed the area cloaked in white, as though by snow.

My house was one of only a couple in our street that wasn't damaged. I had to face it; finding a builder was going to be almost impossible.

Or was it?

Being new to the area, I knew nobody, so I was forced to rely on my instincts. An advert in the local paper caught my eye.

All building work and renovations undertaken.

I phoned the number supplied and spoke to Fred for the first time.

TERIYAKI STEAKS

Asian food of all kinds is extremely popular in Australia. Teriyaki is a Japanese marinade, quite similar to Chinese sweet and sour sauce.

Ingredients (serves 6)

6 pieces rib eye steak

⅓ cup soy sauce

¼ cup red wine

2 cloves garlic, crushed

2 teaspoons grated ginger

2 tablespoons brown sugar

1 tablespoon barbecue sauce

Method

Marinate steaks in soy sauce, wine, garlic, ginger, brown sugar and barbecue sauce for several hours or refrigerate, covered, overnight.

Drain steaks and barbecue or grill on both sides until cooked to your liking.

7

TRADIES

Fred sounded like a decent chap on the phone and very Australian. He explained that he had been a builder in Sydney, but had just moved to the Central Coast and was in the process of setting up his business again. He agreed to inspect the job and give me a quote.

I'd already invited three other builders, but two hadn't turned up, and the third was so young I feared he might need help with his school homework.

Fred promised to come round the following week, but Friday passed without a sign of him. However, he did call and apologise, which was a point in his favour.

"I had a bit of an emergency," he explained.

"Oh, I'm sorry to hear that."

"My house was flooded."

"Oh, right. Plumbing problems."

"Not really, the seal broke on one of my breeding aquariums. Water everywhere and I had to mop it up and sort out a new home for my fish."

"Is everything okay now?"

"I think so, thank you. Dwarf cichlids are fussy blighters so it wasn't easy. They like their water soft and slightly acidic. Sometimes you have to try mimicking the coming of the rainy season with a cool and soft water change."

He'd lost me. I didn't even know what a dwarf cichlid was.

Listening to him on the phone, I imagined Fred to be a large man, perhaps in his mid-thirties, possibly with tattoos, and probably a rugby player. Eventually I would discover I was wrong on all counts.

Around that time, I had an army of tradesmen coming to the door to give me quotes for various jobs. Lola welcomed them all like long-lost friends. They generally tolerated her enthusiasm, but sometimes her unruly behaviour made life difficult for me. I distinctly remember a lady, smartly dressed in a pencil skirt and high heels who arrived to give me a quote for window blinds.

"Would you mind keeping your dog under

control?" she asked politely. She was smiling pleasantly but the smile never quite reached her eyes. "This is a very exacting job and I need to be as accurate as possible."

With that, she produced a pink retractable tape-measure as a signal that she was ready to begin.

"Of course! I'm so sorry, she's just a few months old and hasn't learned any manners yet. I'll shut her in the laundry."

Lola did not accept her banishment lightly. She yapped and scratched the door so loudly that the lady had to shout to make herself heard.

"This is ridiculous!" I said, and reluctantly let Lola back in.

Lola struggled against my grip on her collar, eager to reach the lady and cover her with a thousand unwanted wet licks. The lady continued to talk and take measurements but unfortunately, just for the merest millisecond, I was distracted and loosened my hold on the straining puppy. Lola bounded joyfully over to our visitor, firmly believing she was desperate for another exuberant puppy welcome.

"Ouch!" said the lady as Lola's sharp little claws raked her bare legs.

"I'm so sorry!" I cried and grabbed Lola, but not before she had completely disgraced herself.

In her excitement, Lola lost control. The lady's

white high heels were now standing in a yellow puddle.

"That bloody thing has peed all over my shoes!" she shrieked, all attempts at politeness abandoned.

"I'm so sorry," I gasped, grabbing Lola.

But it was too late. Not only had Lola soaked the lady's shoes, but the puddle had seeped to the samples book laid out on the floor. Even the pink tape-measure hadn't escaped.

"I'm so sorry…" I started to say again, but the lady was taking herself, her wet shoes, her dripping samples book, and pink tape-measure, out of the door.

I didn't blame her.

I told Lola her behaviour had been absolutely appalling and hoped that the lady's pink tape-measure would dry sufficiently to run smoothly again soon.

I didn't invite the lady back and neither did she contact me.

I had learned a lesson: whoever I employed had to accept Lola as part of the deal.

Most tradesmen passed with flying colours, as far as Lola was concerned.

I remember one chap who came to give me a quote for an innovative method of capturing solar energy. His name was Sam and he had an engaging manner. Lola gave him her usual frantic welcome which he accepted, smiling. I offered him a cup of tea, and we sat at the table as he showed me leaflets and talked me through various facts and figures.

After a short while, he shook his head and packed up his paperwork.

"Nope," he said, "I don't think our company can help you. We're geared up for more industrial-type premises. But I'll enjoy this cup of tea with you and Lola, anyway."

A tiny spider walked across the table and he squashed it with one finger.

"Oh, poor thing," I said, "it was just a small one."

"You haven't been in Australia long, have you?" he asked, looking at me sideways.

"Well, no. Just a couple of months, really…"

"Let me tell you, you need to be careful. Take my mum, for instance. She was pegging out her washing, and a white-tailed spider dropped down on her from above and got inside her shirt. She felt something and patted it, and it bit her in the small of her back."

"You are kidding!"

"No, white-tailed spider bites can be really nasty. Anyway, the wound swelled up and festered, and she had to go to the hospital to get it gouged out and cleaned."

"Oh no!"

"Three years later she's still suffering. The wound won't heal, and numerous hospital visits haven't helped. Have you been to the beach yet?"

"Yes, but not to swim. I haven't been here long."

"Take my word for it, swim *only* between the red and yellow flags."

"Right."

"Australian currents are crazy. Have you heard of rips?"

"Yes, but I'm not sure what they are."

"Rip currents can form when waves break near the shoreline. The water piles up between the breaking waves and a narrow stream of water, like a river, can move swiftly away from the shore. It can whip your legs away from under you and drag you out, even if you are only standing knee-high in the water."

My mouth dropped open.

"Seriously. The ocean is a very dangerous place. A couple of years ago, I was out in a boat with some of my mates. We were fishing for lobster. As we were pulling up the pots, a school of humpback whales swam past."

"How wonderful!"

"Yes, they're a common sight around here, but I never get bored with them. Well, I happened to have my underwater camera with me, so I dived into the water to try and get some pictures. Never again."

"Sharks?"

"Nope. Although it could have been. I didn't know then that Great Whites follow the humpbacks, picking off calves, or old, or sick humpbacks."

"So what happened?"

"I had no idea just how fierce the currents were. I did some underwater filming, then looked up and saw I'd drifted quite a long way from the boat. And I was still travelling. I shouted to my mates, telling them I was in trouble. They didn't notice at first. When they did, they sprang into action straight away, but it takes a good five minutes to pull up the anchor with that kind of boat."

"And you were still drifting?"

"Yup! One of my mates just stood in the boat, never taking his eyes off me as I drifted further and further away. I don't mind telling you, I was crying with fright. I thought I was going to die. By the time they weighed anchor and turned the boat round to pick me up, I was probably a kilometre away, and I was more scared than I'd ever been. I was exhausted by the time they reached me. It was a close thing."

Lola gave a little snore under the table and Sam checked his watch.

"Is that the time? I must go! It's been a pleasure chatting and thank you for the tea. I hope you settle in quickly and sorry if I've been rabbiting on."

"No, you haven't! It's been fascinating, thank you, and you've taught me a lot!"

I vowed never to swim anywhere except between the flags. In fact, the talk of sharks and currents made me doubt I'd ever swim in the ocean fearlessly again. I reminded myself that we had our own swimming pool now.

The problem was, the pool was becoming a darker green by the day and definitely wasn't the place to enjoy a swim. It was beginning to resemble spinach soup.

Australian law stipulates that pools must be enclosed by a fence. Mine was, although the metal railings were horribly rusty. However, on my first day at the house, I discovered something very worrying.

Lola was small enough to slip between the railings.

And she did.

The first time it happened, I didn't notice what she had done. What alerted me was hearing a small wet *plop* coming from the pool.

To my absolute horror, I saw Lola had fallen in. A split second later I was at the pool's edge, grabbing her by her fur and rolls of fat. She was underwater, but I had her out in a trice.

"You could have drowned!" I scolded her, and set her down.

Not bothered in the slightest, she launched herself back into the pool.

That day I learned that Lola was a water dog. She added swimming to her list of passions along with tennis balls, visitors, shredding things, and digging.

So we made another trip to Bunnings to buy plastic mesh. I tied it to the pool fence to stop Lola slipping through and swimming without supervision.

By the beginning of December, the weather was hot, but I couldn't cool down in the pool, it was just too dirty.

I knew nothing about swimming pools or their upkeep. The pool had looked wonderful on the day of the house sale, and I was sure I could restore it to its former glory.

I called a pool company for help. Two men promptly turned up and didn't seem too shocked by the murky, green water that looked fit for nothing but hippos. After Lola had finished welcoming them, and stopped trying to scrabble up their legs, they delivered their verdict.

"We can fix the pool and you'll be swimming in it in a week," said one.

"But I'm afraid your pump has seen better days and needs replacing," said the other.

"And your chlorinator doesn't work. You'll have to buy a new one or keep adding chlorine manually every day."

"Honestly," I said to Joe that evening, "I don't believe *anything* works in this house."

Then I reminded myself that my problems were tiny compared with his. I may not have had a working kitchen, or bathroom, and the pool may look as inviting as minestrone soup, but at least I didn't have breathing problems. And I wasn't facing a course of radiotherapy to destroy the prostate cancer that was threatening my life.

I wouldn't have wanted to swap places with Joe.

"How did your first radiotherapy session go?"

"Not too bad. It's just the journey to the hospital and back every day that's going to be such a pain. The bridge is closed so I have to make a detour. It should be a forty minute drive but now it takes me four hours."

"Oh, that's not good."

"The radiotherapy itself was easy. The nurse told me to strip down to my underpants and socks…"

"Socks? Why socks?"

"I don't know. Then she told me to lie on a

very narrow table which I did. I was a bit nervous."

"Why?"

"Because the nurse was huge, with great rippling biceps and a bosom to match. And the table was like an ironing board. 'Don't move,' she said. No fear of that. I wasn't going to argue with her and anyway, I reckoned I'd fall off if I moved."

"Then what?"

"Well, she lumbered out of the door into some sort of outside control room, and her voice suddenly boomed from loudspeakers. 'Don't move and don't be concerned,' she said and then a huge doughnut-shaped machine moved and I felt myself being manoeuvred into the doughnut's hole."

"How odd."

"Yes, it was. Anyway, I lay very still and I guess the zapping started. The beam would have been aimed at those gold seeds they inserted in me before. I didn't feel anything and it only took a few minutes. Then the doughnut backed away. I guessed it was all over so I sat up, which was definitely the wrong thing to do."

"Why?"

"The door flew open and the big nurse came charging in. 'I told you not to move!' she shouted.

That's when I realised that the table had been raised and I was close to the ceiling."

"Oops."

"She wasn't happy. I got a real scolding. She said if I fell off the table and broke my legs I only had myself to blame."

"She was right. She told you not to move."

"I know, I know."

"Oh well, I'm sure you'll be better behaved next time." *Pigs might fly.*

"So you have to attend twenty sessions of radiotherapy and it'll all be over?"

"Hopefully. Monday to Friday, weekends off."

"Only nineteen sessions left, then."

"Yes. And it'll be done by Christmas."

"Good! You'll be here in the new year."

"I can't wait!"

I had a lot to do in one month. Fred, the builder, was due to give me a quote for a new kitchen and bathroom, and Lola was booked to have her final puppy injections. Then she'd start puppy school, not a moment too soon.

Perhaps school would teach her some manners.

LOBSTER AND SUMMER FRUITS SALAD

A delightful, refreshing, colourful lobster dish from www.taste.com.au Enjoy with a glass of chilled chardonnay.

Ingredients

3 baby cos lettuce, leaves separated, torn

1 bunch rocket, trimmed

1 large avocado

½ medium red onion, thinly sliced

½ cup small fresh mint leaves

½ cup small fresh coriander leaves

1 large mango, thinly sliced

150g (4-5oz) fresh raspberries

2 cooked lobster tails, meat removed, sliced

¼ cup lemon juice

2 tablespoons olive oil

2 teaspoons Dijon mustard

Pinch caster sugar

Method

Arrange lettuce and rocket on a platter.

Cut avocado in half and remove the stone. Peel and slice. Arrange over salad with onion, mint, coriander, mango slices and raspberries.

Top with lobster meat.

Whisk juice, oil, mustard and sugar together in a small bowl until combined.

Drizzle over salad.

Serve.

8

NEW FRIENDS

I'd just about given up on Fred, the builder I had booked to give me a quote. He was two hours late and I assumed he wasn't going to show. But then a white tradie ute pulled up and parked outside the house.

The driver's door opened, and out stepped Fred, allowing me to take a good look at him for the first time.

Fred wasn't what I expected at all. He wasn't the athletic rugby type in his mid-thirties that I'd imagined. No. Fred was short for a man, perhaps five feet four inches, not even as tall as me. He was thickset and in his late fifties. Thick-lensed horn-rimmed glasses sat on his nose. He wore heavy boots, the usual tradie neon shirt, and shorts. Later I discovered that he always wore shorts, whatever the weather. Lola hurled herself at him declaring her undying love as I tried to greet him.

"I'm Vicky, thanks for coming out. I'm sorry about the puppy."

"I'm Fred," he said, giving my hand a firm shake. "Pleased to meet you, and I'm sorry I'm late."

Then he crouched down on the doorstep and fussed Lola.

So far, so good. He had passed the first test.

"I'm sorry I was so late today. I was driving along the motorway, and a truck in front of me shed its load. It was carrying cartons of milk. You've never seen such a mess! There was milk everywhere, all over the road — rivers of it. I stopped and helped out because I had brooms on board. All the traffic had to be redirected and we were sweeping milk and trying to clear the cartons."

"Oh my goodness!"

"Eventually the fire brigade arrived. They'd been held up because they'd been attending a bush fire. Bush fires always come before spilt milk here in Aus!"

We both laughed and I was just inviting him in when something appeared at his feet.

"Dinks, how on earth did you get out of the

car?" he said, addressing the strange-looking little dog looking up at him.

"Dinks?" I asked.

"Her name's Fair Dinkum. I rescued her when she was a puppy, but she's getting on a bit now."

Another point in Fred's favour.

Dinkum had a sprinkling of Jack Russell genes somewhere, in addition to a multitude of other breeds which I couldn't even begin to identify. I doubted that she would ever win a dog beauty contest but kept that thought to myself.

In Australia, many tradies own large breeds of dogs, most often of the pitbull variety. These dogs ride in the back of their owners' open-topped utes. I'm not sure why these big, ferocious-looking dogs are so popular with tradies. Maybe the dogs guard the tools, but I think it's more likely that their owners are making a statement.

Fred definitely wasn't making any statement with Dinks. She wagged her tail, then marched into the house ignoring Lola and me and heading straight for Lola's bed. She flopped down and dozed, one eye cracked open and fixed on her master.

"Dinks!" said Fred, catching sight of her relaxing on Lola's bed. "Come here!"

"She's okay," I said, "don't worry."

Fred insisted on removing his boots before entering the house. He set them neatly side by side at the front door. Lola immediately ran off with one of them but he didn't seem to mind.

I took Fred on a guided tour of the house, explaining what needed doing. He snapped heaps of photographs and didn't seem shocked by any of my rather dramatic suggestions.

"Two things really bother me," I explained. "The kitchen, apart from needing to be ripped out and re-done, is much too small."

Fred nodded.

"And we only have one bathroom and that's in a terrible state. I wondered whether we could sacrifice the garage and convert it to a new master bedroom and en suite."

We discussed possible new configurations over a cup of tea. Lola, exhausted by her visitor-welcoming duties, fell asleep under my chair. Dinkum snored on Lola's bed.

"I'll prepare a quote for you," said Fred. "I'll include my licence number so you can check me out."

Business over, we discussed other things. Fred told me about himself. He'd raised two children alone, as his wife had abandoned them all a long time ago when the kids were toddlers. After the children left home, he decided to move from Sydney to the Central Coast, to be near his ageing mother.

I couldn't help but like this man who wore his

heart on his sleeve. I forgave him the broken appointments and decided that, if his quotes were reasonable, I'd give him the job. I was keen to get started. It didn't matter, I reasoned to myself, that Fred didn't actually look like a builder.

"I liked him," I told Joe later that evening. "He looks more like a nerdy accountant than a builder, and his dog won't win any dog shows either. But I think he's a nice bloke. I felt a bit sorry for him, actually."

"Why?"

"Well, I kind of got the impression that he's very lonely. He's not been in the area long and spends most of his spare time looking after his mum. Anyway, he seemed to know his stuff. He made lots of good suggestions."

"Did you believe his milk lorry story?"

"Yes, I did. And when he left, there were two milky stains on the ground where his boots had been standing."

When the quote arrived, I felt it was fair. I contacted Fred and told him he'd got the job. It turned out that my decision was a good one and Fred was a good, competent worker.

However, he was often late and sometimes didn't turn up at all. When this happened, he was most apologetic and his excuses were often unusual. We were to discover that Fred was a man who attracted rather outlandish occurrences.

Bizarre things just seemed to happen to him.

I'd already visited the vet's surgery a couple of times, when I'd registered Lola and booked her into puppy school, so I was familiar with the young lady receptionist. Apart from her, the waiting room was empty when we arrived.

"Hello," I said, "I've brought Lola for her injections."

"Ah yes," she replied, "do take a seat. The vet won't keep you waiting long."

But there was something different about the receptionist today and I couldn't quite put my finger on it. I kept snatching furtive glances at her, trying to work out what it was. I didn't think she'd changed her hairstyle, and her clothes seemed ordinary enough.

And then it clicked. It was her bosom! Surely she hadn't been quite so, um, well-endowed before?

To my embarrassment, she caught me staring at her upper body.

"Ah, you noticed my boobs," she said, grinning.

"Well, I…"

"It's okay. I'm not normally this shape. Come and see."

NEW FRIENDS

I really didn't know how to react. I guessed she'd had surgery, some kind of breast augmentation, and I had absolutely no wish to inspect the results up close. However, it was kind of her to extend the offer. Hiding my reluctance, I trotted up to the desk and obediently peered down the front of her top.

What I saw took my breath away.

"What are they?"

"Two possums. Somebody brought in an adult possum that had been hit by a car. Unfortunately, she died but the vet found these newborn joeys in her pouch."

"Oh my goodness!" I breathed, staring at the baby animals, wrapped in towelling, squirming in her cleavage. "Will they survive?"

"Yes, they should do. It's not the first time we've had to be mum to newborn possums or wallabies."

"Oh, my," I said, gently touching a warm, fuzzy little body with the tip of my finger. It's dark eyes gazed up at me. "I've never seen baby possums before."

"We've got the proper formula to give them, and they should thrive. I'm going to be a double D-cup size for a while though," she said, smiling.

The street door opened behind me. An Asian man entered and I looked over my shoulder, just in time to catch the look of shock on his face. He was clearly surprised to see me leaning over the counter, peering down the receptionist's front, with my hand down her top.

"It's okay, I'm just admiring her little possums," I said, then flushed scarlet.

That didn't sound right at all.

The telephone rang and the receptionist turned to answer it, leaving me to explain. The new arrival was still looking at me strangely. He had an elderly labrador on a leash, and Lola strained to give both dog and master one of her exuberant welcomes.

"I'm sorry, she's very young," I said, trying to restrain her. "We've enrolled her in puppy school, and I'm hoping that will calm her down." I cleared my throat. "Oh, and if you were wondering what I was doing just now…"

The man stared at me, blank-faced. I persevered, keen to clear up the situation.

"The receptionist was just showing me her two little orphans…" Again, I flushed scarlet.

Just then, the vet popped her head out from the surgery.

"Lola?" she asked. "This way."

My moment was lost forever.

"Oh! Must go," I said, and left him, his eyes bulging.

Lola greeted the vet like a long-lost favourite relative and was given her injection. By the time we returned to the waiting-room the man and his labrador had gone and the receptionist was taking another call, her bosom undulating slightly as she talked.

I can only hope that she had explained what was going on to the poor man with the labrador.

I'd never owned a puppy before and, although I was finding it to be utterly delightful, it was extremely hard work. As far as I was concerned, the day of Lola's first puppy class couldn't come soon enough.

Thanks to the crate-training, she was brilliant at night and settled quickly. The crate-training allowed me to go shopping without her, knowing she would snooze until I returned. When I returned, she welcomed me as though I'd been away for weeks, often, in her excitement, leaving a puddle on the floor.

I couldn't leave any paper or cardboard in her reach or she would shred it, scattering numerous tiny pieces all over the floor. Neither was any footwear safe from her needle-sharp puppy teeth. Nor any item of clothing, particularly underwear. Hanging up laundry was a fight because Lola leapt for each item as I pulled it out of the washing basket. And woe betide if I allowed anything to hang within her reach as a glorious game of tug-of-war would ensue. Any dropped pegs were immediately chewed to oblivion.

She drove me to distraction when I showered, scratching at the bathroom door, yapping and crying until I'd finished. Then, before I had a chance to dry myself, she'd burst in and lick all the drops off my legs, making me dance like a possum on a hot tin roof.

Sometimes, when I was trying to write, she was quiet. A little *too* quiet. Like children when they are up to no good. On one occasion, I jumped up to look for her.

"Lola, where are you?"

I searched for her, then glanced out of the window.

I had planned to pave an area in the garden which was muddy and unplanted, but Lola loved it just the way it was.

She adored mud, the wetter the better.

To my horror, her bottom was in the air and her front paws were digging so fast they were almost a blur. Clods of sticky mud were flying into the air.

"LOLA!"

She stopped for a second, just long enough for me to see her black, muddy face.

She's never lost her passion for mud and I have to remember that fact. I choose walking

NEW FRIENDS

routes that avoid puddles. Even now, when I walk her on our local oval, an Aussie term for a sports field, I avoid a particular area which becomes a quagmire after rain. I call it the Ten Dollar Puddle because, if I forget, Lola jumps straight in and executes a kind of commando crawl through the mud. Only a stripe of clean golden coat remains, along her back and the top of her head. The rest of her body is caked with gloop.

Why Ten Dollar Puddle? Because we have to march straight back to Bruce and drive to the nearest dog-wash, which costs ten dollars.

Incredible inventions, those auto dog washes. They've rescued me many a time. I've taken Lola, covered in mud from head to foot after her latest puddle wallow, and fifteen minutes later, after shampoos, conditioner and warm air dryers, I've transformed her into a scented, golden ball of fluffy fur.

But never for long. Only until she finds the next muddy hole to dig, or something disgusting to roll in.

Now that her course of puppy injections was complete, we had much more freedom. I started to walk her up and down the street to accustom her to walking on a lead.

I often walked with my German neighbour, Thea, and her little dog, Nixi. We became good friends.

Nixi and Lola were about the same size, but that's where the similarity ended. Lola was a whirling dervish of energy and naughtiness. One glimpse of Thea and Lola became a frenzy of excitement, jumping and pulling me along to reach her German friend and Nixi. She knew that Thea's pockets were stuffed full of dog treats.

Nixi, the Jack Russell, was not so lively. She was older, more polite and calm, a sweet-natured dog and a huge favourite with local children. She'd trot over to them, wagging her tail happily as she waited for pats, then roll over for tummy rubs.

If one researches the personality traits of the Jack Russell terrier, one discovers they are considered high-energy dogs that need a lot of exercise. They are vocal, feisty and, because of their hunting instinct, have an innate urge to explore.

Nobody told Nixi that. She'd never read the Jack Russell manual.

Unlike any Jack Russell I've ever met, Nixi was neither energetic, nor keen to explore, or even inclined to walk. On the contrary, she'd rather not bother with walks at all. I've often seen Thea throw little treats ahead to encourage Nixi to walk on. The ruse worked, but no doubt contributed to Nixi's expanding waistline.

When Thea pulled out a dog treat from her

pocket, Nixi would sit and wait patiently. Not Lola. She leapt and wriggled, unable to contain her excitement.

"*Donnerwetter!*" Thea would exclaim. "Keep your snoot away! No snatching!"

Treats gobbled up, Lola would dive onto Nixi, trying to initiate a game of rough-and-tumble. But Nixi wanted none of it. Tired of Lola's puppy exuberance, she would roll on her back, wave her stubby paws in the air and expose her very round tummy. It was her signal that she didn't want to play.

But Lola didn't heed signals or requests. She had no manners at all, just an enormous zest for life and everything in it.

The time had come for her to go to school and learn some manners. And as soon as possible. Time was running out because Joe would be joining us in less than a month.

WHITE CHOCOLATE AND MACADAMIA BISCUITS

These cookies from www.kidspot.com.au are very decadent. Rich, crunchy and easy to make, they also make perfect wrapped gifts.

Ingredients

125g (4oz) butter

½ cup white sugar

½ cup brown sugar

1 egg, lightly beaten

1 tsp vanilla extract

¼ tsp salt

¼ cup self-raising flour, sifted

100g (3½oz) white chocolate chips

100g (3½oz) macadamia nuts, chopped roughly

Method

Preheat oven to 180°C (350°F).

Line 3 trays with baking paper.

In a mixing bowl, cream the butter and both sugars with the vanilla extract until fluffy.

Add the egg and mix well.

Add the flour, salt and beat for a minute or two.

Stir in the nuts and chocolate chips.

Roll into tablespoon-size balls and gently press on the baking tray.

Bake for 8-12 minutes.

Leave to cool on a wire rack.

9
PUPPY SCHOOL

Even simple tasks like putting a harness or lead on Lola were a challenge. She thought everything was just one huge game. She bounced about like a fluffy yo-yo and, when I finally succeeded, I then had to wrestle her vaccination papers out of her jaws. Lola and I were the last to arrive at the first session of puppy school.

The teacher took our details and we were asked to sit on chairs in a circle.

"Just tell us your name and a little bit about your puppy," said the teacher, addressing the group. "Perhaps you could share what you'd like your puppy to learn."

I looked around. There was a labrador, a boxer, a staffie, a white terrier like the one from the movie, *Oliver*, and a German shepherd. All were perfectly calm, well-behaved, and sitting nicely at their owners' feet.

And then there was Lola.

Although Lola had grown a lot in the short time I'd had her, she was still the smallest, fluffiest dog there, and by far the most unruly. She wasn't going to sit still for even a second. She was like a hyperactive child, unable to settle, impervious to commands.

We introduced ourselves, while Lola strained this way and that, desperate to reach everyone. I spent all the time apologising and untangling her leash from my neighbours' chair legs.

"And who is this?" the teacher asked the boxer's owner.

"This is Wesley," said the owner. "I'd like Wesley to join me on my jogs and help me get fit. I'm hoping he'll learn to run beside me without tripping me up."

The teacher turned to the anxious-looking lady with the German shepherd.

"Hello, I'm Barb, and this is Jet. His mother is a police dog, so he should be clever. I want to do agility training with him one day."

It was my turn, and Lola was still excited, jumping around like popcorn in the microwave. My wishes seemed trivial compared with those of my classmates.

"I'm Vicky," I said, "and this is Lola. I'd like

Lola to learn not to chew every shoe and piece of paper she encounters. I wish she wouldn't bark at everything and jump up at visitors and complete strangers. I wish she wouldn't steal my underwear or snatch the washing from the clothesline. I'd love it if she didn't jump in muddy puddles. It would also be fantastic if she didn't roll in dead things, or eat beetles. Oh, and I'd be grateful if she'd just be still for a minute."

Lola knew we were talking about her. She panted, tongue lolling and her tail wagged so fast it was a blur. Everybody smiled.

"I take it you've never had a puppy before?" asked the teacher.

I shook my head.

"Honestly," I said to Thea as we walked together one hot day in December. "Lola is easily the naughtiest puppy at puppy school. I was hoping she'd be better behaved by now. Joe will be here after Christmas and I don't think he'll be too thrilled with her bad behaviour."

"After Christmas?"

"Yes, his radiation treatment will be finished by then."

"Good!" she said, adjusting her white hat. "I will bake him a cake."

I was to learn that Thea's cakes were legendary. Apart from tasting delicious, they were produced for a variety of reasons. I was given a cake to welcome me to the neighbourhood, for my birthday, because my family was visiting, and when I wasn't feeling well. Cakes were baked to solve every problem and mark every occasion.

Thea recommended the man who came to mow my lawn, and he blamed his rotund shape on Thea.

"I've been mowing her lawn for years," he told me, patting his stomach, "and whenever I turn up, there's a huge slice of German cake waiting for me. Delicious!"

Thea had other skills beside cake-baking. For instance, she knew exactly what the weather was going to do.

"Take an umbrella, this afternoon it will rain," she would say.

I would look up at the cloudless sky and ignore her warning. Sure enough, it rained, and because I hadn't heeded her advice and armed myself with an umbrella, I was soaked.

Thea was also an excellent visual weather warning. She never went outside without wearing a hat over her silver hair. She owned two, a white one for hot days and a brown, fleecy one for cold days. As she walked, (or dragged) the reluctant Nixi past our house, I knew whether it was a hot or cold day by her headgear. A few consecutive days of brown hats meant that winter was on the way. A week of white hats indicated that spring was in the air.

I rarely missed Thea and Nixi's walk-past: Lola made sure of that. One glimpse of Thea's hat would send her off into a frenzy of barking. One would have thought we were being invaded by a horde of burglars. She hurled herself at the window, scrabbling at the glass until I was afraid it would break.

Lola and I often joined Thea and Nixi on their neighbourhood strolls and I devised a scheme to inform them that Lola and I wished to accompany them. I drew a simple outline of a walking dog on a big piece of cardboard and placed it in the window (out of Lola's reach). This was my signal to Thea to say we'd love to join her and Nixi and prompted her to knock on our door.

I soon discovered that Lola might have been naughty, but she was also extremely bright. She was eager to learn, and I easily taught her the basics, like sit, stay, and lie down. She gave me her paw if I asked for it and rolled over on command. She quickly learned how to pick up her toys and put them away in a bucket, if asked, and ring a bell to go out. I began to run out of things to teach her and googled new tricks.

With such an impressive repertoire of skills,

one would think she was the star pupil at puppy school.

Not so.

Would she sit, stay and lie down on command at school? She would not. Would she come when called, or walk nicely on the lead? No.

All the other puppies showed off their skills, while Lola dashed about, tangling herself in other dogs' leads and making a general nuisance of herself.

"Don't worry," the teacher said, trying to reassure me. "Some pups take longer to learn than others."

"But she does *loads* of clever stuff at home," I protested, perfectly aware that the teacher probably didn't believe me.

"Today, I'm going to give you and your pups extra homework," our teacher announced, handing out sheets of paper. "This is a checklist. I want you to make sure that your puppies are introduced to all the things on this list. I know it may take weeks to get through, but do your best. The more things your puppies encounter early on, the more confident they will be throughout their lives."

There's nothing I like more than a good meaty list. I stared at it with interest, mentally ticking off as many as I could.

Physical Contact

- Being picked up ~ No problem
- Brushed ~ No problem
- Patted ~ No problem
- Nails clipped (or pretend touch) ~ Practice needed
- Teeth examined ~ Practice needed
- Ears examined ~Practice needed

People
- Babies ~ Not tested yet. Must work on that, Indy's new baby sister is due in April
- Children ~ No problem, loves them. Indy and Lola are best friends
- Men ~ Loves them
- Women ~ Loves them
- Groups of people ~ Loves them, the more people to give her attention, the better
- People with hats ~ No problem, she adores Thea whether she is wearing her white or brown hat
- People with glasses ~ No problem
- People with disabilities ~ This one made me stop and recall a recent event.

The family had visited and we'd driven to The Entrance, a favourite place of ours because of the beach, the big children's play area and the daily pelican feeding sessions. I'd stood at the back of the crowd, concerned that Lola's unruliness might unsettle the pelicans. She loved to chase seagulls and I was sure she'd do the same with these birds, in spite of their size.

As usual, Lola bounced and tugged this way and that, making friends, licking hands and thrashing her tail. I was watching the show and listening intently to the commentary from the lady feeding the pelicans when I suddenly realised that Lola was no longer panting or straining.

I hadn't noticed the group of severely disabled adults and children arriving and surrounding us. Some were in wheelchairs, others walked with difficulty, aided by sticks. But it was Lola's behaviour that astonished me. Instead of her usual rowdy boisterousness, she was utterly calm, allowing herself to be patted and stroked by their many faltering hands. All the time, her tail wagged slowly and steadily, so unlike its customary frenzied lashing.

Did she know these people had disabilities and couldn't cope with her usual excessive energy? I'm positive she did because, when the carers wheeled their charges away, Lola returned to her usual unruly self.

One day, I thought, *I'll look into training Lola to be a therapy dog. I think she would take to it like a pelican to water.*

But now, back to the list…
- Elderly people ~ Loves them
- Police officers ~ I don't know

- Men with facial hair ~ No problem
- Postmen ~ No problem

We'd actually had a stroke of luck with these last two. Our postman was a lovely man who weaved his way from mailbox to mailbox, riding a bright green moped. He had a full beard and the first time Lola saw him, she barked with fright. The postman saw this and slowed right down, then stopped. He held his hand out and allowed her to sniff him.

Of course Lola could never resist making a new friend and was soon licking his hand, oblivious of his bushy beard or the revving of his moped. Thanks to the postman's kindness, we could knock three items off our list: men with facial hair, postmen and motorcycles.

Animals

- Dogs (all shapes & sizes) ~ No problem, maybe *too* friendly? Not all dogs like their faces licked at the first meeting
- Cats ~ Oh dear. She seemed to have forgotten those early days, living in Sydney and sharing a house with Bandsaw
- Chickens ~ She used to be okay with them, but now? I wasn't sure.
- Birds ~ Oh dear again. In Lola's opinion, seagulls, magpies, cockatoos, kookaburras, in fact anything feathered, was put on earth for her to chase. Big fail.

PUPPY SCHOOL

- Horses/cattle/sheep/pigs ~ I don't know.

The list went on for another page and included items such as umbrellas, wheelie bins, vacuum cleaners and fireworks. I was lucky, Lola didn't have a problem with any of them.

The final lesson of the course fell on the week before Christmas, and our teacher suggested we dress our pups to look festive. I had a little reindeer costume for Lola, but she shredded it in minutes so I made do with a strand of glittery tinsel around her neck. Wesley, the boxer, won the prize with a Santa outfit.

"Any news?" the teacher asked us, as she always did.

"Wesley has finally got the idea of jogging beside me," said my classmate happily.

Barb, the lady who owned the German shepherd, was also looking pleased, if somewhat tired.

"I've had a bit of a breakthrough with Jet, too," she said. "You know I bought that really nice, expensive outdoor kennel for him?"

We all nodded.

"And he flatly refused to sleep in it? Well, I wasn't going to give up. I decided the only way to force him to try it out was to sleep in the kennel *with* him. I've had three of the most uncomfortable nights of my life, and my husband said I was completely crazy. But it worked! Jet now sleeps outside in the kennel!"

We all clapped and the teacher turned to me.

"Any news?" she asked.

I shook my head. I wasn't going to brag about Lola's accomplishments because I knew she'd never perform in public. I certainly wasn't going to risk asking her to salute or roll over because we'd both look silly when she ignored me.

To be honest, I doubted she had even earned a puppy school graduation certificate, which I knew were being handed out that day. I eyed the stack of papers in the teacher's hand.

"Never mind," she said. "Lola will get there in the end."

THEA'S GERMAN CHEESECAKE
QUARKTORTE

Thea's cheesecake is legendary. She is asked for the recipe so frequently, she has typed it out and printed a stack so that she can hand it out to anyone who asks. The recipe below is copied straight from Thea's sheet.

Ingredients

1kg (35oz) plain yogurt (European style)

6 eggs

250g butter or margarine

375g (14oz) sugar

6 tsp semolina

Lemon peel (chopped to very small pieces)

Lemon juice from 1-2 lemons

Vanilla sugar or a few drops of vanilla extract

A few drops of rum/bitter almond

Some raisins

Some crushed almonds

1½ tsp baking powder

How to do

Put the melted butter in a bowl, add the eggs and sugar and mix with an electric mixer thoroughly.

Add the yogurt and mix.

Add all the other ingredients and mix again.

Prepare your baking form. (I wipe the baking form with a little butter.)

Pour the rather liquid mass into the form and bake for 60 minutes at 180°C or 350°F in a preheated oven or microwave, if you have a microwave with convection.

Enjoy!

Yours,

Thea

10

GRASS

"Right," said the teacher at the end of the lesson. "Let's see which puppies deserve one of these!"

I held my breath as the certificates were handed out. To my relief, Lola was given one. She jumped up on her hind legs and tried to snatch it from my grasp. Another game.

"Oh no you don't, young lady," I said, and held on firmly. After all, she may never be awarded another.

Hola tía Vicky y tío Joe,

I hop you are well. I am well and my sister and family is completely wells but Pollito my little brother he is in big troubles.

My class is studied prehistoric times and we rided on a bus to Los Millares to see the settlement where the very old people lived. We maked notes and we drawed pictures. Pollito he like very much crazy about dinosaurs and saber-toth tiger and he want to go with me and my sister.

One day Pollito is not at home and we are very much worry because he is very bad and sometimes he goes into mountains like that other time he falled in the old mine. This day Mama cried a lot and want to call the Guardia Civil but then Geronimo and my neighbour Paco and his son Paco they find Pollito again. Bad Pollito was in a old sheepherd place my teacher say shelter. It is a place made by stones for when the weather is very terrible.

My mother cry and ask Pollito why for you go to that old sheepherd place. Pollito say he is search for bones from a dinosaur and maybe a saber-toth tiger. My mother she cry more when they find Pollito and she say that Geronimo is the angel guardian of Pollito. My father he say that he will put a big chain on the leg of Pollito so he not go in the mountains alone no more again. My big brothers are not happy because they hop to go in a Guardia Civil helicopter to seek for Pollito.

My *tía* Lola has a new friend from the new

apartments his name is called Esteban. Mama say we not talk about it to father Samuel and it is not the business of children.

I am very sorry you do not have a koala near your house. My teacher say you has redback spider. My big brothers say redback spider kill you.

Felicitations, Catalina xx

I was living on a different continent, in a new country, in a totally strange neighbourhood where I knew nobody. But even though I missed Joe's company, I was never lonely. Thanks to Lola, I made friends wherever I went.

Thea and I often walked together. She showed me places I may not have discovered had I been alone, and introduced me to more people. I also met dog owners at the oval, where I took Lola for her daily run, and so I always had somebody to chat with.

Lola's very best doggy friend at that time was Tilly, another spoodle, the same age but black. When the pair saw each other, they would race around in big circles, tumbling joyously over each other. Exhausted, they'd lie panting side by side in the long grass, gathering up enough energy to do it all over again. It was an absolute delight to watch the puppies having such fun.

I often chatted with Tilly's owner, Sophie. Mostly, we talked about the puppies, comparing notes, but I also learned some surprising facts about Australian fauna and flora from Sophie.

"Does Lola eat mole crickets?" she asked once. "Tilly does."

"Mole crickets? What on earth are they? I've never heard of them."

"Oh, mole crickets are insects, very common and a real pest around here," Sophie explained. "They look a bit strange because the front is like a mole with black beady eyes and forelegs like shovels. But the back end looks like a cricket. And it has wings."

"No way! Where do they live?"

"Underground. They burrow and live on grass roots. They are nocturnal, and you can actually go out into the garden at night and hear them munching. They drive me crazy. Every year my lawn dies because of them."

"Really? Is there any cure?"

"Detergent. I had a really clever idea last week. I redirected my washing machine hose out onto the lawn so that it soaked the grass in soapy water. All the mole crickets came up. It worked a treat. The trouble was, it never occurred to me that Tilly would find mole crickets delicious. She must have eaten dozens of them before I realised what she was doing."

"Did they do her any harm?"

"No. I rang the vet and he said they were harmless to eat. She was fine but her poo looked very peculiar for a couple of days."

Our front lawn was looking very bald and patchy, and I was keen to get it looking a bit better before Joe arrived. There wasn't much I could do about the interior of the house until Fred came and started work, but I could try and improve the look of the front.

Had I been in England, I'd have known what to do. But Australian grass is very different. Instead of just spreading fairly politely, as my lawn in England used to do, this grass threw out great runners. The runners rooted on the drive and across the path, instead of populating the bald areas of the lawn. Not only that, but clover and dandelions made up a large proportion of the green. Another visit to Bunnings was required.

There was plenty of choice, in fact a dazzling display of treatments. I finally settled on a large box of a 'weed 'n' feed' mixture which boasted that it would speedily destroy all weeds and feed and nourish the grass simultaneously.

Perfect!

I applied it exactly as the instructions set out, sprinkling the granular mixture evenly over the area just before wet weather was forecast. Australian weather forecasters are very accurate, and Thea agreed we should expect rain. On cue, we had a good, heavy shower.

Then I waited.

I checked daily, but nothing happened for a week or so. Then I noticed that the weeds were turning brown and dying.

Good!

Unfortunately, it seemed that the grass was also dying. I knew I had followed the instructions to the letter, so I was horrified to see the grass browning and withering in front of my eyes. I was mystified.

"It's as though the whole lawn has been poisoned," I told Sophie. "All the grass is brown. It looks awful!"

Sophie looked puzzled, then put her head on one side.

"Your lawn isn't buffalo grass, is it?" she asked.

"I don't know. What's buffalo grass?"

"It's fast-growing grass, with wide leaf blades, very closely related to weeds. It spreads by shooting out runners."

"Yes! That's what I have, I think."

"Oh dear."

"Why?"

"Well, like I said, buffalo grass is very closely

related to weeds, so it looks as though your weedkiller killed it as well as the weeds."

"Oh no!"

"I think if you read the box carefully, you'll see it says 'not suitable for buffalo grass lawns'. You need a weedkiller that is safe for buffalo grass."

It was too late. Actually, it didn't matter. It turned out that when Fred started work, our front lawn would have died anyway. The numerous garbage skips, piles of rubble, and other building materials heaped on it for months made sure of that.

"I can't believe you'll be here in a couple of weeks," I said to Joe. "Please don't be disappointed by the state of the house. I wish I'd managed to get it more ready for you."

"Don't be silly, Vicky! I'm just delighted that the radiation treatment is over and that I'm free to fly to Australia. I couldn't care less if the place is a complete hovel."

"It is."

"I'm sure you're exaggerating."

"I'm not."

"Never mind, we'll sort it together. I'm not worried about the house at all. But I have to admit I'm quite worried about the journey."

"Why?"

"I'm just not as strong as I used to be. I get out of breath so quickly, and I hope I can cope with my heavy luggage."

"You don't need to bring much! You'll only need to wear shorts and T-shirts and we can easily buy those here."

"I know. I plan to travel light, but I can't help worrying about everything."

I felt sad, remembering how strong Joe used to be and how he never let anything bother him. This illness was taking its toll.

"Well, once you're here, I'll be able to look after you properly."

"Thank you, I know you will. It's so cold here in Britain, but at least I'll be arriving in time to catch the Australian summer. Maybe I'll feel better in the warmth. Maybe I'll find it easier to breathe."

COPD is a terrible, terrible disease. We both knew there is no cure and that it would gradually get worse over time. However, we also knew that we could manage it by maintaining a healthy lifestyle, with good food and plenty of exercise. I was determined to help Joe do all the right things to keep the disease at bay.

"It's a shame you can't be here for Christmas," I commented.

"There were no flights, but actually I think it's

a good thing. I don't think I could cope with a rowdy family Christmas straight after that journey."

It made me sad, but I understood what he meant.

In the days that followed, I tried to look at the house with fresh eyes, to see it as Joe would see it. I secured the services of a floor layer who ripped up the disgusting carpets in two of the three bedrooms. The many litters of puppies, raised by the previous owners, had left the carpets threadbare and stinking of dog urine. It was a massive relief to have them replaced with fresh, clean wood floors.

One of these rooms would soon serve as the main bedroom. I painted the inside of the fitted wardrobe and polished the mirrors on the wardrobe doors. I also painted the walls, bought two bedside tables and bedside lamps, and a new bed. Assembling the bed by myself was a challenge because Lola insisted on washing my face liberally every time I sat on the floor. But I eventually succeeded. I was satisfied that this room was now as clean and fresh as it could be.

It was a start.

The other bedroom, with its new wood floor, I

converted into an office. I painted the walls white and Karly and Cam gave me an old desk they no longer needed.

I couldn't, as yet, extend the new flooring into the living areas because I planned to have walls knocked down, and change the layout of the kitchen and bathroom.

One of the walls I planned to remove belonged to the third bedroom, which I had slept in while I worked on the main bedroom. The third bedroom door was a problem because the previous owners had fixed the door handle so that it could only be opened from the outside. During the day, when I wasn't in the room, I kept the door closed to prevent Lola from getting in. At night, when she was in her crate, I slept with the door wide open.

This room still had its original vile brown carpet and the blanket still hung over the window to block out next door's flashing fairy lights. Now that the main bedroom was finished, I could move out of this nasty room. I wouldn't be sorry not to be sleeping in there any more.

I carried a small tool box into the room, hoping to repair the door handle. Joe would have enjoyed tinkering with it but he was in the UK. Lola ran in and bounded onto the bed as I pulled the linen off. Another game. I tried to grab her but she jumped off and sped towards the half-open door.

"Lola! No!" I shouted, but it was too late. She leapt at the door. It slammed shut.

We were trapped.

I climbed onto the bed and removed the blanket covering the window. I tried to open it but it was painted shut. It probably hadn't been opened in years. I reached for my phone, hoping to call Thea, who lived just a few houses away in the same street. Then I remembered it was on the table on the other side of the door.

I rapped on the window glass with my knuckles.

"Help!" I called.

Nobody heard me.

What to do? Smash the window? That would be a last resort.

Then I remembered the toolbox and fetched a screwdriver. I couldn't use it to fix the door handle because the door needed to be ajar in order to reach the screws. However, I could use it to work away at the window clasp and was rewarded when the window slid open. I say 'slid', but it was more of a jolt than a slide because the channel was filthy, filled with the debris of years.

I leaned out of the window and looked down. I didn't relish setting foot in the dense undergrowth I saw below. It probably hid snakes and giant spiders.

Although the house was single-level, the land

below the window sloped away. It was a considerable drop. If I jumped I might twist my ankle on some unseen rock when I landed. And what if I broke a leg? I would be of no use to Joe then.

"Help!" I called again. "Help! I'm locked in!"

SILVERBEET, BROCCOLINI AND MOZZARELLA PIZZA

This recipe is from Phoebe Wood who says, "Sunday night is pizza night. Enjoy this better-than-takeaway version, filled with healthy gourmet toppings."

Ingredients

1 bunch broccolini

½ bunch silverbeet, finely shredded

1 garlic clove, crushed

Finely grated zest of 1 lemon

1 tablespoon extra virgin olive oil

¼ cup pesto

2 round pizza bases

2 tablespoons finely grated parmesan

250g (9oz) fresh mozzarella or bocconcini, roughly torn

2 bacon rashers, cut into large pieces

Method

Preheat the oven to 200°C (390°F). Line 2 baking trays with baking paper.

Thinly slice the stalks of the broccolini and set aside.

Blanch the broccolini tops in boiling, salted water for 1-2 minutes until just tender, adding the silverbeet for the final 10 seconds. Drain and refresh under cold water.

Combine garlic, lemon zest and oil in a bowl, then toss with drained broccolini tops and silverbeet. Season and set aside.

Spread the pesto over the pizza bases and scatter with the parmesan and sliced broccolini stalks.

Divide the mozzarella, bacon and greens between the pizza bases.

Bake for 12-14 minutes until the crust is golden and crisp, and the cheese has melted.

Cut into slices and serve immediately.

11

NEIGHBOURS

I kneeled on the bed, leaned out of the window and yelled as loudly as I could.

"Help!"

Beside me, Lola stood on the bed on her hind legs, front paws planted on the windowsill. Every time I shouted, she joined in.

It was a weekday, and nobody heard our duet. It seemed none of my neighbours were at home.

Through the gap between the houses, I saw the occasional car flash past. Our house was in a *cul de sac* and there wasn't much traffic.

An hour went by, and my voice was becoming hoarse. As nobody heeded our calls, I considered taking risks. Perhaps I could use the bed linen to lower myself into the undergrowth?

Then I thought of snakes and broken legs. I tried shouting again.

"Help!" I rasped. "Please! I'm locked in…"

No response. A flock of cockatoos flew overhead, screeching. My cries and Lola's yaps were in vain. In despair, I rested my chin in my hands, trying to decide what to do next.

Suddenly, I heard a murmur of voices. Peeping through my fingers, I saw two pale-faced, saucer-eyed ladies peering around the house wall up at me. For a second, I lost all power of speech. Lola, still standing beside me on the bed, front paws on the windowsill, head stuck out next to mine, didn't hesitate. She barked her head off in excitement, her tail thrashing me.

The ladies gaped at us.

"Thank goodness," I croaked. "We're locked in the bedroom."

The ladies looked shocked and didn't move. I tried again, raising my voice over Lola's yaps.

"We're locked in! Please could you go round the house? The front door is locked but you can use the side gate. The glass sliding doors at the back should be open."

The two heads hung for a moment longer, then withdrew. I waited, then heard the side gate rattle and the glass doors slide open. Footsteps entered the house.

It occurred to me that I had just allowed two

complete strangers to enter the house. They could have made off with all my possessions and I couldn't have done a thing about it.

Of course, nothing like that happened.

"We're in here!" I called.

They hurried over to the room we were trapped in and opened the door easily. I could have hugged them, but I didn't need to. Lola treated them to one of her bumper welcomes, regaling them with liberal licks and excited yelps.

The ladies introduced themselves as neighbours from further down the street. I hadn't met them when I first arrived. They had heard my cries for help but couldn't make out where they were coming from. They were about to abandon their search when they saw me. I would have preferred being introduced in less fraught circumstances, but never mind.

I sheepishly explained what had happened, and they were very sympathetic. Like so many others in our street, they had nothing positive to say about the previous owners, and the poor state of the house was of no surprise to them.

"You have got a lot of work to do here," said one, looking around.

I had to agree.

"Have you met many of the neighbours?" asked the other.

"Yes, briefly. There's the lady next door, and

Emma down the road, with her cocker spaniel, Baxter. Lola and I meet Emma and Baxter at the oval sometimes, dog-walking. And there's Thea, who is always bringing me cake. We walk together sometimes, too."

"Have you picked up your invitation to the Christmas street party yet?"

"No! When's that?"

"I don't know the exact date but it's the first Saturday in December. Your next-door neighbours, the couple with all the gnomes and garden ornaments, organise one every year along with the Tongan family. Their house is opposite yours, over the road."

"Sounds good! I'll look forward to that!"

Sure enough, the next time I visited our ancient and dented mailbox that leaned at a dangerous angle and badly needed replacing, I found an invitation to the Christmas street party in it.

"Just bring a bottle, nibbles and a chair," it stated.

Karly, Cam and Indy drove up from Sydney to join me for the street party. We carried out garden chairs and introduced ourselves. Indy instantly made friends with the youngest of the Tongan family's five children. They, and a bunch of other kids, were soon bouncing on the trampoline that was a permanent fixture on the front lawn of the

Tongans' house. The crowd kept growing, and the children ran excitedly from house to house. I smiled. It reminded me of the street parties in our Spanish village.

Lola was supposed to be shut away in our house, but she soon escaped with Indy and the other children, and joined the party.

Tables had been set out and were being laden with all manner of food and nibbles. Thea had baked a cake. I brought out a tray of sausage rolls, intending to put it alongside the other food platters already there.

"Stop!" hissed Karly. "You can't serve them like that!"

"Why not? What's wrong with them?"

"They're nude!"

"Pardon?"

"We're in Australia! You can't just serve them plain. You have to serve them with some type of sauce." said Karly. "Hold on. I'll find something."

She disappeared back inside the house, into my shambles of a kitchen, and came out with a small bowl filled with tomato sauce, for dipping.

"Oh, they look good," said someone, and the sausage rolls and tomato sauce vanished in minutes.

Flocks of cockatoos shrieked overhead, intent on reaching their roosts before dark. The huge, hot Australian sun dipped behind the distant ridge, leaving the sky stained tangerine, peach and orange.

As the sky grew darker, and the cockatoos' shrieks faded, the night shift arrived. The cicadas stopped their grating buzz and were replaced by the more melodic trilling of crickets. Monstrous black silhouettes flapped across the apricot sky on silent wings.

"Look at those huge crows," I commented.

"They're not crows, they're fruit bats," somebody corrected. "They always fly over at about this time. They're leaving their colonies in the bush to head out and search for food."

The moon hung above us and the sky became black velvet studded with stars. It was December. In Spain, we would have been sitting huddled in front of a roaring fire. Here, in Australia, I was wearing short sleeves and rubbing insect repellent on my bare skin to ward off the mosquitoes.

Somebody switched on music. The children played, barefoot, while the adults' voices grew in volume. We met people we hadn't met before and chatted with ones I already knew: Emma, Thea, and her husband, Reinhard.

Then Indy and the younger children were put to bed, protesting, and the party carried on into the night. When I awoke the next morning there was still a jumble of abandoned chairs in the street, and empty bottles stood on tables. I suspect the party continued well after we'd gone to bed.

Before I could blink, Christmas was upon us. Our local shopping village was already blasting out Christmas carols, and the shops were decorated with Christmas bling. When I visited the mall one day, a pen had been set up in the central aisle, housing live reindeer for children to pet.

All the Christmas traditions seemed to match those I remembered in England. There were mince pies for sale, and people decorated their houses inside and out with flashing Christmas lights.

Groups of carol singers came to the door. But, unlike England, where pale-faced, red-nosed carol singers would be wrapped in scarves and woolly hats, these carol singers wore shorts and their hair was bleached and skin bronzed by the Australian sun.

Lola and I spent a wonderful Christmas in Sydney with the family. It was so good to be there and watch Indy open her gifts. As usual, the strict *No Presents for Adults* rule was completely ignored. I reminded myself that Indy's baby sister would be part of the festivities next year. I smiled, knowing that I'd be here, God willing, in Australia for that.

Never again would I need to miss precious family events because I lived in a distant land.

We ate, drank and laughed a lot. Karly, fantastic cook that she is, produced a banquet that was both typically Aussie and totally English. Oysters and seafood began the feast, followed by roast turkey with all the trimmings.

The sun beat down, and I thought of Joe in chilly Britain. It was such a shame he couldn't be here, but it was only a matter of days before he arrived. I joined in the laughter and chatter, but my mind often wandered because Joe was due to land in Australia on New Year's Eve.

"Is everybody coming back here for New Year's Eve?" Karly wanted to know. "You're all invited, of course. Shall we all wear red underwear again and eat a grape for every chime of the clock?"

Everybody laughed. Was it really a whole year since I'd brought that Spanish custom to Australia on my last visit?

"I'll have to miss it this year," I said. "Joe's timing is awful."

Hola tía Vicky y tío Joe,

I hop you are well. My family is completely wells and I am writing you a letter. Now we have no school because it is christmas and we are helping my mother with cookings for christmas. My mother she say if I don't want do cookings i must study because my school statement from my teacher is not so good. I do not like to do study and i do not like to write letters. Mama is not happy i don't like cookings. I like only dancing flamenco and talking with my friends but my mother she say I must study and do cookings like my sister.

Tía Lola and father Samuel they have big loud words in the street. My mother she say to my father that Lola is not knowing when she has the honey on her bread. My sister say it is the fault of Lola and Esteban because Lola she always go to the house of Esteban. My mother say we not talk about it and it is not business for children.

I am very happy that you have redback spider in your house. Pollito say how many peoples your friends they are kill by redback spider.

Felicitations, Catalina xx

The roads were deserted as I drove in Bruce to the railway station. This was hardly surprising because it was New Year's Eve, approaching midnight. I had the radio on, and as the clock struck twelve, the sky was illuminated by fireworks. As rockets exploded in all directions, I thought about the family who would be raising a glass and watching the fabulous Sydney Harbour firework display on TV. Then I thought of Joe, nearing the end of his long journey from the UK.

I glanced at Lola in the back seat, fast asleep, looking like a fluffy mop. What would he think of her? Would her unstoppable energy irritate him? Would he approve of the house I had rushed into buying?

The railway station car park was almost empty. I parked under a lamp post that barely illuminated the parking lot.

"Come on, Lola," I said, opening the back door and unclipping her seat-belt harness. "I want you to be on your very best behaviour. That means no pulling on the lead and no jumping up. I want Joe to be impressed by you."

Of course, I wasted my breath. She sprang out of the car, a ball of hairy excitement, bouncing and tugging this way and that as the train rumbled in and stopped at the platform.

A few doors opened, and suddenly, there he was.

Joe.

I remember he looked tired and pale, and somewhat frail, but mostly I remember his smile as he saw me and the unruly ball of golden, bouncing fur.

And then I was in his arms.

"So this is Lola!" he laughed, as she stood on her hind legs, trying to get in on the act, licking us both frantically. "Hello, Lollipop!"

Lola's tail wagged so hard I thought it would fly off, and from that day, the silly name stuck. Lola answered to the name of Lollipop as readily as she did to her proper name.

The fireworks were dying in the sky as we walked hand in hand back to Bruce, Lola trotting beside us.

"I'm so tired, but it's wonderful to be here at last," said Joe. "So this is Bruce! And I can't wait to see the house."

"Please don't expect too much… It's going to take a lot of work to get right."

"I know. It doesn't matter. We'll sort it out like we always sort everything out. We're a team."

We smiled at each other. He was right.

A brand new year had just begun. Joe was home, and I stopped worrying.

BAKED PUMPKIN RISOTTO

If you like, add in some chopped, cooked chicken about 10 minutes from the end. Also stir in some baby spinach leaves or peas for extra colour.

Ingredients

1 cup arborio rice (or any short grain rice)

2½ cups chicken or vegetable stock

60g (2oz) butter

350g (12oz) jap or butternut pumpkin, peeled and diced into bite-sized pieces

½ cup finely grated parmesan cheese

Cracked black pepper and sea salt

1 tablespoon chopped flat leaf parsley

Method

Preheat oven to 190^0C (375°F)

Place arborio rice, stock, butter and pumpkin into an ovenproof dish and cover tightly with a lid or aluminium foil.

Bake for 30 minutes (although may need up to 50 minutes) until rice is soft.

Stir through parmesan, pepper, salt and parsley and serve garnished with extra parmesan and parsley.

12

BATS

Joe tried to absorb everything as we drove home, but it was dark, and he was exhausted. He didn't even notice the dead, brown area that used to be our front lawn. There would be plenty of time to show him everything in the morning.

When he awoke, rested, I took him on a tour of the house. I showed him the plans I had sketched and described how I hoped the house would look. He'd seen my sketches before, but now that he could actually see the layout, he understood.

"You're very good at this sort of stuff," he said. "I'm sure the house will be brilliant when it's finished. I'm so pleased that you've already organised a builder. Very well done!"

I nodded, privately hoping that, one day, Fred might actually materialise and begin work.

BATS

As the days passed, I showed Joe all the local places I had told him about. Like me, he was in awe of the lake, the white sandy beaches, the wide-open spaces, the bush, and the abundant birdlife. Fabulous colourful parrots often landed in our trees.

Gradually, we fell into a routine. Temperatures were hot, and we would either walk Lola on the beach or at the local oval. We swam in our pool and did odd jobs around the house. Often we just sat drinking coffee in our garden, eating slices of Thea's delicious 'Welcome' cake and chatting. Even though we had managed to keep in touch every day we had been apart, there was still so much catching up to do, so much to discuss.

"Have you had any more news from El Hoyo?" he asked. "You know, from your cute little penpal, the Ufarte twin?"

"Catalina? Yes, didn't I tell you? Hold on. This is the latest." I reached for the iPad and passed it over to him.

Hola tía Vicky y tío Joe,

It is I Catalina your penpall again. I hop you are well again. My family is completely wells again. I am writing you a letter today because my mother she say i must write again a letter.

Pollito my brother he say he is sorry no peoples your friends have kill from a redback.

Pollito he say he now not want to be a scientist for dinosaurs he want to be a detective famous because today he find a diamond ring in the street. My mother say it belong to *tía* Lola and we must carry the ring to her because it is lost. i think the diamond ring not lost because I see *tía* throw when they have loud words and talk about Esteban. My mother say we not talk about it and say it is not business for children.

Pollito say please to tell me if you are seeing a great white shark.

Felicitations, Catalina xx

Joe smiled before commenting. "If I read between the lines, I'd say that Catalina's little brother, Pollito, is still a handful. More importantly, I'd absolutely lay money on the fact that Lola Ufarte hasn't changed her ways one little bit."

"Huh! And you are the one who always accuses *me* of being a gossip!"

"Remind me who Esteban is."

"I don't think we ever met him. He bought one of the apartments in the Monstrosity."

I remembered our horror when the foundations of the new apartment block were laid. As it grew, we named it the Monstrosity, convinced it would ruin the look of our beloved white-washed village. We needn't have worried

BATS

because in time, it blended quite well with the other buildings.

"Ah, right. Poor Father Samuel. I don't think anybody could ever stop Lola Ufarte from misbehaving. Certainly not an ex-priest who's probably had absolutely no experience handling women."

"Poor man. He was so besotted with her, and he dotes on her little daughter. I wonder if he regrets leaving the church for her?"

"It's a wonder nobody warned him."

"They probably did, but we all thought Lola had changed. Perhaps this will pass."

"Well, if they are having 'loud words' in the street and if she's throwing her diamond ring at him, I don't hold out much hope for their future relationship," said Joe drily.

I had to agree.

We were new to Australia, and the mini-beasts we encountered astounded us. Our garden heaved with extraordinary insects. At night, colossal winged creatures battered our window panes, attracted by the light. Something made peculiar chattering, bickering noises outside, causing Lola to growl into the darkness.

By day, huge black, shiny centipedes, with red

legs, marched through the leaf litter. I saw massive ants with jaws that made me flinch, and others as tiny as pinpoints. We rescued delicate insects with lacy wings from the pool, and gawked at giant praying mantises that landed on our windows, inviting scrutiny.

We had never seen stranger creatures. It was as though some joker had been given permission to design the craziest animals imaginable from a mountain of spare parts, and then placed them all in Australia.

Cockroaches were plentiful, but they were three times the size of the cockroaches we had in Spain. Mosquitoes, too, were different from the ones we used to have in England and Spain. Some were tiny, and others were huge. They didn't play fair, either, because they were perfectly happy to suck one's blood in the full glare of daylight, without waiting for the cover of night. Strangely, I discovered that the itching caused by Aussie mosquito bites stopped quite quickly. I recalled that their European cousins' punctures swelled into angry lumps and itched for a full two weeks.

"I guess there's no such thing as paradise," said Joe, as an unusually large cockroach scuttled past his foot.

But I didn't agree. I thought, and still do, that Australia is as close to paradise as one can get. But I felt that about Spain, too.

When I was handed the keys of the house, I discovered a fantastic surprise. I already loved the view from the back of the house and enjoyed seeing flocks of cockatoos rise from it. But the surprise came at dusk.

The back of the house faced west and when the sun set behind the distant and thickly-forested bush, I was treated nightly to the most awesome, breathtaking sunsets imaginable.

About an hour before the sun sank from view, bird activity increased. Great flocks of white cockatoos, their wings tinted pink by the sunset, squawked overhead as they headed for their roosts in the bush. Groups of rainbow lorikeets flashed by at high speed. Loud and hyperactive as always, they darted past, as though dangerously late for some seriously important appointment, shrieking instructions at each other over their shoulders.

"Quick! Quick! We're late! Follow me, hurry up!"

Indian Mynah birds, considered pests and not native to Australia, landed in our palm trees and settled to roost. By day they were regular visitors to our pool and garden. We often saw them teasing visiting magpies and kookaburras by perching alongside them. Their bold behaviour and cheekiness earned them our nickname of The Hooligans.

Then the kookaburras began their twilight laugh-in. Perched on telegraph wires and silhouetted against the orange sky, they exchanged their raucous calls. They are extremely territorial, and that loud laugh is a warning to other kookaburras to stay away. I know now that kookaburras are almost exclusively carnivorous, feeding on mice, snakes, insects, small reptiles, and even the young of other birds.

"Do you remember the first time we saw kookaburras?" I asked Joe.

"Oh yes, when we were camping in Queensland."

"Yes!"

We both smiled at the memory. In 2008, we travelled in a campervan up the east coast of Australia, stopping anywhere we liked. We had a whole month to please ourselves. It was a trip full of adventures, discoveries, and a great sense of freedom.

At one particular campsite, Joe was serving up barbecued sausages. The smell was making me hungry, but I wasn't the only one watching him intently. I happened to look up and caught sight of a kookaburra perched nearby on a low branch, its head on one side, studying Joe.

"I think we've made a new friend," said Joe. "Perhaps he'd like a sausage? I'll put one on that post over there."

He picked up one of the cooling sausages and walked towards the post. But he never reached it. Without warning, the kookaburra left his perch and with a soft whoosh of feathers, swooped past, snatching the sausage from Joe's fingers.

"Wow!" we chorused.

The kookaburra swerved, the sausage still dangling from his beak, and landed on the back of one of our camp chairs. But he didn't immediately gobble down his dinner. He first thrashed the sausage violently and repeatedly against the back of the chair.

"He thinks it's a snake!" I said.

"And now he's dispatching it!" said Joe.

At last the kookaburra was satisfied that he'd knocked the sausage senseless, and that it would give him no further trouble. He gulped it down. Then, having preened himself with an air of self-importance, he flew away. We never forgot the incident.

When the kookaburras had ceased their cackling, twilight cries, the sun vanished. As the orange backdrop darkened to burnt umber, the stage was set for the next show.

At first, just one or two appeared, then more and more, until the sky seemed to be filled with them. Black, silent shapes flapped overhead and only when they flew very low could one hear the whisper of their giant wings. Unless we looked up, we'd be unaware of the fruit bats above.

My first visit to Australia was way back in the early 90s when my son, Shealan, and his little sister, Karly, were still kids. We visited northern Queensland and were experiencing a nature walk through a conservation area within a rain forest. We followed our guide along a twisting specially constructed boardwalk. The area was vast and had been netted to protect the enclosed rescued wildlife. We saw a wombat asleep in his den, and kangaroos in trees. I was surprised to learn that there is a species of kangaroo that climbs and lives in trees.

"Look out for Charles and Diana," said our guide, ducking to avoid a huge fruit bat dangling upside down from a branch above our path. "I see Charles has chosen a rather silly place to snooze today. Don't worry. He won't harm you."

The whole party filed past Charles, who regarded us with big dark eyes. I couldn't see Diana.

We were the last to pass, Shealan bringing up the rear and perhaps stopping to stare at Charles a little too long. Without warning, Charles dropped and wrapped himself around our son.

We gaped for a second and then attempted to gently detach Charles from Shealan. But Charles was thoroughly enjoying his new perch, and it was proving impossible to remove him. In addition to wrapping his enormous wings around my son, Charles also clung with the hooks on his wings. As fast as we unhooked him, he found a new hookhold, wrapping Shealan in a cosy embrace. Shealan wasn't in the least bit concerned.

"I think we need help," I said. "Karly, run on ahead and tell the guide."

Off she ran, her feet pattering on the wooden boardwalk. The guide was busy explaining how the eco-system of the rainforest worked and how it was affected by the seasons. Karly came to a halt in front of him and looked up. He didn't pause with his explanation, so she tapped him lightly on his leg with her knuckles. He looked down in surprise.

"Excuse me," she said, flushed but polite. "A fruit bat's got my bruvver."

Everyone stared, then swung around and smiled. Now the guide understood and trotted back to rescue Shealan from Charles's enveloping embrace. He succeeded and hung Charles on a nearby branch, well away from the boardwalk.

"Now behave," he told Charles. "No more dropping down on unsuspecting visitors."

Unfortunately, many Australians dislike fruit bats. They believe the bats will raid fruit harvests, unaware that they prefer pollen, nectar and bush fruit, in that order. As usual, it is a problem of diminishing habitat. The bush has been cleared to make room for the ever-growing human population. Existing bat colonies have been lost to new housing schemes and farms. Farm-grown fruit is bound to attract hungry flying foxes, even though they prefer bush fruit to the cultivated hybrid varieties.

The problem is severe, and flying fox numbers are in sharp decline. These native 'gardeners of the sky' have a crucial part to play. They help regenerate by spreading seeds which develop into new forests.

There are other reasons why fruit bats get a bad press. Their colonies are noisy and give off a terrible smell of ammonia. Fruit bats don't smell at all, they are fastidious creatures, but the stench of their guano and urine, which collects on the ground below their colonies, is overpowering.

I didn't appreciate this until Joe and I encountered our first fruit bat colony in Queensland. We'd parked the campervan on a grass verge and got out to stretch our legs. Cars sped past us on the road and beyond the verge was typical Australian bushland, edged with tall trees.

That's when the stench hit us.

"Boy, that's a *horrendous* smell," said Joe,

clapping his hand over his nose. "It's enough to make my nose-hair shrivel and die."

"Every cloud has a silver lining," I said.

"Where's the smell coming from?"

We looked around, and then we saw the source.

"Over there! Bats! Quick, grab the binoculars, let's go and look!"

FIG AND WALNUT BREAKFAST LOAF

Delicious when topped with cream cheese and sliced strawberries. From newideafood.com.au

Ingredients

125g (4oz) unsalted butter, chopped

1½ cups water

250g (8½oz) dried figs, chopped

½ cup buttermilk

2 eggs, beaten

1¼ cups brown sugar

2 cups white spelt flour, sifted

2 teaspoons baking powder

1 teaspoon mixed spice

1 cup walnuts, chopped

½ cup desiccated coconut

Method

Grease and line a non-stick loaf tin and set aside.

Place butter and water in a large saucepan and heat over medium heat.

When butter is melted, add figs.

Bring to the boil and remove from heat.

Transfer figs and butter mixture to a large bowl and allow to cool.

Add buttermilk, eggs, brown sugar, flour, baking powder and mixed spice to bowl and stir to combine.

Add walnuts and coconut and stir one last time.

Pour into prepared tin.

Bake in 160°C (320°F) oven for 90 minutes.

Slice and serve.

13

A BANANA AND BEETLES

"Look out for snakes," said Joe as we stumbled through the long grass and headed towards the trees.

"Make lots of noise and they'll slither away."

"I think the bats are making enough noise for both of us!"

We could see the colony ahead of us, each individual hanging upside-down from a branch, encased in its leathery wings. Sometimes they stretched out a wing or changed branches. They chattered, jabbered, and bickered with their neighbours.

"There must be hundreds of them!"

"Thousands!"

And there were. Some branches had as many as ten bats hanging from it, others only one. But there were dozens and dozens of them. We didn't want to scare them away by getting too close, but an all-pervading smell and a deep ditch kept us at a distance.

We raised our binoculars and stared. I focused on a particularly large, restless specimen.

"I didn't realise they had such bulgy black eyes and long dangly noses," I commented.

Joe said nothing for a moment and appeared to be thinking.

"Long dangly noses? I don't think so. They're called flying foxes because they have faces like foxes. And foxes don't have long dangly noses."

"Well, the one I'm looking at has. Focus on that big one, on the high branch on its own, with the family of about six under him."

"Ah yes, I see it…"

"Well?"

"Honestly, Vicky!"

"What?"

"I can see what you're looking at, and it isn't his face."

"It isn't?"

"No, it's a particularly well-endowed specimen of a male fruit bat. You're not looking at his face at all."

"Oh."

As though aware of our scrutiny, the bat scratched himself.

"Oh, he's scratching himself. Now, who does that remind me of, I wonder..." I commented.

"Humph!"

Scratching his nethers is a horrible habit I have never managed to cure Joe from doing.

For a long time we watched the bats bicker, gibber, scratch and snooze.

"Let's come back at dusk and watch them fly out," I suggested.

"Great idea!" said Joe.

That evening we managed to park a little closer to the colony, but far enough away not to be overpowered by the stench. As the sun dipped, we barbecued our dinner, keeping an eye on the colony. It may have appeared a strange spot to choose to cook one's dinner, but the roadside gave us a perfect vantage point, and we were rewarded.

As the sky darkened, the bats grew more restless and twitchy. They stretched and flapped their wings, and the noise level rose. One sensed a mounting excitement.

First one bat dropped from its perch and rose into the sky, followed by a few more. Then more lifted into the air, flying in ones and twos, then groups, then dozens. Eventually the evening sky was almost black with bats.

"They're all heading in the same direction," Joe remarked.

"Yes, I read somewhere that they can smell ripe fruit from three miles away."

We finished our meal and watched until the last bat launched into the sky. Then we drove back to our campsite, delighted with our evening's entertainment.

The next day, we were discussing fruit bats when a nugget of previously forgotten information jumped into my head.

"Did you know that fruit bats don't actually bite, chew and swallow as we do?"

"Don't they? What do they do then?"

"They crush the fruit against the roof of their mouths, suck out the juice, then spit out all the fibrous remains."

"Really?"

"Yes, really."

"We could test that theory," said Joe. "I'm sure they eat bananas. Why don't we leave a banana out and watch it tonight?"

"How would the fruit bats find it?"

"You said they could smell ripe fruit from three miles away. I bet they'd easily find our banana."

"Where would we put it?"

"Hmm… Up one of these trees, I reckon," said Joe, looking up at the tall pine trees surrounding our campervan. "Nice and high."

"Don't be ridiculous! Are you suggesting we

climb one of these trees and put a banana up there?"

Joe was deep in thought, absent-mindedly scratching himself down below.

"No, of course not. We've got a big ball of string, haven't we?"

"Yes..."

"Well, we could attach a stone to the string and throw it up over a high branch. Then we lower the stone, and exchange the stone for a banana. Then we pull the banana up."

"Are you serious?"

"Yes, of course."

"Right..."

The first throw proved nowhere near high enough. The second one hit the trunk of the tree, ricocheted and nearly took Joe's eye out. The third throw sailed over the branch, precisely as planned.

"There you go, easy!" said Joe, rubbing his eye.

He lowered the stone, exchanged it for our banana, and pulled on the string until the banana swung high in the air above us. It looked very odd.

"Perfect!" said Joe, securing the string to another branch.

"Now what?"

"Well, we sit outside tonight and watch the

banana. A fruit bat is bound to come along and find it."

That evening, we set up our camp chairs, opened a bottle of wine, and waited. We watched bush turkeys flap into the trees to roost for the night. We heard owls and a dozen strange noises, including the chitter of bats, but saw nothing else. The yellow banana swung high over our heads in the moonlight.

Eventually we gave up and went to bed, confident that some fortunate bat would devour the banana during the night.

But none did.

We left that campsite two days later and the banana was still hanging there, untouched. I wondered whether any future campers might notice it and scratch their heads, asking themselves why anybody would want to dangle a banana high in a tree.

We'd driven about a hundred kilometres towards our next destination when another thought occurred to me. What if the banana rotted and fell on somebody's head? I doubt they would ever solve the mystery of the banana that fell from a pine tree.

Joe had been in Australia a few weeks and still hadn't met our builder, Fred. We had no working kitchen but we were coping, cooking on a camp stove and using a microwave. It wasn't worth investing in a proper cooker yet, not before the kitchen was remodelled.

The bathroom was dire, but everything worked, and one could enjoy a proper shower if one averted one's eyes from the deeply ingrained mould, the cracked tiles and dripping taps.

At last, Fred got in touch and arranged to come over. I introduced him (and Dinkum) to Joe, and as they shook hands, I noticed cuts and scratches on Fred's forearms.

"Sorry I'm late," he said, "I've just rescued a puppy, and he's a bit of a handful."

"Oh, really? What kind of puppy?"

"He's a Great Dane. He doesn't take no for an answer when he wants to play. Actually, he grabs my arm with his teeth and drags me into the garden."

He rolled up his sleeves to reveal more cuts and grazes.

"Oh my goodness," I said, shocked. "What does Dinkum make of him?"

"Dinks is fine; she's the boss. She can control Hulk better than I can."

Dinkum had already marched in and plonked

herself on Lola's bed. I tried to picture this small dog and the Great Dane together and failed.

"Lola's grown a lot since I last saw her," he said, patting her as she gave him her usual exuberant welcome.

It was true. Lola was growing very fast. She was a lot bigger than Thea's dog, Nixi, and was even taller than Emma's cocker spaniel, Baxter, down the road. I had thought Lola would be a small dog, but she was still growing. Later, I checked her papers and was surprised to discover that one of her parents was a standard poodle. That would explain a great deal because standard poodles are big dogs.

"Have you any idea when you'll start work, Fred?" Joe asked.

I held my breath.

"Well, that's one of the reasons why I've come around today. It seems to me that we'll have to go about it all in a certain order."

"How do you mean?"

Dinkum snored, opened her eyes a crack to check her master was still there, then went back to her slumbers.

"I'm desperate for a decent kitchen and bathroom," I said, trying not to whine.

"Yes, but we can't start with the kitchen because of the kitchen wall that needs knocking down. And we can't start with the bathroom, or you'll have no toilet or shower for quite a long time. So it makes sense to start with the new bedroom and en suite. That'll give you a bathroom to use when we knock the other one down."

Joe and I looked at each other, then back at Fred.

"I suppose that makes sense," I said.

"Yes, I see," said Joe. "So when can you start?"

"First we'll need to get planning permission. I'll leave you with the name of an architect. You can make an appointment with him."

"An architect?" spluttered Joe. "Planning permission? We only want to convert the garage into a bedroom with en suite."

"I'm afraid it's necessary," explained Fred. "And we'll need to set up things like termite protection."

We were a bit depressed when Fred and Dinkum left. Things were going to take a lot longer than we'd planned.

It's hard to stay depressed in Australia when the sky is bluer than a roll of washed denim, the sun shines nearly every day, and your puppy wants to romp on the beach with you.

We began to explore further afield and fell in

love with the area more and more. Thea showed us a beautiful lakeside path which soon became a favourite walk. There were clifftop lookouts from which we planned to watch the whale migration, and more beaches than one can count on two hands.

And, as if that wasn't enough, we had our pool, although that wasn't without its problems. Thank goodness for our friend Emma, Baxter's owner, because she worked in a pool shop and could answer our numerous questions.

One summer day we were taking a dip. It was an excellent place to be because of the heat. Pelicans flew in formation overhead, and a gentle breeze fanned the palm fronds above us.

"Ouch! That hurt!" I said.

"What's the matter?"

"Something nipped me!"

"What sort of something?"

"I don't know!" I said, peering into the water.

Actually, it crossed my mind that it could be a funnel-web spider, because I knew they sometimes lurked in swimming pools, having fallen in when searching for a mate.

Thankfully, it wasn't a funnel-web; it was something entirely unexpected.

"I see it! It's a water beetle!"

"A water beetle? Don't be ridiculous. The pool

has chlorine in it, how could a water beetle survive in it?"

"I don't know! Look, there's another! And another…"

"Ow!"

Joe had just discovered that, not only were there indeed water beetles in our pool, but that they were armed with surprisingly powerful jaws. We jumped out of the water.

"Look, there are *hundreds* of them," I said, pointing at the pool filter where dozens of little black beetles were merrily swimming in and out.

"Oh, you've got them, too?" asked Emma when I told her about it. "We've had loads of calls from customers who've found beetles in their pools recently. Seems there's some kind of water beetle epidemic going on."

"How can they survive in chlorinated pool water?"

"I don't know. Chlorine will kill them, but you'd have to put so much in that you won't be able to swim."

"Oh no! I don't want to do that. Is there anything else we can do?"

"Well, there is a chemical you can add, but lots of our customers have complained that it doesn't work."

I reported the conversation back to Joe, who wasn't pleased.

A BANANA AND BEETLES

"Don't worry," I said. "I've got an idea."

Without telling him where I was going, I shot off to the nearest dollar store and purchased two children's shrimping nets, the type with very fine mesh.

"Correct me if I'm wrong, Vicky, but are you suggesting we catch all those beetles with these nets?"

"Yes."

"Don't be ridiculous."

"Have you got a better idea?"

"No, but do you realise how many there are? I think they've been holding some kind of beetle love-in because I'm sure there are hundreds more since I last looked."

"Never mind, it'll be fun. And then we can release them into the wild."

"Excuse me? Do what?"

"Well, as we catch them, we can put them into this Tupperware box. Then we can take them to the lake and set them free."

"Now I know you are crazy."

We added a new activity to our list of hobbies: beetle catching. It might not have been as good as swimming, but it was surprisingly entertaining. We set ourselves small targets, like how many could we catch in one scoop of the net. On the eighth day, we caught the last one and swam in the pool to celebrate.

Lola had no idea why we didn't use our pool for a week, but she enjoyed the lake visits. We emptied our daily catch into the water, and the beetles scooted off to hide in the reeds. Perhaps the lake water wasn't their natural habitat, but we'd given them a chance, and I'm sure the local frogs, fish and egrets enjoyed snacking on them.

Slowly, as summer slipped away, the water in our pool became too cool to swim in. It was essential that Joe continued to exercise and keep his lungs as active as possible. He joined a local gym that also offered a decent, very warm, indoor swimming pool. He began a daily regime of a workout in the gym followed by a swim in the pool.

How could we know that this place was to change our lives? We can't be sure, but we suspect that this innocent gym subscription was the cause of a catastrophe waiting to happen in the not too distant future.

CREAMY CAMEMBERT POTATOES

A delicious vegetarian side dish for any meal or barbecue. This recipe came from a 20-year-old Australian Women's Weekly magazine.

Ingredients

750g (1½lb) potatoes

2 tbs sour cream

15g (½oz) butter

1 clove garlic

125g (5oz) camembert

salt, pepper

2 tbs chopped chives

Method

Boil or steam potatoes in the usual way until tender. Drain.

Mash with sour cream until smooth.

Remove rind from cheese, chop cheese roughly.

Melt butter in pan.

Add crushed garlic and cheese, stir over a low heat until the cheese melts, then add to potato.

Season with salt and pepper then stir through the chives and serve hot.

14

CLONES AND A RUSSIAN

The architect came and took measurements. He drew plans to convert our garage into a bedroom with an en suite bathroom. We submitted the proposals to the council and waited for permission to be granted.

Lola continued to grow, and so did her hair. She didn't shed at all, which was a blessing, but every three months her curly coat needed clipping or it would begin to mat. It surprised me that she was such an enthusiastic swimmer and puddle-splasher, yet she wasn't very fond of being bathed. And she was even less keen on having her fur dried with a hairdryer.

But Lola had no choice, and a very nice lady regularly visited our house with her mobile dog-wash salon. She parked the trailer in our drive and set to work on Lola. She lathered her, dried her, trimmed her coat, cut her nails, until Lola looked and smelled delicious. That was until her next muddy puddle paddle or roadkill encounter. She loved to roll in anything that stank, and the stinkier the better. A rotting fish on the beach, a dead bird riddled with maggots, whatever. Sometimes she stayed clean and perfumed for no more than an hour.

I couldn't really blame Lola for not enjoying her salon experience. I don't enjoy visiting a hair salon either. When I first arrived in Australia, I was quite excited, knowing that I'd be able to chat with a hairdresser in my own language. In Spain, I always took my English-Spanish pocket dictionary with me, in case I forgot essential words like 'fringe' or 'layers' or phrases like 'low maintenance'.

I was still living in Sydney when I made my first hair appointment. The receptionist led me to a chair and introduced me to my stylist.

"This is Li Na," she said, and a delicate Chinese girl smiled at me and bowed her head respectfully.

I hadn't expected that, although I shouldn't have been surprised. Australia is exceptionally multi-cultural and Asians are the largest ethnic group to settle and start new lives here, followed by the British.

CLONES AND A RUSSIAN

We didn't talk much, although Li Na smiled a lot and told me her name meant 'elegant'. I didn't know the word for 'fringe' or indeed anything at all in Mandarin, so I gave her free rein. She did an excellent job and seemed to understand the sign language I had perfected in Spain. Although we couldn't chat, I was very satisfied with the result.

The next salon I visited was near my new home and only employed Australian staff. Communication wouldn't be a problem. When I arrived and gave my name, the receptionist looked at me strangely. She stared intently at the appointment book. Her eyes narrowed. Adjusting her spectacles, she checked the book again.

"Is there a problem?" I asked.

"Well, no, not really," she said. "It's just I think we've got some client names mixed up."

"Well, my name is Vicky. Vicky Twead."

"Yes, that's what I have written down here." She lowered her voice to a whisper. "The strange thing is, the lady in the chair over there is also named Twead."

"Twead with an EA instead of double E?"

"Yes."

"You're kidding! It's a really unusual name. Apart from family, I don't believe I've ever met any other Tweads."

"Oh, I expect we've made a mistake in the

appointment book," she said, leading me to the empty chair beside the other Ms Twead.

But they hadn't made a mistake. As soon as I was settled, and my stylist had begun her work, I couldn't resist starting a conversation with the lady next to me. She was roughly my age and seemed friendly.

"Hello," I said. "Excuse me for asking, but I wondered whether your surname really is Twead, like mine? With an A? That would be such a coincidence if it was!"

"Good heavens! Really? Yes, I'm Val Twead. Twead with an A. My husband is an only child, and I've never met any other Tweads."

"Me neither! How extraordinary! I'm Vicky so both our names begin with V. Do you get called V often? I do."

"All the time!"

As the stylists mixed colour and snipped, we chatted on, making discovery after discovery. I was beginning to think I had entered some kind of twilight zone or alternative universe.

"I can hear from your accent that you're English," said Val. "So am I! I've been here for over forty years, but I originally came from Dorset."

"Dorset? No way! So did I! When's your birthday?"

"February."

"So's mine!"

We gaped at each other, then carried on firing questions to and fro. A few details were different, but the vast majority were staggeringly similar.

"Do you have any grandchildren?"

"Yes, a granddaughter, and another one due in April."

"I have two granddaughters! The eldest is called India and the one-year-old is called Summer."

I didn't yet know the name of Indy's new baby sister who would be born that coming April. But India and Indy were undoubtedly very similar names.

By this time, the staff members were equally fascinated and joined in the conversation, firing more questions and comparing answers. Val and I drove similar cars, liked similar foods, we both had a dog, although she also had a cat.

And so it went on. It was one of the most surreal hair appointments I have ever attended. Readers may remember I had another, more unnerving experience, in Spain before emigrating to Australia. I documented that one in *Two Old Fools in Turmoil*, and it still causes shivers to run down my spine when I recall it.

Val left before me, and I never saw her again because the salon changed hands soon after and closed. In fact, the incident slipped my mind until

Indy's baby sister was born. When her parents finally decided on a name, I was profoundly shocked. The name they announced was so similar to that of Val's youngest granddaughter, Summer, that I wondered whether I had imagined the whole episode.

"It just isn't possible," said Joe, always the cynic. "I don't believe in *doppelgängers*, and I think you dreamed the whole thing."

I didn't dream it. And it *did* happen. I did meet a lady called Val Twead, and we definitely shared numerous personal details.

But I can't prove it.

So if you know somebody called Val Twead, do tell me. And if Val ever reads this book, please do get in touch so that I can prove to Joe that the salon incident was not a figment of my imagination.

Oh, and Val, I wonder if you can guess what name my daughter and son-in-law chose for my youngest granddaughter that April?

Meanwhile, another problem was distracting us. Australia's National Broadcast Network (NBN) was being rolled out across the country, designed to provide fast broadband Internet for all businesses and households. It was a government sponsored scheme and I had to apply for it through an Internet provider. I chose a popular one from a list of many and, when I moved into our house, I visited their outlet in the shopping village.

"The NBN is coming to this district," an assistant informed me, checking my address.

"That's good to hear," I said happily. "When is it coming?"

"We're not exactly sure. It will probably be several months."

That was disappointing, but I was pleased that it was definitely on its way. Fast Internet access was vital to me.

"Can I arrange for ordinary cable Internet to be set up? To tide me over until the NBN arrives?"

The assistant checked his computer, and his voice was solemn.

"I'm sorry, we're not allowed to install that service to your address."

"Why ever not?"

"Because the NBN is coming to your district. There's no point setting you up for cable Internet because you will soon be getting NBN."

"Yes, but it's not coming quite yet?"

"That's right. Not yet."

"So how do I get Internet access until then?"

"You'll need to use your phone as a hotspot and pay as you go."

That was double-Dutch to me but I had no choice. I knew I'd have to master it and rely on that until the NBN arrived.

"I've checked the system. I can now see the NBN should be available for you in December."

"Good, thank you. I guess that's not too long to wait."

"Would you like to put your name down for it?"

"Yes please."

In December, I phoned to see if there was any NBN news, and they admitted to having lost my order. The next date I was given was February. This was a blow because the pay-as-you-go system was proving to be expensive.

It also meant that my beautiful new flat-screen TV that Karly had so valiantly fought for, was useless. It could only pick up two local channels, one of which was dedicated to horse-racing. Not my personal viewing choice. It was probably just as well that I didn't want to watch horse-racing because the horses were blurry and disappeared at the slightest breeze.

When Joe arrived in Australia, he was horrified.

"What? Only two channels? Well, only one really as I have no intention of spending my evenings watching a pack of ghost horses galloping around a track. And that's only if the weather is good."

He called out a TV aerial expert who marched outside and looked up.

"Is that your TV aerial?" asked Mr Aussie Aerials, his eyes wide.

"Er, yes. That's what the previous owners left behind."

"Well, no wonder you've been having trouble. That's a caravan aerial, and I'm surprised you receive any TV channels at all. I doubt whether that thing could catch a cold, let alone a signal. It's about as useful as a glass door on a dunny."

Ah, another new Aussie word to add to my growing collection. Dunny: Australian/New Zealand slang for toilet or WC.

The flimsy TV aerial shook and wobbled, as though seriously affronted.

Mr Aussie Aerials erected a much more robust model, and hey presto, we had a dozen new TV channels.

Nothing happened in February, but in March, we received fantastic news. The NBN had arrived in our suburb. A team of workers attached a box to the outside of our house, and we were told somebody would soon appear to connect it to a smaller box inside.

We were given a date and at seven-thirty in the morning, a burly technician arrived carrying a toolbox and an assortment of levels, drills and square plastic tubing. Everything looked suspiciously shiny and new.

"I am Vladimir," he said, bowing slightly. "I am from Russia."

"Come in, Vladimir," said Joe cheerily. "We'd like to have the box put up in the office, please. It's very close to the outside box so there shouldn't be any problem connecting them through the wall. I suggest that if you run the tube along the wall just under the edge of the desktop, it'll be hidden."

Vladimir's lips stretched into a smile, but the smile never quite reached his eyes. I wondered whether he had actually understood us and if he'd ever done this job before.

"Would you like a cup of coffee or tea?" I asked.

"I am Vladimir," he said, bowing slightly.

"Oh dear. Let's leave Vladimir to get on with it, shall we?" said Joe, backing out of the office. "I'm sure he knows what he's doing."

Before long, we heard the clatter of tools and the encouraging sounds of industrious drilling.

"How wonderful!" I yelled above the noise. "We'll soon have fast Internet access! Would you mind holding the fort while I take Lola for a quick walk around the block?"

"No, you go ahead. I'll keep an eye on things

here," shouted Joe over the deafening sound of brickwork and masonry under duress.

The closed office door was vibrating as I walked past, and in the bedroom the noise, if possible, was even louder. I wanted my favourite cardigan and opened the sliding doors of the wardrobe.

What I saw inside made me gasp.

SPEEDY BEEF STROGANOFF

Delicious when poured over pasta or creamy mashed potatoes. From Taste.com.au

Ingredients (serves 4)

300g (10½oz) dried spiral pasta

600g (1¼lb) beef rump steak, trimmed, thinly sliced

2 tablespoons plain (all-purpose) flour

2 tablespoons olive oil

1 large brown onion, thinly sliced

200g (7oz) button mushrooms, thinly sliced

2 garlic cloves, crushed

2 teaspoons sweet paprika

1 tablespoon tomato paste

2 teaspoons dijon mustard

2 teaspoons Worcestershire sauce

½ cup beef stock

185ml (7fl oz) can light and creamy evaporated milk

Chopped fresh flat-leaf parsley leaves, to serve

Method

Cook pasta in a saucepan of boiling, salted water following packet directions, until tender. Drain.

Meanwhile, place steak in a large bowl. Add flour. Season with salt and pepper. Toss to coat.

Heat oil in a large, deep frying pan over medium-high heat. Cook beef, in batches, for 2 to 3 minutes or until browned. Transfer to a bowl.

Add onion to pan. Cook, stirring, for 5 minutes or until softened.

Add mushrooms and garlic. Cook for 5 minutes or until mushrooms are tender.

Return beef to pan and add paprika. Cook for 1 minute or until fragrant.

Add tomato paste, mustard, Worcestershire sauce and stock. Bring to the boil then reduce heat to low. Simmer for 5 minutes or until slightly thickened.

Remove from heat.

Stir in milk.

Divide pasta between plates.

Spoon over stroganoff mixture.

Sprinkle with parsley. Serve.

15

TERRY

I clapped my hands over my ears to muffle the roar of the drill, but I STILL couldn't believe my eyes. Surely this wasn't my neat, orderly wardrobe?

Vladimir had missed the outside wall entirely. The NBN technician had drilled through the office wall straight into our bedroom wardrobe.

Worse still, brick dust coated my hanging clothes and chunks of brick filled my shoes. I could see something soft and ragged wrapped around the drill bit, spinning crazily.

My favourite cardigan had suffered a terrible fate.

"Stop!" I yelled.

In the office, Vladimir didn't hear me, but Joe came running.

"What the..."

He turned back and burst into the office where our Russian friend was still drilling purposefully. Joe tapped him on the shoulder and the Russian stopped abruptly, but looked puzzled when he found he couldn't withdraw the drill from the wall.

"Are you aware that you're drilling into our wardrobe?" asked Joe, his voice calm but icy, a mirthless smile on his lips. "You can't pull your drill out of the wall because my wife's cardigan is wrapped around it."

Vladimir looked nervous.

"I am Vladimir," he said, bowing his head slightly.

"I know you are..." said Joe, but then caught sight of the box fixed to the wall.

"What the..."

Even an inebriated wombat would never have declared that box to be level. And as if that wasn't bad enough, the cable that led to the box was fixed to the wall in full view. It ran merrily along for at least a metre, halfway up the wall. And it wasn't level either.

I sensed Joe might implode and quickly intervened.

"Vladimir, come with me," I said, grabbing his sleeve and pulling him into the bedroom. It briefly crossed my mind that this was the first time I had *ever* dragged a man into a bedroom, let alone a burly young Russian.

Vladimir was goggle-eyed and even more shocked when I pointed at the debris and ugly hole in the wardrobe. His eyes nearly popped out when he saw my shredded cardigan wrapped in a ball around the end of his drill.

Back we marched to the office to find Joe busy herding our technician's tools into a heap.

"What are you doing?" I asked.

Joe knows two words of Russian, 'Hello' and 'Goodbye', and he was about to employ one of them for the first time in his life.

"I don't believe I have ever, EVER, seen a worse job," he said grimly. "I'm just gathering up these shiny new tools which have *clearly* never been used before. Then we're going to say Прощай (pronounced *proshchay*) to Vlad the Impaler, because he is leaving now."

Vladimir jumped. He may not have understood much English, but Joe's tone and expression, and the word Прощай, left him in no doubt. Grabbing his tools, he made a hasty exit. He might have left even faster had he not been delayed by needing to cut away my balled-up cardigan from his drill before he could extract it from the wall.

Poor man. I could see his hands shaking as he ripped away the last shreds.

Probably wisely, he didn't stop to say *Прощай*.

Next, we made numerous phone calls. These were fielded by helpful, polite representatives called Rashid or Sanjay, who were based in a call centre in Mumbai. Each listened sympathetically. Finally, we were invited to submit emails with attached photographic evidence of the disaster in the wardrobe, and the crooked NBN box.

Countless phone calls and emails later, a proper, skilled technician arrived and put everything right. Of course, he couldn't re-knit my favourite cardigan. Our Internet Provider gave us a router that we connected to the internal NBN box. Then, one happy day, a remote switch was flicked, and the little red and green lights on the router lit up and blinked cheerily. We finally had fast Internet access.

I danced with joy.

It seemed everybody had their own NBN horror story to tell. Our tale wasn't unique. We heard of telegraph poles falling without warning, and holes left in walls that allowed armies of insects to march into people's houses. We heard of installed NBN suddenly dropping out, and streets where houses on only one side had access to the Internet.

It was enough to make us quite twitchy.

One day, while driving down our street, we saw a parked NBN truck. A bunch of workmen were poring over an NBN switchboard located in a roadside electrical box. Joe stopped Bruce.

"Don't you dare mess with our NBN," he called out of the window.

The workmen stared at him.

"There, that's told them!" said Joe, satisfied, and drove off.

I've mentioned before that I don't enjoy visiting a hair salon, but that changed when I met Terry. The closure of the salon where I had met my clone, Val Twead, meant I needed to find another hairdresser, and one of my new dog-walking pals suggested Terry's place.

"I've been going there for years," she said. "You'll love Terry."

She gave me directions to the salon, and I drove slowly past. It wasn't in the smartest district of town, and empty shops flanked the building, but I parked Bruce and entered the salon.

Inside, it looked as though time had stood still and nothing had changed very much in the last twenty years or more. It didn't boast the flashy decor one often sees in modern salons. There were no vivid colours or posters of lithe young models sporting edgy hairstyles.

TERRY

Nevertheless, this salon had a unique attraction of its own. It was clean and homely, and there were little displays of lovingly-knitted toys and homemade cot quilts. Greetings cards were being sold for charity. It reminded me of a bygone England, when Women's Institutes thrived, before we began importing everything from China.

But what I caught sight of, in a corner, convinced me to make an appointment. It was an overflowing bookcase with shelves bowed into crescents by the weight of stacked books.

A tiny, blonde lady detached herself from her customer and smiled at me. I judged her to be in her sixties, like me, and couldn't help noticing she had a gap between her front teeth, exactly like my own.

"Hello, can I help you?"

"Are you, Terry?"

"I am."

"Oh good! A friend recommended you. I wonder whether I could make an appointment, please?"

"Of course," she said, pulling out a big, dog-eared appointment book and thumbing through the pages. No fancy computer system here. "When would suit you?"

My first session with Terry was a delight. She was perfectly satisfied with my request of 'just a tidy-up, please' and didn't attempt to convince me I needed 'foils' or other baffling hair treatments. Instead, we had a good old-fashioned gossip, and I left feeling I'd made a new friend, not just acquired a new hairdresser.

As we nattered, ladies would come in, and Terry would look up.

"Hi, Beryl, how are you?"

"Good, thanks, Terry. I'm just bringing in a few new books and returning that one you recommended. I really enjoyed it."

"Oh good, I thought you would. There's another one by that author on the second shelf somewhere. Unless somebody else borrowed it."

A steady stream of readers arrived to swap and donate books. I feared for the shelves that groaned beneath the weight of each new book.

Terry knew everybody, and I began to understand why her appointment book bulged.

"I don't think I'll ever retire," she said, shaking her blonde tresses. "It's not like going to work. It's like meeting friends. I've known some of my clients for more than twenty-five years."

I felt relaxed and was actually enjoying my appointment. We had plenty in common, like our love of wildlife.

"I have two Indian mynah birds in my garden," she said, "I call them Heckle and Jeckle."

Most Australians dislike the Indian mynah bird, perhaps not without reason. This cheeky chap should not be confused with the Noisy Mynah, which is an Australian native, grey in colour and much better behaved.

Deliberately introduced in the 1860s to keep insects down in Melbourne's market gardens, Indian mynahs thrived and multiplied, reaching almost epidemic proportions and making life difficult for native species. Apart from competing for food, the mynahs take over the native birds' traditional nesting hollows, and their ability to multiply is breathtaking. One bird can lay six eggs in one clutch, and they often breed three times a year. It has been estimated that one breeding pair could potentially be responsible for 13,000 birds within five years.

Scary.

Often called 'flying rats' or even 'cane toads of the sky' they have earned a place on the list of the world's 100 most invasive species.

I guess it's understandable that some councils have taken steps to keep the numbers down. I read that Bundaberg Regional Council, in Queensland, offers a bounty of two dollars per head for Indian mynahs, delivered alive and unharmed. It kills them humanely, and some are sent to the *Snakes Down Under Reptile Park* in Childers, where crocodiles regularly snack on them.

Of course, we can't blame the mynah birds for

being so successful. It was man's fault for meddling and introducing them to Australia in the first place. Like the disastrous introduction of rabbits and cane toads. And, like Terry, I couldn't help liking these bold, mischievous birds. The gang we had christened The Hooligans entertained us greatly.

"Oh my stars!" exclaimed Terry. "You wouldn't believe how cheeky Heckle and Jeckle are! If the door is open, the pair of them march straight into our laundry and help themselves to the dog's kibble out of her bowl. And Bridie just watches them!"

I laughed.

"And you know what? My husband got a different brand of kibble and Heckle and Jeckle just turned their beaks up at it. So when he went shopping again, I asked him to get the usual stuff. 'Why?' he asks, 'doesn't Bridie like the new brand?' 'Nah,' I said, 'Heckle and Jeckle don't like it.' Well, he just rolled his eyes at me."

We chatted on, and I discovered other things about Terry. For instance, although Australian through and through, she was a staunch royalist and her knowledge of the British royal family put me to shame. The year 2016 was quite a busy one for the Royals, and Terry followed their every move. She celebrated the Queen's 90th birthday and was delighted when Prince Harry made headlines by confirming he was dating Meghan Markle. She knew what outfits were worn at what official occasions, and the names of all the little princes and princesses. The very mention of Princess Diana made Terry's eyes mist over.

"I remember it like it was yesterday," she said. "I couldn't stop crying. Then, when the day came to lay Diana to rest, I said to my family, 'Listen, I'm going into the lounge room with a scotch to attend a funeral. Do not disturb on any account.'"

Not only was Terry an avid reader and Royal Family watcher, but she could tell stories that held me spellbound. We were discussing Australian wildlife once when Terry recalled an incident.

"Oh my stars! I remember when my daughter was a baby, and I was making our bed. She was crawling around the floor by my feet when she lost her toy. I think it went under the bed and we couldn't reach it. So I moved the bed back from the wall and peered down. Oh my stars! Something was moving!"

"What was it?"

"Well, it was dark down there so I couldn't make it out at first. I know it's crazy, but I thought it might be a turtle or a lizard. When it moved again, it suddenly dawned on me. Oh my stars, it was a snake! So I grabbed the baby and flew out of the room. Then I rolled up some towels to block the gap under the door. I don't think it could have come out, but I wanted to be sure. I thought it was probably harmless, but I didn't know what sort of snake it was and I certainly wasn't going to risk it."

"Wow! What did you do then?"

"I ran over to a neighbour and left the baby with her, and then I didn't know what to do. It was the days before mobile phones, and my husband was away and couldn't be reached. I thought of ringing my dad, but he was an hour away. Anyway, my neighbour's husband said he'd go and have a look and when he came back, he'd gone pale. 'Did you see it?' I asked him. 'Yes,' he says, 'it's a five and a half foot red-bellied black snake.' Well, I nearly died!"

Red-bellied black snakes are beautiful creatures, but highly venomous. They have forward-facing fangs and although their bite is rarely fatal, anyone bitten must seek immediate hospital attention. They are very common along the eastern coast of Australia and usually hide in moist vegetation. They can climb trees and are excellent swimmers, being able to stay underwater for twenty minutes or more.

"What on earth was it doing in your bedroom?"

"I have no idea."

"How do you think it got in?"

"I don't know!"

"I wonder how long it had been there?"

"Who knows? In the end, I called out the council, and a ranger came. He said they hibernate in cold weather. We might have been sleeping in that bed, with a red-bellied black snake underneath us, for weeks!"

"Did he take it away?"

"No, he killed it."

I was sorry to hear that. I think we are a little wiser nowadays. Had it happened today, the snake would probably be relocated to a place where it wouldn't be a nuisance.

When Terry's husband came home, he thought the whole tale was just a huge prank. He refused to believe they had been slumbering blissfully between the sheets, unaware of the red-bellied black snake that lay under their bed.

FAST FOOD MINESTRONE

With stock in the freezer and a few veggies in the fridge, you can make this steaming bowl of minestrone in just under half an hour.

Ingredients

2 cups prepared chicken stock

2 cups water

1 tin tomatoes

1-1½ cups small macaroni

2 zucchini (courgette) sliced

2 carrots, peeled and sliced

Handful of frozen peas

1 can red kidney beans, drained

2 tablespoons tomato paste

½ bunch spinach or 1 small packet frozen spinach

Parmesan cheese then salt and ground black pepper to taste

Method

Bring the stock and water to the boil.

Chop the tinned tomatoes a little and add to the stock with macaroni and tomato paste.

Simmer for about 10 minutes.

While that is simmering, chop the spinach, then add carrots, zucchini and kidney beans.

Simmer for a further 10 minutes or so until carrots are tender.

Add salt and pepper to taste.

Stir in the spinach and peas, cook for a minute or two, then serve.

16
HOSTIBALS

Hola tía Vicky y tío Joe,

It is I Catalina your penpall again. I hop you are well again. My family is completely wells. I do not know what things I can write but my mother say to tell you here are many almond flowers on the trees today and everybody say we will have good lots of almonds. Valentina say if she marry Geronimo she will make a dress the same colour of almond flowers and she want Geronimo wear a necktie of blue colour same of sky above mountains.

I ask Valentina if she marrys Geronimo soon because I want to dance flamenco at the weeding. But Valentina she say no because first she must hit Geronimo into a shape. I do not understand hit Geronimo into a shape. I like the shape of Geronimo. I say Valentina that my mother she say Geronimo is a guardian angel because he always save my little brother Pollito from dead. Valentina she laughs much but she not very happy. She say me if Geronimo is a angel why he not fly out of the valley more??? She say if Geronimo has wings he can see some more of the world.

I say the words of Valentina to my mother and she say we not talk about it and say it is not business for children. But she say me that Valentina has visit many places in the world. Perhaps she wish Geronimo come with her for some travellings.

I say Geronimo I care for his donkey with straw then he can make travels with Valentina. Then he be the right shape for Valentina. Then they can marrys and I can dance flamenco at the weeding. Geronimo make an noise like PAH then say he like Andalucía much and why for he want see more???

Pollito say you not remember write if you have great white shark near your house.

Felicitations, Catalina xx

Before we knew it, summer tiptoed out, and autumn crept in. The water in our pool cooled but

Lola, the water-dog that she was, didn't care. I'm sure she'd be willing to break through ice to have a swim, although I've yet to see frost in our part of Australia.

It was April, the month when, in Spain, the almond blossom petals would litter the ground like confetti, to be replaced by new leaves in the branches overhead. Our grapevine in Spain was, no doubt, bursting into life. But here, in Australia, the forests turned red and gold.

We still had no kitchen or a decent bathroom. Neither did we have a date when the promised work would begin.

But that April a very exciting thing happened which took our minds off such trivia.

At dawn on the 25th of April, 1915, armed forces from France, Great Britain, and the British Empire, including Australia and New Zealand, landed on the Gallipoli peninsula. Battles raged, and many lives were lost on both sides. More than 8,000 Australian soldiers were killed.

A year later, in 1916, the 25th of April was officially named Anzac Day. ANZAC is an abbreviation for Australian and New Zealand Army Corps. Declared a public holiday, it became the day on which Australians remember the sacrifice of those who died in the Great War. Every year, on the 25th of April, memorial services are held at dawn, the time of the original landing in Gallipoli.

One hundred and one years later, in 2016, Anzac Day fell on a Monday and saw me driving to Sydney. I'd left Joe at home to look after Lola. I would be looking after Indy in Sydney. But this wasn't an ordinary babysitting engagement.

"Are you ready to go?" I asked when I arrived at Karly and Cam's house and had finished hugging Indy.

"I think so!" said Karly. "My case is all packed. I've left a list on the table of what Indy can have for meals, and Cam will be back late tonight. Help yourself to anything."

"Gosh, so exciting! This time tomorrow, I'll have another granddaughter."

Karly and Cam left, and I had Indy all to myself.

"Do you know where your mummy and daddy have gone?" I asked her.

She looked back at me with those wise, wide three-and-a-half-year-old blue eyes fringed with thick lashes.

"Yes."

"Where are they?"

"Hostibal."

"That's right! And why have they gone to hostibal?"

"To get my new sister!" she squealed, clapping her hands.

And that's precisely what the plan was. Karly was booked to go into hospital to be induced, and we all expected the baby to be born the next day.

It was exciting going to sleep that night knowing that the new day would bring another little person into our lives.

In the morning there was no news, and I tried to concentrate on playing Princesses with Indy, but my heart wasn't in it. The morning wore on, and I drove us over to Cam's parents' house so that we could all wait for news together. A gathering of the clan was always fun, but this time we were all breathless with expectancy.

"Have they decided on a name yet?" somebody asked.

"No, they have a shortlist, but they haven't picked one yet."

How slowly the time crawled by. Had the baby been born? Was everything okay?

At last, the telephone call came through. The baby had arrived, and mother and daughter were both doing well.

"Indy, your new baby sister is here! She's in the hospital!"

"Can we go and get her?"

"Not yet, Mummy and Daddy will bring her home soon, but we can go and see her."

HOSTIBALS

We bundled into our cars and drove to the hospital. We shared a lift to the third floor with an elderly couple.

"Oh," they said to Indy, noting her costume and tiara, "are you a princess?"

"Yes, and I've got a baby and its name is called Dragon."

"Oh, that's nice…"

Cam was in the waiting area, grinning.

"Everything's great," he said, "it all went really well. Karly's tired but doing fine and the baby's perfect."

"Still no name yet?"

"My baby's name is called Dragon," announced Indy.

"Hmm, maybe…" said her daddy, smiling down at her. Then he turned to all of us. "Now, I hope you don't mind, but I'd like to take Indy in first, on her own, to meet her baby sister."

We all nodded.

"Of course!"

We understood this was a very special family moment and watched, moist-eyed, as the pair walked away, hand in hand, up the corridor. Cam, tall, strong and capable, holding the princess's little hand in his big one. Her long blonde hair streamed out behind her as she ran alongside him, three of her steps matching his single stride. In her other hand, she clutched a soft little teddy, a gift for her new sister.

"Well, we'll never forget this baby's birthday," I said, while we waited. "The day after Anzac Day."

Then, at last, they appeared, coming back towards us down the corridor, Cam marching while his eldest daughter skipped beside him. We all stood.

"Did you see your new sister?" I asked Indy.

"Yes!"

"Oooh! Have you got a new baby sister?" asked a passing nurse, overhearing the conversation. "What's her name?"

"Her name is called Dragon."

The nurse smiled and walked on.

A weary but radiant Karly, with her new daughter, were in a little side room. We all flooded in. Of course, the baby was perfect and slept through the whole experience of being examined, and cooed over, and passed from family member to family member.

"She's got heaps of hair," said Karly, "and she's quite a lot darker than Indy was. We still haven't decided on a name."

Meanwhile, Indy and her little cousin, who had just arrived, discovered that if they pressed individual buttons on a remote control, the bed would rise or lower, or tip this way and that. They almost folded poor Karly in half. Probably wisely, she escaped the levitating mattress by vacating the bed. I heard later that the bed eventually broke, but the hospital was very nice about it. They claimed it must have been faulty, and quickly replaced it with a new one.

It wasn't until a couple of days later that Cam and Karly finally settled on a name for their baby daughter. We were all delighted that it wasn't Dragon.

"We're going to call her Winter," Karly said. "She'll always remind us of when Cam and I met in the snow."

Having lived so many years in Spain, I was aware that I had neglected routine medical procedures that I might have been encouraged to pursue had I been living in the UK. I received no reminders for bowel cancer tests or mammograms; neither did I ever have my blood routinely tested. Now, as an Australian permanent resident, all that would change.

I registered Joe and myself at the local Medical Centre and was delighted with my new doctor. Dr Sarah happened to be English, and she was one of those special people who listen to you as though you are the only person in the world. I immediately felt at ease, and I trusted all the advice she gave me. If she didn't know the answer, she said so, and never made me feel I was wasting her time.

Joe's doctor was South African, a man who didn't make small talk and called a spade a spade. Joe liked him very much, so we were both happy.

Dr Sarah conducted a smear test, which pronounced me clear of cervical cancer. Dr Botha kept an eye on Joe's high blood pressure and prescribed medication for that, and his COPD and prostate cancer.

I received a parcel in the mail. I ripped it open to find that it was a 'self-administer' bowel cancer test kit. I'd never heard of such a thing in Spain. I followed the instructions and found it a straightforward process, in spite of my horror at the thought of it. I labelled my specimen and sent it off in the envelope provided. In due course, I was thrilled to be told that no evidence of bowel cancer had been detected.

One day, I noticed a huge pink van parked in our local shopping centre car park, with the legend *BreastScreen NSW* painted in enormous letters on the side. *Book your free mammogram*, it invited.

I nervously climbed the steps, entered the little waiting room and made an appointment.

It was the first time I had ever had a

mammogram, and I now understand why women don't like it very much. I had no idea that breasts can be squeezed and compressed so dramatically. Bread dough being flattened under a rolling-pin springs to mind. The actual compression only lasts a few seconds and is utterly necessary, but I was heartily glad when it was all over.

"We'll be in touch," said the receptionist as I left.

I put it out of my mind until I received an ominous letter.

> *Thank you for attending your appointment at Breast Screening, New South Wales. We would like you to return to have further tests to complete your screening. This appointment usually takes from two to four hours, however, occasionally an appointment can take longer. It is therefore recommended that you commit the day to your visit just in case.*

I checked in and was directed to a waiting room. I remember thinking it must be tea-break time because there was a bunch of ladies in blue overalls already seated there, some with white cups and saucers, sipping tea.

A nurse bobbed up from nowhere.

"Victoria? If you'd like to go into one of those cubicles over there, you'll find a pile of gowns on the bench. Just pick one that's your size and change into it. Pop all your clothes and personal items into one of those lockers."

Ah. So the other ladies weren't cleaners or hospital staff. Like me, they were patients.

"Thank you," I said and made my way to a cubicle.

A pile of neatly folded gowns awaited me on the bench, and I selected one marked *Medium to Large* because I didn't want anything too skimpy. Then I struggled with the crossover ties, trying to work out how they were supposed to hold the gown together. By the time I'd just about fathomed it, I realised that the gown was far too big for me and threatened to reveal large portions of my naked self unless I kept it clamped together with a firm grip. It was too late to exchange it for a smaller one because I heard my name being called. I bundled my clothes and handbag into a locker and hurried back out into the waiting room to join the seven other ladies.

ANZAC BISCUITS

ANZAC biscuits were originally made by the wives and mothers of soldiers fighting in World War 1 and were sent to them in packages. From bakeplaysmile.com

Ingredients (serves 2)

110g (4½oz) rolled oats

150g (5oz) plain flour

125g (4½oz) brown sugar

70g (2½oz) desiccated coconut

125g (4½oz) butter

2 tbs golden syrup

½ tsp bicarbonate of soda

Method

Preheat oven to 160°C (fan-forced) or 320°F. Grease and line three flat baking trays with baking paper.

Combine the rolled oats, flour, brown sugar and coconut in a bowl.

Place butter, golden syrup and 2 tablespoons cold water into a microwave-safe bowl and heat for 3 minutes, 50% power or until melted.

Stir through the bicarbonate of soda.

Pour the butter mixture over the oat mixture and stir to combine.

Roll level tablespoons of mixture into balls.

Place on trays, 5cm (2 inches) apart and flatten slightly.

For chewy biscuits, bake for 10 to 12 minutes or until light golden. For crunchy biscuits, increase cooking time to 12-15 minutes.

Leave on the baking trays for 5 minutes before transferring to a wire rack to cool completely.

17

CATS AND DOGS

I was taken to a little side room where the doctor asked me lots of questions. She ticked boxes on her forms.

"We called you back because we noticed a shadow on one x-ray," she explained. "It's probably nothing, but we need to check it out and investigate further."

She pointed to an area on the screen. I peered at it, but it wasn't obvious to my untrained eye.

"We'll run a few different types of tests to check your breasts in more detail," she continued. "A specialist will give you a thorough examination, both visually and by manipulation. She'll be feeling for abnormalities. We'll give you a second mammogram, and we'll also conduct an ultrasound scan. This uses harmless sound waves.

The test is done by moving a probe over the surface of your skin, and it's completely painless."

"That's a lot of tests," I remarked.

"Yes, I'm afraid it's going to be a long day for you. Now, if you'd like to return to the waiting room, we'll call you when we're ready for the first test."

I joined the gown-clad ladies and waited, probably wearing the same anxious expression as all the others. Gradually, the ice began to break and some ladies chatted. A few flicked the pages of magazines or concentrated on finding pieces of a giant jigsaw puzzle that lay partially finished on a table.

At regular intervals, a nurse popped her head around the door and called out a name. That person would stand and follow the nurse to carry out the next test.

I grabbed some multi-coloured knitting out of a basket. I hadn't knitted for years, but it would keep my hands busy. I looked at the rows knitted so far. It was evident that this square had been taken up by a variety of knitters. Some rows were tighter than others, some of the stitches smaller or looser. There were plenty of dropped stitches. I wondered how many anxious women had added rows to this misshapen woollen piece. I hoped that none of them had to hear those words all women dread.

It was a strange day. Gradually, the eight of us were whittled down as individuals were given a clean bill of health and sent home. They dressed and waved a cheery goodbye, wishing the remaining few the best of luck.

By late in the afternoon, there were only two of us left. Barbara was in her forties and had discovered a lump when taking a shower. And there was me.

Why hadn't I been sent home already? What had they found? My fingers knitted furiously, row after row.

"Victoria? Sorry to keep you waiting, but would you mind coming through for another mammogram?"

"Another one?"

"Yes, we just want to repeat the sideways section on the right side. The doctor felt it wasn't clear enough."

My heart lurched. Had they found something?

"Good luck!" called Barbara as I trotted after the nurse.

I was already feeling somewhat bruised and tender after all the other tests, but I followed her. The top plate descended and squashed me, holding me firmly in place for the x-ray.

Another interval in the waiting room. Another four rows of knitting.

Then the nurse returned.

"Victoria? The doctor is happy with your x-rays now. We can't see any problems. You can get dressed and go home. Expect a letter from us in due course confirming that all is well."

"Oh, thank you!" I was beaming from ear to ear.

"I'm very pleased for you!" said a voice at my elbow.

I'd forgotten Barbara, the only remaining patient, and my smile vanished.

"Oh, I'm sure that any minute now they'll come in and say the same thing to you," I said quickly.

I retrieved my clothes and dressed. When I came out, the waiting room was empty. Barbara wasn't there.

Perhaps she'd been called in for another test, or maybe she been given good news, like me, and was getting dressed.

I sometimes think about Barbara. Had she been declared clear, or did she have to listen to those words that none of us ever want to hear?

I'll never know.

The month of June brought the shock news that Britain was leaving the European Union. In a referendum, held on 23 June 2016 in the UK, 51.9

per cent of voters supported leaving the EU. Brexit, a combination of the words 'Britain' and 'exit', was dominating the news headlines.

Everybody we knew seemed to have a passionate opinion on the matter, and I was surprised that my friends and family in the UK were also split on the issue.

Me? I have no head for politics and couldn't substantiate any argument, for or against. I hadn't lived in England since 2004, and didn't feel qualified to vote. However, although I'm aware of being hopelessly naïve and over-simplifying the matter horribly, I dream of a world with no borders, no wars, and mankind living at peace with each other. Somehow, leaving the EU feels like we are taking a step backwards.

"Hear! Hear!" said Joe when he read these words over my shoulder.

July in Australia is midwinter, and we were delighted that the temperature didn't drop very low. In fact, when there was no southerly wind, and the sun shone, it was as warm as a British summer's day. The only complaint we had was that our house seemed to be much colder inside than out.

Most Australian houses are not built to combat

cold temperatures. I have yet to see double-glazed windows, and cavity-wall insulation is not automatically installed.

"We'll make sure we get insulation put in the roof when the reno starts," I said.

"Reno?"

"That's Aussie for 'renovation'."

"Oh. You mean *if* the reno ever starts. We've got the planning permission in place, what's holding Fred up?"

Fred did contact me that week, although not in quite the way we had expected.

Out of the blue, a text appeared on my phone. I read it, and my eyes popped.

> *U sound lovely. Would u like to meet up some time? I've not been well but I'm ready for some fun now.*

"Who's texting you?" asked Joe.

"Fred," I answered, and passed him the phone. We both started laughing.

"I think he sent that message to the wrong person," I said. "What shall I do?"

"Nothing. Don't embarrass him. At least we know why he hasn't been in touch, anyway."

I followed Joe's advice, and sure enough, Fred phoned the following day.

"Sorry I've been a bit delayed. I've actually been in hospital. They're not sure what was wrong with me, except for being diagnosed as diabetic, but I'm okay again now."

"Oh, that's good."

"Right, expect a bin to arrive on Monday morning. They'll put it on your front grass. Then I'll be coming later with building materials and my plumber. He'll be mapping out how your new en suite bathroom plumbing will be laid."

"So, what fantastic excuse did he come up with this time?" asked Joe, ever the cynic. "Did aliens whisk him away and experiment on him?"

"No. As we suspected, he was crook."

"What? He was what?"

"Crook. It's Aussie for 'unwell'."

"Oh."

"Anyway, work begins on Monday."

"Hmm... I'll believe that when I see it."

Very early on Monday morning, before I'd even finished my first cup of coffee, the rubbish skip arrived. Lola barked so hard I feared she would give herself a sore throat. And she didn't stop, even after the skip had been lowered onto our front lawn and the lorry had driven off. She carried on barking at the skip until I took her outside and introduced her to it. When she understood that it wasn't a huge yellow intruder, she calmed down.

"That dog never stops barking," said Joe. "She

barks at everything. Can't you do something about it?"

"Like what?"

"I don't know. She barks at people walking past the house, birds, cats, everything."

Actually, he was right. She spent much of her time peering through the living room window studying the goings-on in our street. Anybody passing got a good barking at. If The Hooligans, or any other birds, invaded the front lawn, they were barked at. And cats infuriated her.

The rascally cats knew how to wind her up. They would deliberately preen themselves just a few feet beyond the window, in full view of Lola, sending her into a frenzy. Memories of the days when she was a tiny puppy and friends with Bandsaw in Sydney, had apparently faded away.

"She's only a puppy…"

"Well, you need to get it sorted now before she gets any older."

Joe was right, of course. We had three cats living next door, and several more in the street. At night a tomcat roamed, howling at the moon. The thought of Lola forevermore going berserk every time she saw or heard a cat was not pleasant.

What to do? Consult the Internet, of course.

Apparently, desensitisation is the answer. Get one's dog so accustomed to whatever sets them off that they eventually cease to notice it.

I couldn't physically introduce Lola to a hoard of cats, but I could do the next best thing. I could expose her to cats meowing. I found a soundtrack on Youtube called *12 hours of cats meowing*, or something like that, and warned Joe.

"Now, before I start this therapy, I want your promise that you won't interfere, and you won't tell me to stop."

"What are you going to do?"

"I'm going to play a soundtrack I found, and it's twelve hours long."

"Twelve hours? What is it, music?"

"Um, no, not really. Not unless you're a cat, I suppose."

"Go on, then, if it cures Lola's barking, it'll be worth it. I promise not to interfere."

I slipped my phone out of my pocket and pressed Play. The unearthly sound of a cat yowling filled the room and Lola went ballistic. She barked and rushed around searching every room and nook and cranny for cats.

Joe and I looked at each other.

"Are you sure?" shouted Joe, scratching.

To be honest, I'd had enough after one minute. The never-ending howling of the cats combined with Lola's hysterical barking was almost unbearable. But we had to give this therapy a chance to work.

"Let's just carry on as normal, and she should start to ignore it soon."

Actually, it did work. After five minutes of searching for the noisy feline invaders, Lola gave up and went to sleep. I wondered what she dreamed of as the soundtrack continued with litters of kittens mewling and tomcats singing. Joe had shut himself away and clamped earphones over his ears, enjoying Beatles' songs, and successfully drowning out the caterwauling. I tried to write, but I couldn't string any coherent thoughts together.

Hour after hour, the cats howled, nearly driving me insane. Occasionally, when they changed note, Lola would begin to bark, then lost interest. I felt the treatment was working.

There was a knock on the door, and I opened it to Fred who had brought the plumber. Joe heard nothing because he was still shut away with the Beatles. I held Lola back as she tried to give both men her usual enthusiastic welcome. Dinkum marched in and stole her bed while Lola was otherwise occupied. The sound of meows didn't bother Dinks in the slightest.

"Have you got some new kittens?" asked the plumber.

"I was going to ask the same thing," said Fred.

"No," I replied and explained. "Lola barks every time she hears a cat. I'm playing a soundtrack of cats meowing so that she learns to ignore it."

"She isn't barking now so perhaps it's working." the plumber commented.

"Yes, I hope so."

We discussed pipes and water pressure for a while, then Fred and the plumber left. I looked at my watch. It was time to take Lola for her run on the oval so I gathered her up, shouted goodbye to Joe and drove away. I put my phone in my pocket, the cat soundtrack still running.

As I got out of the car, a mum passed with a toddler.

"Mummy, where are the pussy cats?"

"What pussy cats? There are no pussy cats here, silly!"

In the distance, I could see some of my dog-walking pals and Lola raced over to greet them. Frankie was an elderly lady who had never lost her Scottish accent despite having moved to Australia more than fifty years ago. She had two little white fluffy rescue dogs.

I met so many people through Lola, and many of them had stories to tell about their dogs.

For instance, there was Monty, or Mounty as I called him privately. Monty was an ancient, black, miniature poodle, greying around the face. He was quiet and relaxed until he saw another dog. Then his demeanour would change. Suddenly he became an ardent lover with just one thing on his mind.

His owner admitted that it didn't matter to Monty whether the other dog was male or female.

"In fact, it doesn't even have to be a dog; he humps everything. He humps cushions, legs, anything. We had him de-sexed, but it made no difference."

"Oh dear!"

"He has a favourite soft toy at home which he won't leave alone. Even the kids accept it. We call it Tigger-time."

I couldn't help laughing.

"I know! He's a pedigree, and he was supposed to be a stud dog at a breeder's place. But he didn't do the business so they gave him away. We reckon he's spending the rest of his life making up for it. He's got something to prove."

Monty always tried his luck with Lola but she just shrugged him off. No doubt she was baffled by his advances.

Another owner, Chris, had a pug named Riley, and he had a very different story to tell. He paid $1000 for Riley but when he got him home, he discovered his dog was riddled with worms. However, medication sorted the problem, and all was well.

Until the day Riley disappeared.

HOME-MADE DOG BISCUITS

I had to wait until I actually had a kitchen with a working oven before I could try this recipe. It's good to know what goes into your dog's treats, and they didn't taste too bad to me, either.

Ingredients

Dog Biscuits

1 cup cooked pumpkin

½ cup peanut butter

2 eggs

¼ cup cooking oil

2½ cups of wholewheat flour

1 tsp baking powder

Glaze

2 tablespoons of bacon grease or similar

¼ cup of smooth peanut butter

Method

Preheat oven to 350°C (650°F)

Combine pumpkin, peanut butter, eggs and oil in a bowl. Add baking powder and flour and stir until a stiff dough forms.

Knead or mix dough until all the flour is incorporated.

Roll out the dough with a rolling pin and use a cookie cutter to cut out dog bone shapes, or just bake in little circles like cookies.

Bake for 15 minutes.

Whisk the bacon grease and peanut butter until very smooth. Drizzle over the treats and cool in the fridge until the glaze sets.

18

MORE CATS AND DOGS

"Riley disappeared? Was he stolen?"

"No," said Chris. "He was just a puppy at the time, and he was always into mischief. I don't know how he managed to get out through a tiny hole under the fence, but he did. I was beside myself! I looked for him everywhere and went to three local vets in case he'd been handed in. They asked if Riley was microchipped and I told them he was."

"So what happened?"

"Then I got a call from one of the vets saying somebody had found a pug and that it seemed to fit Riley's description. The vet said that the people who found him were bringing him in to get the microchip checked. The vet would phone me back as soon as that was done."

"Oh, thank goodness for that!"

"I was overjoyed! But that wasn't the end of the story."

"Why? Wasn't the puppy they found Riley?"

"Well, that's the thing! The vet called me back, as he promised, but he said there was a problem. They'd scanned the microchip and looked it up, and it belonged to a seven-year-old black German shepherd. That dog was registered at a breeder's address in a town several miles away. The vet phoned the breeder and was told that there must have been a mix-up with the microchip. But they said Riley belonged to them."

"Belonged to who? The breeder?"

"Yes."

"That's very odd!"

"I know, and the story nearly had a horrible ending!"

"Why?"

"The vet gave the finder's address to the breeder, and they said they were setting off straight away to collect Riley. I jumped in my car and drove around to the finder's address, too, praying that I'd get there before the breeder did. As it happened, we arrived at exactly the same time. The breeder was just walking up the path to the finder's front door. I saw the finder looking out of the window, and then the front door opened. Riley burst out and charged down the path. He swerved straight past the breeder and his wife and jumped up at me, giving me a massive welcome."

"Wow!"

"Yup, there wasn't any doubt that it was Riley! Or that I was the genuine owner. The breeder couldn't leave fast enough. Thank goodness I arrived in time because they would have taken him and resold him, I'm sure of it."

I heaved a sigh of relief, hearing the end of the story. That had been a close call.

At the oval I joined my dog-walking pals, Frankie, with her two fluffy rescue dogs, and Jean, who owned another pug named Bella.

"Can you hear cats in the distance?" asked Jean. "Kind of muffled?"

"No," said Frankie, "but I am rather deaf."

"I'm sorry, but the cats are my fault," I said, sighing. I explained, pulling out my phone from my pocket.

Frankie and Jean laughed. We chatted and watched the dogs play, ignoring the sounds of the cats which kept up their infernal meowing.

Eventually, it was time to go home, and I was pleased that Lola was no longer showing any interest in the cats' chorus. I parked Bruce and was about to enter the house when I saw a large white card tucked into the screen door. It said:

Council Ranger Section

We visited this property at 15.30 on urgent business. Please contact us as soon as possible using the above telephone number. Fines may apply if you disregard this notice.

"Joe? What's this card on the door? What do they mean?"

Joe was making himself a coffee and examined the card.

"I have no idea! I didn't hear anybody come to the door. I've been listening to music with my earphones on. Ranger? Urgent business? Whatever do they mean?" He scratched below, deep in thought. "What are Australian rangers responsible for, anyway?"

"Um, litter, bush fire matters, animal control…"

"That's it!"

"What? Lola hardly needs controlling!"

"Not Lollipop. It's the cats! Somebody has complained about the incessant cat noises coming from this address! And I don't blame them either! Hours and hours of continuous yowling? I bet you've been driving our poor neighbours insane!"

"You don't think…"

"You mark my words, our neighbours have had enough. They probably think we're cat hoarders and have cats in every room. Not to mention the litters and litters of kittens and marauding tomcats!"

"Oh, don't be ridiculous…"

But his words struck home, and I hastily switched off the cats' chorus. I called the number on the card.

"Ah yes, we called today, thank you for getting in touch."

"What exactly is the problem?" I asked nervously.

"Our records show you have a number of dogs on the premises."

"A number? We have just one."

"Our records indicate that you have three mastiffs. Two females and a male…"

"Excuse me, can I just stop you there?"

"…and that none of these dogs has been properly registered."

"No! We just…"

"In New South Wales, all cats and dogs, other than exempt cats and dogs, must be microchipped by twelve weeks of age, or before being sold or given away, whichever happens first."

"Yes, I know, but…"

"Are they exempt? Perhaps they are guide

dogs? Although that would be most unusual as mastiffs are very large and don't make good guide dogs."

"No! We have just *one* dog, and she's not a guide dog. Or a mastiff, for that matter. She's a cross between a cocker spaniel and a poodle. And she's microchipped and registered. I think your records need updating because I believe the previous owners of this house had mastiffs. And they had heaps of puppies, too."

I went back to Joe with a smile on my face, delighted that my cats' chorus recording wasn't to blame. However, I had no wish to hear the cats any longer and never pressed 'Play' again.

I'm sorry to report that Lola still reacts when she hears a cat, but I refuse to resume the caterwauling therapy. And Joe's next suggestion hardly deserved a reply.

"Here's an idea! Why don't we make a load of cardboard cut-outs of cats? We could attach them to a string and keep pulling them past the window for Lola to see. Then maybe she'll lose interest and won't bark when she sees a real cat."

"Don't be ridiculous."

I guess we'll just have to accept that she'll always bark at cats.

As for the previous owners of our house, I have no idea where they went, or whether they still have heaps of unregistered mastiffs. I do know that, even now, we get a constant stream of mail for them from Foxtel, Mastercard, utility companies, and various debt-collecting agencies, all demanding money.

That August we celebrated Indy's fourth birthday.

"You can choose any theme you like," said her mother. "What sort of party would you like? A princess party?"

"A cat party, please," said Indy, carrying a long-suffering Bandsaw.

"Are you sure?"

"Yes, I love cats."

A cat party? Easy!

Karly had lots of ideas. I reverted to infant-teacher mode and thoroughly enjoyed myself making preparations.

Everything was cat-themed. The cake was a cat, there were blue jellies with little fish set in them, cat-shaped cookies and sandwiches, and I made some strawberry mice with long liquorice tails.

The toilets had signs saying, 'Litter Tray'. Karly set up games including 'Pin the Tail on the Cat' and 'Find the Prize' in a (new) litter tray using a poop scoop. There were stick-on cat tattoos and a host of other feline activities.

While her four-month-old baby sister slept, Indy's little friends arrived, and the party began. I'd made a cat collar, using wide ribbon and velcro, for each child to wear. Attached to the collar, like a pet tag, was a disc with the child's name on it. Karly also presented each child with a set of cat ears and a tail.

The birthday party was a huge success.

By August, work had begun in earnest on our house, although, as Joe pointed out at regular intervals, *ad nauseum*, they weren't exactly racing along.

We couldn't argue with the quality of Fred's work; it was consistently good. But everything moved at a snail's pace. Fred and Dinkum never arrived early, which we understood because we knew he had his elderly mother to look after. However, he was often extremely late, and although his excuses were probably genuine, they were colourful.

"I'd have been here earlier, but Hulk chewed the sole off one of my work boots. I had to stop and get some more."

"Hulk?" asked Joe, eyebrows high.

"You remember, the Great Dane Fred rescued," I reminded him.

"Ah. Yes."

Another time it was:

"I'm sorry I'm late, but Hulk ate Mum's medication, and I had to take him to the vet for a stomach pump."

"I suppose we should be grateful he doesn't bring Hulk here," said Joe. "At least Dinkum just walks in and makes herself at home on Lola's bed."

Dinkum was never any trouble, but Lola was dreadful. She dug holes in sand piles, destined for making cement, scattering it all over the place. She dived into the sacks of plaster, sending up great white clouds that made us all cough, poor Joe in particular.

Once, when the rubbish skip was too full to take any more, Lola discovered the best toy ever. A huge roll of disgusting old carpet was left unattended. She found that if she pulled and worried a ragged end, the ancient, smelly carpet, amidst loud ripping noises, fell apart. She would have happily unravelled that carpet all day had I let her.

It was no wonder that Joe escaped to the gym every day. Apart from needing to maintain his exercise regime, there was too much dust, noise and activity at home.

The doctors had always impressed on us how vital exercise is to patients suffering from Chronic

Obstructive Pulmonary Disease. COPD is a condition in which the air sacs of the lungs are damaged and enlarged, causing breathlessness. Therefore, any exercise that strengthens the heart and lungs may improve the body's ability to use oxygen. We knew there was no cure, but exercise would definitely slow down the inevitable and cruel progress of the disease.

I didn't stay at home much, either. My lovely German neighbour, Thea, and her dog, Nixi, often accompanied Lola and me on walks beside the lake.

Thea was great company and always made me smile.

"No! You can't park there," she would say as I searched for a car parking space. "That's for the limping ones."

She was warning me not to park in a slot reserved for the disabled.

Or, when telling me about a detective show she had watched on the TV the night before. "It is about a policeman wearing clean clothes."

That had me thinking for a moment until I realised she was referring to a plain-clothes policeman.

It was impossible to wear Lola out, but poor Nixi was older and stouter with much shorter legs. She often sat down and refused to walk any further.

"Are you sure she's a dog?" I would ask Thea. "I think she might be a guinea pig."

Thea would throw treats in front of her to encourage her to keep moving. But only when we turned around and headed for home did she show any spring in her step.

The lake path is many kilometres in length. It is flat and meanders as it hugs the shore. At intervals there are children's play areas and shelters with barbecues and benches. In typical Aussie style, families hold their children's parties there, decorating the shelters with bunting and balloons, and bringing party food.

The lake was also a favourite place for cyclists, joggers and dog walkers. You never knew who you were going to meet, or what strange sight you might see. I once met a young couple walking their pet dingo. They told me its mother had been killed in Queensland. The litter of puppies she'd left behind had been rescued and given to suitable homes. Lola was very interested in saying hello to the young dingo, but it was extremely shy.

It is believed that primitive man brought the dingo to Australia around 15,000 years ago. Dingoes hunt alone or in packs, and prey on small animals such as rabbits, birds, lizards, and rodents. They are usually shy creatures, avoiding humans, and they choose a mate for life. When a dingo's partner dies, it is not uncommon for the living mate to pine away.

Dingoes are also known to be great tree climbers, which astonishes me. Imagine going for a stroll and seeing a dingo up a tree.

One day, Thea and I met a tall, thin man with long black hair, his face hidden behind sunglasses. Accompanying him were three giant white standard poodles, each wearing little booties.

Both Thea and I avoid big dogs whenever possible because both Nixi and Lola are very submissive. If a large dog approaches Lola, she throws herself on her back, cringing and frantically wagging her tail, showing the other dog she is no threat. Nixi does the same.

Therefore, when both Lola, and the usually placid Nixi, began to strain on their leashes, pulling us towards the three giants, we were rather taken aback.

The three poodles were male and rather haughty, quite disdainful of Lola and Nixi who were both displaying embarrassingly skittish behaviour.

Dogs are instant ice-breakers, and we were soon chatting to the poodles' owner. The poodles were beautifully trained and perfectly behaved, unlike Lola, who was wild with excitement. They sniffed her politely, then looked down their long noses at her, maintaining their dignity, even while wearing the little booties.

The booties, their owner told us, were to protect the dogs' pads from pine needles. The whole incident was a little surreal.

But it was the birdlife at the lake that really took my breath away. Pelicans flew overhead or sailed like galleons on the water. White and grey egrets stood motionless in the water, apart from one particularly magnificent specimen that frequently flapped up to perch on a parked car's roof. Sulphur-crested cockatoos screeched overhead. Pink and grey galahs sat in rows on telegraph wires. Rainbow lorikeets swooped and shrieked through the trees.

On the several jetties that stretched out into the lake, cormorants stood with outspread wings, drying off, allowing one to approach quite close before launching themselves and flapping away. In the water, fish jumped, breaking the surface. I saw fish of all sizes, huge stingrays and little needlefish. I saw jellyfish the size of dinner plates feeding on the weed. There was so much life, both in the water and out.

"Huh," said Joe when he joined me for a walk one day. "I wish there was this much activity going on at our house."

STRAWBERRY MICE

These mice are simple to make and were a big hit at Indy's cat-themed birthday party. Each strawberry makes one mouse.

Ingredients

Strawberries

Black writing-icing

Silver or coloured cake decoration balls

Mini chocolate chips

Almond flakes

A few straps of black or raspberry liquorice

Swiss cheese for garnish, optional

Method

Remove the green stems from each strawberry. Slice a small slice from one side of each strawberry so it will sit flat on the plate.

Use the black writing-icing to stick a choc chip on the pointy end as a nose.

Use the writing-icing to create eyes and push in a silver ball while still wet.

Poke 2 slots with a sharp knife and slide in 2 almond flakes as ears per mouse.

Use a skewer to poke a hole into the berry and slide in the liquorice as a tail.

Cut the cheese into little wedges and serve with the strawberry mice.

19

WATER BALLET

I had to agree with Joe. Things were not moving very fast at all, and each tradie that arrived seemed to be odder than the last. The only thing they seemed to have in common was that they were all aged 55 or older. That didn't matter to us, but we wondered whether Fred deliberately employed older tradies, or if it was just coincidence.

Fred's attendance was erratic, but his work was of a high standard, and he remained polite and respectful. For instance, he insisted on removing his boots before entering the house. This was probably a waste of time because our old, chipped white floor tiles were destined to be replaced soon.

Fred would place his boots, side by side, at the front door. The moment he turned his back, Lola would charge in and drag one of them away. Then there would be a mighty tug of war between Fred and Lola, which was one of Lola's favourite games. Fred would pretend to be cross with her, but he was laughing at the same time, and it was hard to decide who enjoyed the game more.

Every day, Fred revealed more details about Hulk, his Great Dane puppy. Apparently, even though he already weighed 80kg (176 pounds, well over 12 stone), he was an absolute coward. He was frightened of everything, even his own reflection in a puddle. A manhole cover in the pavement sent him bolting in the opposite direction. Poor Fred, who weighed less than his dog, had to hang on for dear life. Bicycles and motorbikes terrified Hulk. The sight of a helmet strapped to a parked motorcycle by the side of the road spooked him so violently, he knocked Fred and a passerby over in his attempt to flee.

Apart from recapturing his work boots from Lola, Fred had his work cut out overseeing all the other trades. Work was being carried out on both inside and outside the house and I wanted the drive to be widened to allow two cars to park, side by side.

"Why would we want to park two cars?"

asked Joe. "We only have Bruce. Surely a narrow drive is enough for us?"

"What about when the family visit? They will need a place to park."

"Yes, I suppose so."

"And if we ever bought a boat or a caravan, there'd easily be enough space to keep it."

"I can't see us ever buying a boat! Hmm. A caravan could be a possibility, though. I'd love to see more of Australia and that might be a rather fun way of doing it."

Aha! I'd succeeded in sowing a little seed in Joe's mind. I'd always loved the idea of travelling around Australia in a caravan.

"And the wide drive would be a good selling point if we ever sell. Also, it's all cracked and breaking up! While they are digging it up and re-laying it, they may as well widen it."

"Okay, okay, you've made your point. Let's go with the double drive."

At the back of the house, the area outside the sliding patio doors was a mixture of poorly-laid paving and grass. Lola easily identified where the grass was thinnest and loved to excavate, leaving a moonscape of holes. Stepping out, we had to wade through mud, particularly when it rained. This area, and that around the pool, needed to be concreted in preparation for laying pavers.

I couldn't wait for the concrete to be laid.

WATER BALLET

There are not many people I dislike on sight, but I confess that Seth, the concreter, was one of them. I guess he was in his mid-sixties, but his skin was so shrivelled and sun-dried, it was hard to tell what age he was. He was covered in tattoos. Huge likenesses of his children's faces decorated his chest. But the giant features had puckered and dropped over time, making them look like evil, deformed monsters. Every square inch of his remaining flesh was covered with vast swathes of roses and rolls of barbed-wire, phoenixes and mermaids. He never wore a shirt and constant exposure to the Australian sun had turned his skin to dirty brown parchment.

"Don't you ever protect your skin at all?" I asked him, one particularly hot day.

"Nope! And if I find any new lumps and bumps, I just cut 'em out meself, or burn 'em with me cigarette. That's all a doctor would do, anyways."

It wasn't the tattoos or how he looked that made me dislike him so much; it was his attitude. He was small and sly, and had the habit of creeping up on me unnoticed. Then he'd peer at whatever I was doing and pass an opinion on a better way to do it, whether it was painting, planting, or whatever.

"Oh, you don't want to use *that* paintbrush for

corners. Get yourself one of those cut-away ones. You're wasting your time using *that*."

Another time, I was gardening.

"You're not thinking of planting *that* there, are you? You might as well throw your money in the bin. It won't like *that* spot at all," he said. Then he turned the label over and read the price on it. "What? Did you pay $25 for *that*? You were robbed. You should have asked me, I've got a mate who sells those for half that."

A mate? Personally, I found him so objectionable that I was surprised he had any mates at all.

When we discussed the job, I told him what I'd like done. His response was predictable.

"Oh, you don't want to do it like *that*."

I'm rarely rude to people, but Seth brought out the worst in me. I took a deep breath.

"I do, actually. That's exactly how I'd like it done."

"Well, don't say I haven't warned you. It's your money. If you ask me, *that* just won't work."

When I told Joe about it, he was circumspect.

"I know he's rather an irritating little man, but just ignore him. The sooner he gets on with the job, the sooner he leaves. Perhaps you should pass on any instructions through Fred. That way you won't have to deal with him directly."

Easier said than done, because often Fred

wasn't around. But it was good advice, and I promised to behave myself.

Seth often worked alone, and despite his age and size, he was very strong. Even in the baking sun, he dug up yards of soil and ripped up old paving slabs as though they were made of polystyrene. Shouldering two at once, he dropped them into the waiting skip.

Sometimes he'd bring an assistant labourer, who he called Simp, which I assumed was short for Simpson. Simp was in his twenties and twice the size of his boss, Seth. He was also shockingly lazy, and I often caught him hiding down the side of the house, puffing away on a cigarette or busy on his mobile phone.

"I just twisted my ankle," he said quickly, when I caught him one day. "Giving myself a bit of a break."

Or his excuse was the heat.

"The sun's so hot, it was making me dizzy. Just cooling off for a moment."

I couldn't decide whether Simp was a delicate little blossom, or just lazy and fabricated stories to get out of doing any work. Whichever it was, I don't believe I've ever met a grown man, let alone a labourer, who was more of a whining hypochondriac.

One day somebody knocked on the back door.

I opened it to see Simp the Wimp holding up a finger.

"I think the shovel is giving me a blister," he said. "Have you got any band-aids?"

I invited him in, of course, and found a plaster, which I offered him.

"Thank you," he said, "could you put it on for me, please?"

What could I say? I was forced to put the plaster on his finger while he screwed his face up in pain. Joe sniggered in the background.

"Vicky is really good at getting splinters out, too," Joe volunteered.

I could have kicked him.

But there was one time when Seth and his labourer, Simp the Wimp, had me laughing until I cried. It could have developed into something more serious, definitely no laughing matter, but the memory makes me laugh even now, just thinking about it.

Seth had arranged for a man to dig out our driveway, using a JCB digger and loader, in preparation for the laying of concrete. I watched from inside the house as the digger gouged the ground before the shovel swung in and removed the excess soil.

All was going well. The JCB toiled away. Seth yelled instructions to the driver while Simp the

Wimp leaned on his shovel, no doubt resting his exhausted body.

"More to the right," yelled Seth, waving his arms. "Yeah, that's it! Deeper than *that*, for —sake, we're goin' to be here all week otherwise!"

I was just thinking how rude Seth was, and how there was no need to curse, when something unexpected happened. A spout of water shot up into the air.

"You — idiot! Not like *that*!" Seth roared. "You've bloody dug up the mains water pipe!"

The Wimp gaped. From inside, I gaped. The driver gaped and shut off his engine.

Thinking quickly, Seth put his foot on the pipe, temporarily blocking the hole. But the water pressure was too powerful and was lifting his foot off the pipe.

"Simp, come here! I'm going to have to stand on it with both feet. I need you to steady me."

Reluctantly, Simp stepped forward, offering Seth his shoulders so the older man could balance himself while standing with both feet on the pipe.

"Dan, call the bloody council!" Seth roared at the digger driver who was still watching events with his mouth hanging open. "This is an emergency! If I take me bloody feet off, the road will flood!"

Dan jumped to it, jabbing the keys on his mobile phone.

Seth was heroically stemming the flow. However, the occasional spout of cold water still managed to escape, drenching him, and his leaning post, Simp.

"Get a b-bloody m-move on!" shouted Seth, his teeth beginning to chatter. "This water is freezing!"

"The council is asking whether the break in the pipe is within the nature strip," Dan announced.

I didn't know this before, but in Australia, a 'nature strip' is the name given to the council-owned land located between a constructed road and private property. In England, I believe the property holder owns and maintains the verge, all the way from the property down to the street. In Australia, this area is council-owned, although most residents maintain the strip themselves. I knew this because I had to get planning permission for our drive as it would pass through council property.

"Nah, the leak's on p-p-private p-p-property," said Seth. "C-c-call an emergency p-plumber."

Seth was shivering, and I took pity on him.

"I'll take him some towels," I said to Joe. I grabbed a pile and hurried outside.

"Me b-b-bloody feet have gone numb," Seth was saying. "S-S-Simp, you're going to have to t-take over."

"What?"

WATER BALLET

"Listen," said his boss, "p-put your hands on me shoulders and I'll keep m-m-mine on yours. When I say 'now', I'm going to s-s-step back. And you're going to take a step f-f-forward and take me place on the p-p-pipe."

Simp had gone pale and looked horrified.

"S-s-o on 'one', I take me f-f-foot off the hole, and 'two', you put your f-f-foot *over* the hole. Then 'one' I s-s-step off the pipe and 'two' you s-s-step on. Only after I s-s-say 'now'. G-g-geddit?' "

His bottom lip trembled. But Seth had no pity.

"G-Geddit?"

"Yes, I think so."

"It has to be quick and smooth, or we'll b-b-both get satched."

I'd never heard that word before, but I looked it up later. Apparently it's one of those new words creeping into our language.

Satched: To be soaked through or drenched to the skin.

"S-S-Simp, you r-r-eady?"

"Yep."

The two men tensed and took deep breaths, tightening their grip on each other's shoulders and concentrating on their feet.

"NOW! Back one-two, forward one-two!"

Any competition ballroom dancer would have been proud of the fancy footwork those two men executed. My face ached from trying not to laugh.

I didn't dare look at Dan, the digger driver. If he was laughing, I would have lost control.

Just one small burst of water escaped, squirting Simp in the face, but the operation was mostly successful. Now Simp was balanced, feet glued to the pipe, while Seth supported him.

"Plumber will be here in twenty minutes," said Dan gruffly, his face deadpan. I was sure he found it as funny as I did.

"Towels for you," I said, handing them to Seth who slung one round his naked shoulders, mercifully covering his hideous tattoos. "I'll bring out some more."

It was an excuse to get away, really. I couldn't keep a straight face.

Every few minutes, the pair repeated their dancing duet. Back one-two, forward one-two. We watched, hidden, from inside the house and I laughed so hard my ribs became painful. Joe became breathless with laughter and had to turn away.

I was almost sorry when the emergency plumber arrived.

It wasn't our last broken pipe; we had two more. One was caused again by Seth, this time in the back garden when he severed a swimming pool pipe, and the other was in the bathroom when a tradie drilled through a cold water pipe.

But neither incident came close to being as

entertaining or memorable as Simp and Seth performing the spellbinding Dance of the Shattered Water Pipe.

By the end of August, we were seeing signs of spring.

Welcome as spring always is, there is one significant downside in Australia. Magpies, a perfectly well-behaved, intelligent species during all other seasons, turn into monsters in spring. Once their eggs hatch, magpies will swoop and attack any child, adult or animal that gets too close to their nests.

I haven't been attacked yet, but I guess it's just a question of time. I've seen other people being swooped, especially when I take Lola for a run. Magpies on the ground or sitting on fences are not a threat. It's the hidden ones high in the trees who attack if anyone, however unknowingly, dares to approach their nests. I've often seen small boys innocently playing football being chased off the pitch by angry magpies.

In September, Karly was due to take her Australian Citizenship exam.

"I'm so nervous," she said. "I've been studying loads, but what if I fail?"

"You won't fail. You were always the same

when you were at school. You used to work really hard and worry yourself sick that you'd fail. But you never did!"

"Yes, but this time it's different."

"You always used to say that, too! But you still got straight A's for most subjects and ended up with a degree in Law."

"I know, but…"

DEAD-EASY DAMPER

Damper is a traditional Australian soda bread, historically prepared by swagmen, drovers, stockmen and other travellers.

Ingredients

250g (9oz) self-raising flour

½ tsp salt

25g (1oz) unsalted butter, chilled and cubed

175ml (6floz) milk

Method

Mix the flour with the salt in a large bowl. Add the butter and rub it into the flour with the tips of your fingers, until it resembles fine crumbs.

Stir in the milk with a round blade knife (butter knife) to make a soft, but not sticky dough.

Turn out onto a lightly-floured work surface and shape into a soft, smooth ball.

Set the ball of dough onto a tray or baking sheet and flatten gently to make a round about 17cm (7in) across. Cut a deep cross in the dough and brush lightly with milk.

Bake at 190°C (375°F) for 30 minutes until golden.

Serve warm or at room temperature.

20

DEBBIE REYNOLDS

When the results of the Australian Citizenship exam were announced, nobody was surprised except Karly.

"What did you get?" I asked.

"Um, 100%."

"There! Didn't I tell you? I knew you had nothing to worry about!"

I was very proud of my daughter. There would be a ceremony in Sydney where Karly, and many others who had passed the exam, would be officially awarded citizenship.

A few days before the ceremony, Karly rang me.

"I'm not sure I want to be an Australian citizen, after all," she said.

"What? Why ever not?"

"Well, I was out walking LJ, and I got dive-bombed by a magpie. That wouldn't happen in England!"

We both laughed. She was right.

With the renovations going on, there were a million things to do every day. In Spain, when we renovated our cottage, Joe and I did most of the work. Joe did all the plumbing and electrical stuff, and I did the tiling and carpentry. We both painted and attempted to plaster. The results were rustic which suited the ambience, luckily.

In Australia, we were handing most of the jobs over to skilled workmen instead of tackling them ourselves. However, there were decisions to be made, items to order, and I undertook all the exterior and interior painting. Joe couldn't be exposed to dust or paint fumes and, frankly, he didn't know a travertine paver from a slab of toffee. So I made most of the design decisions.

He helped out, assuming the shopping and cooking duties, which was an enormous help. We still had no kitchen, but we had a microwave and portable gas stove, and as the weather improved, we cooked our food outside.

In addition to all these tasks, Joe forced himself to visit the gym as the doctors insisted he should.

And Lola needed a good walk every day, which was my responsibility.

Lola and I visited the oval regularly and always enjoyed a chat with the other dog owners. It was rare not to see somebody we knew.

Sometimes it was Jean, with her pug, Bella. Bella and Lola liked each other, but Bella had a mischievous streak. She wasn't as fast as Lola, but she was patient. When I threw Lola's ball, Bella would rarely join Lola in running for it. Instead, she'd watch and wait for Lola's attention to wander. Sure enough, an opportunity arose, and Bella would snatch the ball and race off with it. Then she hunched over it and shredded it to pieces.

Lola would watch, heartbroken, but wasn't the type of dog to stand up for herself and fight for her possessions.

"Bella!" Jean would shout. "Drop it! Leave it! Give it back! That's Lola's ball!"

But it was usually too late. Bella, the ball thief, had struck again and another tennis ball was reduced to green strips.

It didn't matter one bit because I kept a supply of balls for Lola in the car. Lola soon learnt never to leave her ball unattended near Bella. Even when she drank water from a bowl, she would first drop the ball in the bowl and drink round it, never leaving her precious toy unguarded or open to theft.

Sometimes Frankie was there, with her two white fluffy dogs, Sandy and Suzy. Both were rescue dogs, both lucky to end up with Frankie. Suzy was tiny and terribly timid. Not really surprising as Suzy had been rescued from a breeder who kept her permanently confined in a cage producing litter after litter of puppies.

The result of this horrific treatment was that Suzy's hips were deformed and she had no idea how to be a dog or how to interact with humans.

Frankie's heart went out to her, and she adopted her. It was a long haul, but, after expensive surgery on her hips, Suzy gradually healed, mentally and physically. She adored Frankie, who was the only person she allowed to touch her. She learned how to walk, then run and even became confident enough to yap at visitors. In future years, Suzy's health failed prematurely, but that didn't stop Frankie from taking her out. She bought a dog stroller and took her out in that instead.

We often saw an older man with two terriers whose routine was utterly cast in stone. Privately, I called him Mr Grunt. He parked in the same space, at the same time, every day. Then he opened his car door, and the terriers tumbled out. Pulling on a wide-brimmed hat, he'd walk around the three ovals, always anti-clockwise, never taking his eyes off the ground in front of him, or deviating from his daily route.

If their paths crossed, Lola and the dogs always greeted each other briefly, which was more than I ever got from their owner.

"Beautiful day!" I would sing out when we passed.

But, other than a grunt, I never received a response.

Sometimes I saw Scottish Irene, who didn't actually own a dog herself. Irene, like Frankie, still retained her strong Scottish accent, despite moving to Australia decades ago. She was excellent company, and I always enjoyed our chats as we walked.

Sometimes I wouldn't see Irene for ages, but then she would reappear. This was because Irene looked after Bella, an elderly golden retriever owned by locum doctors, who were often called away to work in other parts of Australia.

Big Bella, as we called her to differentiate her from Bella, the pug, was gentle and in her nineties, if one calculated her age in dog years. However, she and Lola liked each other and Bella became quite frisky when they met up, which was lovely to see.

Although older than me, Irene kept fit by swimming across the bay at some unearthly hour every morning. The fact that she could be sharing the water with sharks bothered her not at all. Her idea of an annual holiday was to cycle across Eastern Europe, and I sometimes met her when she was in training, cycling by the lake. She was easy to spot because her cycling helmet was adorned with a bunch of cable ties that pointed skyward.

"What are they for?" I asked, not having been in Australia very long.

"They are supposed to discourage the magpies from swooping me," she explained.

Apart from her obvious love of dogs, and the fuss she made of Lola every time we met, there was another aspect of her personality that endeared Irene to me. I love gadgets, apps, computers and labour-saving devices. Irene was the exact opposite.

"I'm a Luddite," she confessed. "I don't own a microwave. I don't have a mobile phone or a computer. Personally, I don't like technology, and it isn't something I want to learn. I won't even use the self-checkout at the supermarket; I'd rather queue and be served by a human."

As Irene and I walked around the oval, chatting, I clipped Lola's lead on her when we approached the Ten Dollar Puddle.

"I don't want her jumping in that," I said, "or we'll have to go straight to the dog wash."

"The what?" asked Irene, "you mean take her home for a bath?"

"No, the automatic dog wash. It's fantastic! Have you never used one?"

"No. How does it work?"

"Well, it's a coin-operated kiosk with a dog bath in it. The dog hops in. When it starts, there's a dial with options like 'Shampoo', 'Conditioner', 'Rinse', and then 'Dryer'. The water is warm and controlled by a soft-touch gun. Lola quite likes it. If she's rolled in something disgusting, I can get her clean and dry in ten minutes. Worth every cent."

"You're joking!" said technophobe Irene in disbelief. "I'd like to see that in action!"

So, one day, I took her with me to the dog wash. I even put her in charge of the dial.

"Oh my!" she said, thoroughly impressed.

"Conditioner, please!" I said, then, "Rinse!"

Irene dutifully turned the dial and may have been more in touch with her techy self that day than she'd ever been in her life.

On one particular day, I was in such deep conversation with Irene that I forgot about the Ten Dollar Puddle. Too late to stop her, Lola threw herself into it and happily splashed and commando-crawled through the mud.

"Lola!" I cried in horror, and she bounded over to me.

I had Lola's ball in my hand and she spotted it. She jumped up and, moments later, I, too, was plastered with mud.

Irene managed to get a photo of the subsequent disaster which you'll see if you browse the Down Under photo book on my website.

One day, I met Debbie Reynolds.

Lola and I were walking around the oval when I noticed a lady on the far side. She appeared to have a dog that was very similar to Lola.

I always keep to the outer edge of the oval, throwing the ball for Lola to fetch as I walk along. By the time I reached the lady, she had seated herself on one of the wooden benches. Her dog was panting in the shade beneath it. Lola, as she always did when she saw another dog, rushed up to say hello. The two dogs wagged tails, touched noses and decided they liked each other.

"Hello!" I said, to both the cute Lola look-alike and her owner.

"Hello," she answered, smiling.

It's strange how one can meet dozens of random people and like them all. Then, for no reason you can explain, you meet someone and connect on a different, special level. Somehow you know that you have much in common and that you will become close friends. That's how it was with Deb.

Of course, it helped that Lola and Molly were the same breed and of a similar age, so we had plenty of doggy details to discuss. Both were spoodles, both had boundless energy, and both loved running after a ball. They also both had a passion for beach walks.

"Do you go to the beach much?" asked Molly's owner.

"Not very much," I said, resisting the urge to explain about Joe and how he struggled to walk far. "I don't know the area very well yet."

"Molly and I'll show you," offered the lady, "if you'd like."

"Lola and I would love that!" I said, delighted to be asked.

We chatted on until it was time to leave.

"Let's exchange numbers then we can sort out a beach date," she said. "I'm Deb, by the way."

"And I'm Vicky," I said, fiddling with the Add Contacts app on my phone. "What's your surname?"

"Reynolds."

"Debbie Reynolds?"

"Yup. My mum had a sense of humour."

Our first doggie date was perfect, as I knew it would be. Deb and I had already risen above the polite 'just met' level, and we were now confiding in each other, sharing our hopes, fears, and future plans.

We strolled along the beach, enjoying miles of deserted white sand lapped by frothy waves. The dogs galloped together, running so closely across the sand that their footprints were entwined.

Meanwhile, Deb and I chatted. I told her that I was a writer, a fact I rarely mention to people I meet. I also told her about my family and Joe's illness.

In return, Deb told me about her family and the fact that she'd recently overcome breast cancer. She explained she was looking for a job, and how difficult life was at that time because her sister had been diagnosed with cancer.

"I drive up north at least once a week to see her and help out," she said. "I spend a fortune at Doggy Day Care centres. Molly can't handle being left alone."

It seemed both dogs shared the same traits, like separation anxiety, although poor Molly appeared to have more than her share of it.

"It's a real problem," Deb said, sighing. "I installed one of those pet minder apps on my phone to see what happened when I went out. It's like a baby alarm, but for dogs."

"Did she bark?"

"Worse than that. I tested it by driving around

the corner. I knew she'd be anxious, but I expected her just to wait and watch out of the window until I came home."

"What did she do?"

"She lifted her nose to the sky, and she howled. She didn't stop until I came home. And that's what she does every time I go out."

"Oh no! Poor thing."

"I know. I can't bear to think she's so distressed, and the noise probably drives the neighbours crazy. That's why I'd rather drop her off at a Doggy Day Care centre. She's fine as long as she's with a human. She just can't bear to be alone."

"That's so sad."

"I know. But what am I going to do when I go back to work?"

I shook my head. I didn't know what to suggest. I would love to have offered to look after Molly, but I knew that was impractical. Our house was a shambles, and Joe could never have coped with another dog in the house, especially one with issues. He'd only just accepted Lola, and he had done that reluctantly.

DEBBIE REYNOLD'S MUM'S PAVLOVA

"Hellooooo! Here is Mum's pavlova recipe.

It's been our family's celebration dessert for as long as I can remember and I think of my wonderful Mum every time I make it." — Deb

Ingredients

4 egg whites, room temperature

1½ cups caster sugar

1 dessertspoon cornflour

1 teaspoon vanilla essence

1 teaspoon white vinegar

Whipped cream and fruit for decoration (any combination of strawberries, blueberries, raspberries, mango slices, pineapple pieces or for a Christmassy theme, strawberries and kiwi fruit are lovely).

Method

Preheat oven to 150°C (300°F).

Line a large oven tray (such as a biscuit/cookie tray) with baking paper.

Beat egg whites until just stiff, then add sugar a dessertspoon at a time, beating well after each addition. Beat until the sugar is dissolved so there is no "grit" in the mixture.

Add cornflour, vanilla essence, white vinegar and mix in lightly but thoroughly.

Spoon mixture onto the oven tray in a round. Turn oven down to 110°C (230°F).

Bake 1½ hours then leave to cool in oven with door open. (If you close the oven door the pavlova will be flat and sticky!)

Decorate with whipped cream and your chosen fruit, maybe with either passionfruit pulp or chocolate grated over the top.

21

A FRIGHT

Meeting up with Deb and Molly became a regular event. She showed me beaches in our area that I had never heard of, so stunning they almost hurt my eyes. Molly and Lola ran together on endless pristine stretches of sand, before stopping to dig a hole, or roll, or chase each other down to the sea's edge.

Meanwhile, Deb and I chatted non-stop. For me, it was a wonderful break from house renovations, and I'm guessing it took Deb's mind off her own problems. Her sister's health wasn't improving. Deb was dividing her time between driving up to see her and hunting for a part-time job. She needed to find work that would allow her enough free time to visit her sister. Meanwhile, Molly was a regular Doggy Day Care attendee.

A FRIGHT

"I don't know what you two find to talk about," Joe often said when Lola and I returned from a walk. I suspect he was a little jealous of our friendship, but Deb and I never ran dry.

Nor did Molly and Lola ever tire of running on the sand together.

Our tiler arrived and measured up the jobs in hand, namely the en suite bathroom and the outside patio and pool areas. We needed to choose tiles.

Reg, the tiler, was in his sixties with a rather red, flushed complexion. He had a lot of hair of which he was clearly very proud, and dyed it strawberry blond. He always sported a sharp haircut. He informed us that his son, Kurt, would sometimes be joining him on the job.

At first, I quite liked Reg, although that sentiment would gradually change to a hearty dislike for a number of reasons, later on.

"There's a tile shop up the road on the industrial estate," said Reg. "I know the owner. His name's Jonas, tell him I sent you. He'll look after you."

We headed off happily to the tile shop, intent on finding precisely the right tile for our new en suite bathroom. We found the store easily and entered.

When shopping, I prefer to browse in peace, considering each item carefully. I dislike feeling rushed into purchase decisions. Joe is the opposite; he'll grab the first thing he sees, hoping to curtail the painful shopping experience.

Unfortunately for me, we seemed to be the only customers in the shop. This meant that we had the undivided attention of the man behind the counter and it would have been rude not to speak to him.

"Hello, how are you?" I asked. "Our tiler, Reg, sent us. Are you Jonas?"

"I certainly am! What can I help you with today?"

"Oh, we're just browsing really…"

"We need to order some tiles," interrupted Joe.

Oh dear. No preamble. Joe didn't want to discuss the merits of matte versus glossy tiles, or colour schemes.

Jonas leaned forward, getting so close I could see the pores on his nose.

"And what are the tiles for exactly?" he asked.

"Oh, just the en suite bathroom," I said, stepping back pretending to examine a display of coloured grouts and trying to hide the fact I was backing away from him.

A FRIGHT

Jonas darted out from behind the counter.

"I have just the thing! Follow me," he ordered.

We trailed behind. Well, I trailed, but Joe trotted along like an enthusiastic little pony, no doubt imagining that our tile quest would be over in a trice, if we stuck close to our new friend, Jonas.

"Here we are!" said Jonas, triumphantly. "Wall tiles and matching non-slip floor tiles."

"I like these," said Joe hopefully, pointing at the nearest tile which happened to be a garish pink colour.

"Very fashionable," Jonas chimed in. "I have those in my downstairs bathroom at home."

"Gosh! What do you think, Vicky?"

"Our bathroom is a very small space," I said. "I don't think a bright pink tile would do at all."

Joe looked disappointed.

"I think I'd prefer to go for something more classic. Like a white marble, perhaps?" I said, thinking aloud.

"Good choice," said Jonas, leaning in and seriously invading my personal space. "I have those in my guest en suite at home."

"Gosh!" said Joe, perking up.

"Can you show us the different sizes, please?" I asked, and Joe sighed.

Jonas pulled out some samples, and I deliberated over the bewildering array of choices.

At last, when I sensed that Joe was losing the will to live, I made my choice.

"Excellent," said Jonas, rubbing his hands together. "Exactly the sizes I have in my home."

Really?

"Is that it, then?" asked Joe, smiling again.

"Niches," said Jonas.

"Pardon?"

"I was suggesting you might consider shower niches. Everybody has them now. I have them in my home."

But of course.

"A niche is a storage space in the wall of your shower to put your soap and shampoo bottles. You can use the same tile to line it or choose something ornamental like these little mosaic tiles."

Joe groaned and I gave him one of my Looks.

"I think that's a very nice idea," I said and began to browse the ornamental tile section, eventually picking a grey and white mosaic that tied in well with the marble.

"Excellent choice," said Jonas, copying down the reference number. "I have those in my bathroom niches at home."

What a surprise…

"Good," said Joe. "That's it, then, isn't it? All done."

A FRIGHT

"Except for the grout colour. I think I'd like white for the wall tiles and black for the floor."

"Oh yes," said Jonas, adding those to the order. "Very stylish. That's what we did in our laundry at home."

Naturally.

Mission complete. The order was successfully placed, and Joe and I exited with a spring in our steps.

"Careful!" I squeaked, pointing. "Don't step in that!"

"Yuk! I nearly did! Why don't people clean up after their dogs?"

"Do you think I should go back in and tell Jonas there's a massive pile of dog poo on his path?"

"No, I wouldn't. He'll just say he's got one of those at home."

We were still laughing when we drove off.

On Monday, the 26th September, Joe complained that he wasn't feeling great and he skipped his gym session, which was unusual for him.

"We'll make an appointment at the medical centre in the morning if you don't feel any better," I suggested.

The next day, he looked a strange colour and said he had no energy. He said he felt nauseous and was more breathless than usual. In fact, he kept closing his eyes and drifting off. I know nothing about medical matters, but I thought it was a good thing he was having a snooze. Perhaps he needed the rest. Nevertheless, I made an appointment for him.

"They can see you later this morning," I told him. "Do you want me to drive you there?"

"No, I'll be fine. I'll see what Dr Botha says then I'll come straight home."

He later told me that he hardly remembered the drive to the medical centre. He parked and made his way into the building and headed for the receptionists' desk. The staff took one look at him and summoned a doctor, who shot out of his consulting room, leaving behind an astonished patient who was in mid-sentence.

Joe was helped through the waiting room and into the treatment room where the doctor immediately gave him oxygen. Slowly, Joe's breathing began to ease, and his colour improved.

"I'm sorry," said the doctor, a young visiting locum, "but I'm not happy with the state of you. You need to go to the hospital."

"Hospital?"

"Definitely. I don't mind telling you, it's a very good thing you came into the surgery when you

A FRIGHT

did, because you may have died if we hadn't given you oxygen. You say you've been drifting off recently?"

"Yes. I just seem to doze off…"

"You were losing consciousness. When you get to the hospital, they'll give you proper tests."

"Can I call my wife?"

"Of course. Now, how did you get here?"

"I drove."

"You are kidding! I'm amazed you got here in one piece."

While Joe was away, I had decided to take the opportunity to do some small painting jobs. I had barely prepared an area and picked up a brush when the phone rang.

"Joe? Are you okay?"

"Well, no. I don't think I am."

"What?"

"I'm in the medical centre. The doctor here seems to think I'm not at all well, and I need to go straight to the hospital."

"What?" My paintbrush dropped to the ground.

"They're giving me oxygen. I'm not allowed to drive, of course, and we're waiting for an ambulance. Do you think you could grab a few wash-things for me? Toothbrush, a change of underwear, that sort of thing?"

"Right! Of course! I'm on my way!" I said,

utterly horrified by the news, but glad to be given an important job to do.

I rushed around collecting bits and pieces and throwing them into his holdall. Lola watched me with interest, but I was too busy to give her any attention. I couldn't pack any pyjamas because Joe didn't possess any. Until I could buy him some, I hoped the hospital might provide something temporary.

There were no workmen at our house that day, but, by now, Lola was accustomed to being left alone for a few hours.

I was ready. I reached for the car keys, but they weren't on their usual hook. And then I remembered. Joe had driven Bruce to the medical centre.

What to do?

"I'll be home soon," I said to Lola, and flew out of the door.

Luckily, my friend and neighbour, Thea, was at home. I knew she didn't drive, but her husband, Reinhard, did.

I gabbled my story and Reinhard didn't hesitate.

"Jump in," he said, and very kindly drove me to the medical centre.

"I'll bake a cake for Joe when he comes home," promised Thea as we left.

It was a shock to see Joe wearing a nasal

A FRIGHT

cannula (a word I'd never heard before) attached to an oxygen tank. He smiled when he saw me, and I sat down beside him. He reached for my hand.

"It's okay," he said, "I'm in the best place here in the medical centre. And when I get to the hospital, they'll be able to work out what's going wrong."

A smiling nurse clipped an oximeter onto one of his fingertips and studied it.

"That's a better number, Mr Twead," she said. "You had us all worried earlier."

We sat quietly for a little while until the ambulance arrived. The nurses brought the two female paramedics up to speed.

"May I go with him in the ambulance?" I asked.

"You can if you like," said the paramedic. "Your husband may have to wait in Emergency for a while, and then I imagine they might want to keep him in, which means he'll need to be allocated a bed. It's quite often a lengthy process."

"No, I think you should go home," said Joe. "I'll be fine now. There's so much to do at home, so it's silly wasting time sitting around in waiting rooms. Anyway, if you come with me in the ambulance, you'll be stranded without a car. And you can't leave Lola alone for too long."

"Okay. I'll see to Lola and buy you some

pyjamas," I said. "I don't want you making a spectacle of yourself in front of all those nurses. Keep in touch, and I'll be right over as soon as you phone me. I think the hospital is only forty minutes away."

Hola tía Vicky y tío Joe,

It is I Catalina your penpall again. I hop you are well again. My family is entirely wells but i am much unhappy. My grandmother is wells.

Every person in El Hoyo is occupied because we must take the grapes for the wine. My neighbour Paco he say it is best year for his wine but he always say it is best year for his wine.

Next month I am dancing flamenco with my sister at the *fiesta*.

Valentina say she will holidays in London after the *fiesta* and if Geronimo not accompany then she not have an weeding. I am much unhappy. i want dance flamenco at the weeding.

Felicitations, Catalina xx

I bought a couple of pairs of pyjamas and a bathrobe and slippers and waited for Joe's phone

A FRIGHT

call. The day wore on but I heard nothing from him.

At last, my phone rang.

TROUT WITH LEMON PARSLEY BUTTER

There is no need to bother to de-scale fish when cooked this way because the skin will peel away easily with the aluminium foil.

Ingredients

2 trout (serves 2 people)

60g (2oz) butter

1 teaspoon grated lemon rind

1 small clove garlic

1 tablespoon chopped parsley

1 tablespoon lemon juice

Salt and pepper

Method

Wash and dry the trout.

Fold a large piece of aluminium foil in half for extra strength. Lay the fish on the foil so it is completely enclosed, wrapping tightly.

Bake on a tray in a moderately hot oven for 20 minutes. The fish can also be cooked on a barbecue, turning the parcel regularly.

Blend softened butter with lemon rind, crushed garlic, parsley and lemon juice. season with salt and pepper and mix well.

Serve fish topped with the lemon butter.

22

BREATHLESS

"Joe? How are you?"

"Hello sweetheart, I'm not bad at all, but they want to keep me in for a day or so for observation."

"Are you in a general ward now?"

"Yes, they've put me in the respiratory ward."

"Are you okay? Are you still on oxygen?"

"No, I seem to be coping by myself at the moment. I'm a bit breathless, but not too bad."

"I bought some pyjamas. Shall I come over now?"

"No, Vicky, don't worry about it tonight. I've been lent some pyjamas for the time being, so I can manage. I'm exhausted, so I think I'll just go to sleep now. Anyway, I know you can't see a thing when you drive at night. It's getting dark, so you'd better not drive."

Joe was right. I suffer from night blindness, and it would have been foolish to drive in the dark to an address I'd never been to before.

"Well, if you're sure. I'll come tomorrow morning."

"Yes, that'll be best. The doctors will come on their rounds tomorrow, and perhaps they can shed some light on what happened to me. Have you got a busy day planned tomorrow?"

"Oh, nothing to worry about. I'll let you sleep and we can talk properly tomorrow. Goodnight."

It was a bit of a white lie. I was expecting the wardrobe fitter, the pool man, and the plumber. I asked Fred to handle it, and, thankfully, he agreed. He also kindly agreed to make sure Lola was okay, which was a relief. I didn't want her 'helping' the wardrobe fitter, pool man or plumber. Fred was accustomed to her foibles.

I phoned the family to keep them up to date. Then I sorted myself and Lola out and dropped into bed.

The weather was beautiful the next day as I drove to the hospital. I'd already given Lola a run on the oval, and I knew Fred could cope with the day's agenda. I hoped Joe was feeling better this morning.

I found him sitting up in bed, looking quite

cheery. He was definitely a better colour than he had been the day before.

We chatted, and he told me a little about the other patients in his ward. Some were extremely ill and lay still; I never even saw their faces. Others were more lively, like the flatulent old gentleman called Brian, in the opposite bed, who kept letting off a stream of muffled explosions under his bedclothes.

"So what did the doctor say?" I asked. "Has he shed any light on what happened?"

"No, not at all. Not yet. They want me to stay a little longer, but I think I may be allowed home soon."

"Oh, that's good news. At least the pyjamas I brought you won't be wasted."

Joe grinned. He knew I was joking.

Just then, a little girl ran into the ward, blonde hair and toy stethoscope swinging as she turned her head looking for someone.

"Grumps!" she called. "Where are you?"

"She looks just like Indy!" said Joe, astonished.

"It is Indy!"

Indy caught sight of us and cantered over.

"Grumps! I got my stethes-poke and my doctor bag. I'll make you all better!"

Karly and Cam, carrying baby Winter, were hot on her heels and hugs were exchanged all round.

"I can't believe you're all here," said Joe. "You shouldn't have taken the trouble to drive all the way from Sydney! I'm much better; I think I'll be going home soon."

"Oh, we had to come. Indy needed to try out her new doctor's kit."

It was a lovely visit. Indy climbed up on the bed and subjected Joe to a series of extensive medical tests, including having his ears examined and giving him several injections. We laughed and joked and generally shattered the peace in the ward.

At one point, Brian, in the bed opposite, let off a particularly violent explosion of wind. It sounded like a gunshot. We all politely ignored it, looking away avoiding any eye contact with each other.

"Pop goes the weasel," Joe said quietly, his face deadpan, and we all lost it.

Karly and I laughed so much our sides ached. It was probably just a reaction to the potentially serious situation, but it did us all a lot of good.

I stayed for another hour or so after the family left. When I finally left, Joe was cheerful and waved me goodbye.

The next day was packed with events, and I scarcely had time to catch my breath. Fred had texted me to say that he couldn't come to work because he needed to take his elderly mother to a hospital appointment. The bathroom tiles were scheduled to be delivered, and the man was arriving to measure up for the shower screen and a glass fence for the pool. Thea had kindly offered to take Lola for a while, but I didn't want Lola to outstay her welcome. Consequently, I couldn't stay long during my visit to the hospital.

"It's okay," said Joe, "I'm absolutely sure they'll discharge me tomorrow. I'm feeling so much better, and they all seem pleased with my progress. Off you go, and pat Lola for me. And do thank Thea."

I shot off and arrived home just in time to receive and sign for the tiles. It was going to be a frantic day.

I had no idea that the next day would turn into an utter nightmare.

I arrived at the hospital early the next morning looking forward to bringing Joe home.

As I passed the nurses' station, the sister in charge looked up, then dropped the papers she was holding on the desk.

"Mrs Twead?" she asked, darting out.

"Yes," I smiled. "Is my husband being discharged today? I've brought some more clothes and shoes."

"Er, I was just about to call you, Mrs Twead. Would you mind coming into the Relatives' Room for a moment, then I can explain everything."

"Shall I drop this off with him first?" I asked, holding up the bag containing Joe's clothes.

"No, bring it with you."

I stared at her dumbly.

Relatives' Room?

I've watched enough TV medical dramas to know that if a doctor or nurse calls you into the Relatives' Room, things were serious. They were not about to hand out good news.

My legs began to shake. My mouth went dry. She was already heading off, so I followed like a lamb to slaughter. A thousand questions jumped into my head, but I couldn't form any words.

The little room had some comfy chairs, a low coffee table and a couch. The window looked down onto a car park. I felt detached, as though I was floating above.

I saw somebody helping a young man into a wheelchair. Some distance away, a little family hurried towards the hospital entrance. The father held the little girl's hand, and she clutched the string of a pink helium balloon which bobbed as she walked.

Little dramas were taking place wherever I looked. It dawned on me that Joe, the sister, and I, were about to star in one of them.

"I'm afraid your husband has literally just been moved, no more than half an hour ago. He isn't in this ward anymore," she said.

"Where is he? Why has he been moved?"

"The doctor is on his way, he'll be able to explain everything. Would you like a cup of tea or coffee?"

"No, thank you. Can you tell me…"

"Doctor will be along in a minute," she said with a smile, as though talking to a child. But I could see pity in her eyes.

"But…"

Then she uttered that ghastly phrase guaranteed to make one frantic with worry.

"Try not to worry."

The doctor was a tall, pleasant-faced, white-haired man, although I imagine he was no more than fifty. He wore his shirt sleeves rolled up and his handshake was firm.

"I'm Gordon," he said, "the doctor in charge of the ICU."

Did I mishear? Did he say ICU? Doesn't that mean Intensive Care Unit?

I opened my mouth to speak, but absolutely nothing came out. The sister excused herself and backed out of the door.

It's strange how trivial, irrelevant, unbidden thoughts crowd into one's mind at the most stressful moments in our lives. Perhaps it's a kind of safety valve. I remember thinking, *That's a nice necktie. Goes well with the shirt. I wonder if his wife chose it for him?*

"Mrs Twead."

"Vicky, call me Vicky."

"Vicky, let me try to explain what's happened," said Gordon, gently.

Gordon? Whoever addresses one of the most prominent doctors in the hospital by his first name? We wouldn't dream of doing that in England…

I tried to concentrate on Gordon's words.

"Your husband ate well last evening then had a good night. However, something happened this morning. He couldn't breathe, and he lost consciousness."

I gasped.

"Normally, we use a type of non-invasive ventilator in cases like this. We call them BiPAPs. This BiPAP machine is designed to increase the pressure when you inhale. To prevent the airways in the nose and throat from closing. Have you heard of sleep apnea and a CPAP machine?"

"Yes."

"Well, it's similar to that except it provides help with both inhalation and exhalation. The patient wears a mask, and the machine pushes air into his airways. It helps open the lungs with air pressure."

I nodded.

"So we set up a BiPAP which usually helps immediately. However, in Joe's case, he didn't respond. We had to act quickly."

I could hear the muffled noises of a hospital day beyond the closed door in the corridor. Somebody was laughing. Outside, a flock of white cockatoos screeched as they swooped over the hospital car park.

"So he's been taken to the Intensive Care Unit?"

"Yes. We thought it best to put your husband into an induced coma. We are getting him settled now. We have set him up on a ventilator that will breathe for him until we know what's happening."

"A ventilator? A life-support machine?"

"Yes…"

"He can't breathe for himself at all?"

"No, not at the moment, but we're hoping this is a temporary situation."

"Does he know what's happening? Is he in any pain?"

"No, he's asleep. He won't have any pain, and he wouldn't have been aware of the intubation."

"Intubation?"

"That's what we call the insertion of a tube into a patient's body, especially that of an artificial ventilation tube into the trachea. He would have known nothing about it."

"I don't understand. What would have caused all this so suddenly? He seemed so much better. We thought he was coming home today."

"We'll be running tests. People with COPD are very susceptible to viruses. It could be a virus. We'll know more later."

A hundred other questions that I could have asked, popped into my mind later, but for now, I was numb.

"Can I see him?" I managed to say.

"I suggest you go home," Gordon said gently. "There's nothing more you can do here today. He's in the best hands. You can phone the ICU later on, and the staff will be able to let you know how he's doing."

I drove home in a daze, my hands gripping the steering-wheel far too tightly. Somehow, I greeted Fred and the other tradies and served them a tray of tea and biscuits. I felt like a zombie. I didn't tell them what was happening in the hospital. Then I went into our bedroom with Lola and locked the door.

I couldn't function properly. All I could think of was Joe on a life support machine. Joe with a tube down his throat.

I leaned my back against the wall. Lola, sensing something wasn't right, watched me with her head on one side. Her tail waved slowly, uncertainly. I slid down the wall, put my arms around her, buried my face in her soft coat, and wept.

For once, Lola didn't bounce or wriggle. She didn't tug my clothes or roll on her back. Instead, she sat quite still, occasionally licking my hand, allowing me to soak her with my tears.

I phoned the hospital later and was put through to the ICU. The nurse in charge informed me that there was no discernible change.

"We do have the results of the tests, though," she said. "Your husband definitely contracted a virus, and that's what caused this to happen. At least we have that information now, and can treat the virus accordingly."

"If I come over, will I be allowed to see him? Will he know I'm there?"

"Yes, of course you can come if you like, but I'm afraid he won't know you are there. He's still in an induced coma to give his body a rest. He's settled now. He'll have a nurse at his bedside the whole time, day and night. You may decide to wait and visit him tomorrow."

"I see."

"Do phone us in the morning. If you come in then, you'll be able to have a chat with the doctor."

I had an early night, but sleep eluded me for a long time. Finally, I drifted off, but the scenes my mind created were far from restful.

BREATHLESS

I entered a world where the Spanish village *fiesta* was in full swing. The stage was set up in the square, just as it always was every year when we lived there. Coloured lights hung in the trees, but they were swinging dangerously low, forcing villagers to duck out of their reach or be struck on the head. The twins danced flamenco, but the music was all wrong. The band was playing, and the dancing villagers gyrated around something in the middle of the stage. I saw Paco and Carmen, then caught a glimpse of Geronimo and Valentina. I think I saw Lola Ufarte but Father Samuel was not among the throng of dancers. Everybody looked solemn. And then, as the dancers parted momentarily, I saw what everybody was ignoring, but dancing around.

It was Joe, laid out on a hospital bed.

SPINACH AND FETA QUICHE

A lovely vegetarian quiche, hot or cold. If you prefer, use half a pack of frozen spinach, defrosted and drained of water.

Ingredients

3 eggs

100g (3½oz) feta cheese, crumbled

125g (4½oz) spinach

½ cup self-raising flour

1½ cups skim milk

½ cup cheese, grated

1 onion thinly sliced

200g (7oz) mushrooms

Method

Sauté onion and mushrooms until just cooked.

Mix flour, eggs, cheese and milk together in a bowl.

Add the feta to the spinach and combine with the onion and egg mixtures.

Spray a quiche dish with non-stick spray.

Pour mixture into dish and bake at 180°C (350°F) for 30-35 minutes.

23

BED NUMBER FIVE

As soon as I had shaken off the disturbing dream, I phoned the hospital and was put through to the ICU.

"Your husband has had a reasonable night," said the nurse. "There hasn't been much change. We're trying to give him the lowest dose of sedation possible, and he's doing okay. If you are planning to come in today, I know the doctor would like to ask you a few questions."

"Yes, of course, I'll be in as soon as I can."

I was so lucky to have such fantastic neighbours. Thea had already helped me out, and that morning, when I gave Lola a quick run on the oval, I met up with Emma and her cocker spaniel, Baxter. I told her what was going on.

"Leave Lola with me," she said, "I'm not going

into work today so she can hang out with Baxter. I'll have her any time. And if you're stuck when I'm at work, I'll just pick her up from your house when I get back."

I could have hugged her. I'd been worried because I couldn't always expect Fred to look after Lola when I was away. Neither could I trust the workmen to remember to keep the garden gate and front door closed all the time. If either one was left open, Lola would be out faster than a rat up a drainpipe, searching for me. Thea had already been so kind. I couldn't keep asking her to look after a boisterous puppy. Emma's offer was heaven sent.

I headed for the hospital. Now that Lola was sorted, and I'd left keys and instructions for Fred, I could focus on the day ahead.

And I was absolutely terrified.

I'd never entered an intensive care unit before. Apart from scenes in television dramas, I'd never seen a patient on a life support machine. And now I had to steel myself to see Joe hooked up on one.

Could I cope? Could I bear to see Joe like that? What if I broke down?

Parking in the multi-storey car park wasn't easy, and I wasted twenty minutes slowly driving from floor to floor, waiting for somebody to leave. All the time, my heart was hammering in my chest.

I was directed to the ICU, and my feet felt like lumps of lead as I made my way along the corridor until it forked.

No Entry - Staff Only, ordered one sign. *Visitors - This Way*, pointed the other.

I pushed the door open and found myself in a gloomy, windowless waiting room, with a wall-hung television screen flickering away to nobody. A middle-aged lady seemed to be demonstrating some kind of cooking device, but the volume was off, so she was wasting her time here.

I caught sight of a telephone with a notice beside it, inviting visitors to call the ward, after which someone would arrive to escort me in. I dialled the number.

"I've come to see Joe Twead," I said. I was struggling to keep the tremble out of my voice.

"And you are?"

"Vicky. His wife."

"Ah, yes. Bed number five. I have a note in Joe's file to say that the doctor would like a word with you. Could you please wait, and I'll let her know you're here."

I didn't have to wait long. A door I hadn't noticed before swung open to admit a young lady doctor into the waiting room.

"Mrs Twead? May I call you Vicky? I'm Cherry, the doctor in charge today. Thank you for coming in."

The door behind me opened, and an elderly couple entered, pain etched on their faces. Above their heads, the silent chef lady was still demonstrating her cookware.

Cherry put her hand on my arm.

"Would you mind following me to the Relatives' Room?" she asked. "We won't be disturbed there."

My heart lurched. Not again! *Please, not the Relatives' Room!* There must be more bad news because that's the place where distressing news is delivered.

She kept her hand on my arm, and I allowed myself to be led away. The Relatives' Room was very similar to the one off the respiratory ward. The walls were painted a soothing soft green and comfy chairs were placed around a low coffee table. There was no window.

"I know how hard this is for you," said Cherry, looking into my face. "Your husband is quite stable. Now that we know what we're dealing with, we can make headway. It's best that Joe remains sedated for the moment. The machine will breathe for him, which will put much less strain on his heart. Before we go on, do you have any questions?"

I nodded. "Can you tell me more about the virus?"

"Well, actually, we discovered that he

contracted *two* viruses. Neither is very serious; in fact, one is similar to babies' croup. That particular virus leads to the swelling of the larynx and windpipe. Although they are fairly minor viruses, it's very serious for him as his lung disease is quite advanced."

"I wonder where he could have caught them?"

"Oh, it could be anywhere. Any public places, like supermarkets. Quite often these sort of viruses are picked up in gyms or swimming pools. Coughs and sneezes spread them."

Perhaps I am being unfair, but I've always blamed Joe's gym. It never seemed very clean to me, and the indoor pool water was always exceptionally warm.

"How will you know when he's able to breathe by himself again?"

"We'll be monitoring him very closely. We'll be checking his heart, and we'll be waiting for these viruses to abate. Which brings me to a couple of questions."

"Yes?"

"Do we have your permission to include Joe in a clinical trial? There are two sedation drugs we'd like to use. There's no risk involved, but the data would be very useful for our research."

I didn't have to think very hard about that one. Joe has donated gallons of blood in his time, earning himself all sorts of awards. He's always declared that, after death, he'd like to gift his entire body to medical research, if it was useful, and medical science were welcome to any organs they fancied. I was positive he'd be delighted to be part of a clinical trial.

"Yes, that's fine."

"Thank you so much. I'll get the relevant papers prepared for you to sign. There's just one more thing I need to discuss with you before I take you to him."

I could feel my hands still shaking, but the chat with the doctor had calmed me. She hadn't delivered any additional terrible news. Was she going to do that now?

And then it came. Cherry's brown eyes watched me as she spoke.

"Vicky, in the course of our examinations, we discovered a mass in Joe's pituitary gland. Was he aware of it before?"

"What? A mass? Do you mean a tumour?"

"Yes, but it's not necessarily anything sinister or aggressive."

"No! We knew nothing about any tumour! Are you saying he has cancer?"

"No, in over 99% of patients, this is not a cancer; it is benign. Actually, it's surprisingly common."

Poor Joe. He already had high blood pressure, COPD, and prostate cancer to deal with, and now life had thrown him another curveball. A tumour, for goodness sake.

"Where and what is the pituitary gland, exactly?"

"The pituitary gland is a tiny organ," explained Cherry, "no bigger than a pea. It's found at the base of the brain. It makes or stores many different hormones."

"So, what happens now?"

"I'm going to request an MRI for him. Although the tumour is more than likely harmless, we need an image of it now, so we can compare it with future images and check that it's not growing."

"And if it *is* growing?"

"Well, although a tumour may be benign, it can cause problems if it grows. It can cause loss of vision, for instance, or headaches."

"What sort of treatmen…" I began, but I never finished the sentence because I was interrupted by an urgent-sounding rap on the door.

A nurse stuck her head around the door.

"Cherry, could you please attend to bed number five as soon as you can? We have a little problem."

Cherry jumped up. "Vicky, would you mind waiting? I'll just go and see what's needed and then I'll be right back."

I leant back in the armchair and replayed our

conversation in my head. All in all, it didn't sound *too* negative, I told myself. If all went according to plan, the viruses would be dealt with; Joe would emerge from the coma and get his strength back. The tumour was a shock, but Cherry didn't seem unduly worried. Or was she just pacifying me?

I'm ashamed to admit that my next worry was utterly selfish. I was terrified of being taken to Joe's bedside and not being able to handle what I would see. I never watch medical procedures on television, and I turn away when receiving routine injections. How would I cope with seeing Joe on a life-support machine? I closed my eyes and took a deep breath. In a minute, I would be tested.

Suddenly, a shocking thought occurred to me. Had the nurse just said *bed number five*? Wasn't that the bed number the other nurse on the phone had said that Joe was occupying?

If I was right, something was happening to Joe in the ICU.

Right now. This minute.

With that realisation, my fears flew away. Now I was desperate to see Joe, life-support machine or not. I sprang up and began pacing back and forth, back and forth, waiting for Cherry to return.

At last, the door opened, and Cherry walked in.

"Everything's fine," she said, reading my expression. "We've been keeping Joe on the lowest possible dose of sedatives, and perhaps it was too low. He suddenly became very agitated and was attempting to pull out the ventilation tube from his trachea."

I stared at her, shocked.

"So we had to increase the dose, I'm afraid. Don't worry, this often happens. Would you like to see him now?"

I nodded.

I stared straight ahead, refusing to glance at the other beds we passed. Each bed was occupied, I knew, and a nurse was attending every patient.

Cherry pulled back the cubicle curtain surrounding bed number five, to reveal Joe. A nurse stepped forward.

"I'm Katrina," she said. "Are you okay?"

I knew all the colour had drained from my face, but I *was* okay.

Just.

I had never seen so much medical equipment in all my life. Monitors flashed coloured numbers and graphs. Tubes, drips, cables, plugs, machines on wheels, lights on stands, shelves laden with more equipment. Strange beeps and hums kept up a constant background noise.

And in the middle of it all was Joe.

Lifeless, laid out like a shop display dummy,

he was mostly covered by a white sheet. Both his arms were lying outside the sheet, but I couldn't see much of them because they were wrapped in bandages from which lines and tubes led to machines and drips.

I forced myself to look at his head. Electrodes were taped to his skull and forehead. Worst of all, his mouth was open and his dry lips were parted to allow entry for a fat plastic tube.

"Here," said Katrina, "use this gel to sterilise your hands. He's doing fine, don't worry."

Cherry smiled reassuringly. "Will you be alright now?" she asked. "Stay as long as you like, and you can touch him. I must go now, but remember, you can phone any time of day or night."

I thanked her, and she left.

Katrina had pulled up a chair for me. I sat down and slowly reached out for Joe's hand. It was reassuringly warm in mine. I wasn't frightened any more.

"Hello, Joe," I said quietly. "I'm here."

Katrina smiled approvingly.

"Does he know anything of what's going on?" I asked.

"No, I doubt it. He was having a temper tantrum earlier. He was determined to pull out that tube so he's quite heavily sedated for now."

Temper tantrum? Yup, that would be Joe.

I sat there for a long time, holding his hand. Katrina busied herself with charts and dials, frequently checking her watch and recording readouts. The ward was calm. Every cubicle held a human in crisis, but there was very little noise apart from footsteps and machines.

There was nothing I could do except sit with him. As time ticked away, I sat there, watching him, stroking his fingers.

GERMAN BUTTER CAKE (BUTTERKUCHEN)

This is perfect with a cup of coffee. (From thespruceeats.com)

Ingredients

The Sponge

4½ cups plain (all-purpose) flour, divided

2½ teaspoons dry yeast

1 cup lukewarm milk

Pinch of sugar

The Yeast Cake

½ teaspoon salt

1 large room-temperature egg

225g (8oz) room-temperature butter, divided

1 ¼ cups sugar, divided

2 teaspoons cinnamon

Method

The Sponge

Place 4 cups of flour in a large mixing bowl or stand mixer and make a hollow in it with the back of a spoon.

Sprinkle dry yeast in the hollow and fill with the lukewarm milk. Add a pinch of sugar and mix a little to incorporate some of the flour.

Let the sponge sit in a warm place for 15 minutes.

The Cake Batter

After the yeast is activated and showing strong growth, add the salt, egg, 7 tablespoons of the softened butter and ¾cup of the sugar to the yeast mixture.

Mix until the dough is smooth and forms a ball. Add up to ½ cup additional flour if necessary. Form dough into a ball, place in a greased bowl, turning the dough once and cover. Let rise 15 to 30 minutes.

Roll the dough out to 1cm (½ inch) thickness on a lightly floured board and transfer to a baking sheet with edges, like a jellyroll pan. (Approx. 30 x 25cm or 10 x 15 inches.) Let it rest again for 15 minutes while heating oven to 190°C (375°F).

Dimple the top of the dough all over, using your fingers or the back of a wooden spoon.

Mix remaining ½ cup of sugar and 2 teaspoons of cinnamon together and sprinkle evenly over dough. Cut remaining 9 tablespoons of butter into small pieces and spread it evenly over the dough.

Bake the Cake

Bake for 25 minutes, or until cake is done and the sugar/cinnamon mixture has melted together and caramelised a little.

Optional: Mix ¼ cup of sugar with enough water (¼ to ½ cup) to dissolve the sugar and brush this sugar water on the hot cake right after you take it out of the oven.

This cake freezes well. After defrosting, crisp it up for a few minutes in a 175°C (350°F) oven. Top this *butterkuchen* with sliced, blanched (or toasted) almonds.

24

ROLLERCOASTER

During those early days of October, I felt as though I needed to split myself into two, with separate heads. I had a 'House' head and a 'Hospital' head. Both required my undivided attention, and every night I went to bed drained and exhausted.

Only when I walked Lola could I relax to some degree. If we could arrange it, Deb and I would walk the full length of the beach, stopping for coffee at a cafe before walking back. Lola and Molly sniffed at seaweed and ran together along the wet sand, frothy waves erasing their paw prints.

We were in the middle of spring, and the weather was already balmy. Thea wore her white hat, and the magpies' babies had grown into awkward teenagers. They were easy to spot, hopping after their parents, because their plumage was grey and black. As they grew older, the grey feathers would turn white.

Australian magpie youngsters are hilarious to watch. The ones I observed that spring followed their parents in flight, their flying skills already impressive. However, they still had a lot to learn when it came to landing.

Instead of slowing down before reaching their target, they would come in much too fast, consequently crashing into the tree. With a loud shriek and a flurry of feathers, they scrabbled to grab a branch with their claws. Often they spun upside down, hanging like a circus acrobat, before righting themselves with the help of their beaks. There they would stand, swaying and hanging on for dear life. Mum or Dad could be seen on a branch nearby, rolling their eyes in exasperation as their offspring steadied themselves. Then Mum and Dad would swoop away, and the kids were forced to relaunch or be left behind. With an indignant squawk, they would take off only to repeat the performance and crash-land into yet another tree.

As strange as it sounds, magpie parents actually play with their youngsters. Joe and I have seen teenage magpies lying on their backs while their parents appear to be tickling their tummies.

We've seen siblings on their backs, side by side, play-fighting like puppies. They are remarkable birds, extremely intelligent with long memories.

"Pooh! Magpies never bother me," Thea told me. "When I walk with Nixi, I throw some dog treats to them. When spring comes, magpies never swoop me. I think they know my hat."

Then there are the plovers. These large, common and conspicuous creatures are arguably some of the most bad-tempered birds in Australia. Magpies only lose their patience during their breeding season, but plovers seem to spend their whole life in a rage. Most streets and ovals in our area have pairs of patrolling plovers, and if anybody gets too close, they scream abuse before flying away in a shrieking fury.

In my opinion, the plover, or masked lapwing, isn't a pretty bird. It has a white stomach and brown back, a dangly yellow wattle, black scalp and long skinny legs. It never tolerates interference, but during the breeding season, it becomes a menace. Plovers lay their eggs on almost any stretch of open ground, including front gardens, school ovals, and even supermarket carparks. Woe betide any unsuspecting human or creature that dares approach. Hurling abuse, the plover parents will swoop and attack.

One spring, poor Jean, one of my dog-walking pals, was unable to leave her house to walk Bella.

Plovers had made a nest and laid eggs in her front garden. Every time Jean and Bella attempted to leave the house, they were attacked.

However over-zealous the plover parents might be, it is impossible not to love plover chicks. The babies can leave the nest and feed themselves a few hours after hatching and are extremely cute. Like round, fluffy pom-poms on knitting-needle legs, they scuttle after their parents who zealously guard them.

Such scenes warmed my heart during those dark, dark days when Joe fought for his life in hospital, and our home was a demolition site.

The first thing I did when I awoke every morning was phone the hospital, which, by now, was on speed-dial. I was usually put through to the nurse currently in charge of Joe's care. It was never the same person.

On 2nd October, I phoned the hospital and was told Joe had enjoyed a restful night. I arrived, expecting to sit quietly at his bedside, watching the machines breathe for him, as I always did.

"Hello, I'm Nita," said his nurse. She glanced at her notes. "You must be Vicky?"

"Yes, that's right."

"Good, I'm sure he'll be pleased you are here."

"Really? Is he awake?"

I looked at Joe, and he seemed the same. He lay motionless, eyes closed, the tube still inserted into his mouth, breathing for him. The machines hummed and beeped. Numbers flickered.

"Well, he's still sedated, but he definitely knows what's going on around him. You'll see."

I sat down quickly and reached for his hand, taking care not to dislodge the confusion of plastic lines taped to it.

"Speak to him," said Nita.

"Joe. Joe, can you hear me?"

Nothing.

"Joe? It's me."

Slowly, slowly, Joe's heavy eyelids lifted. His eyes looked straight ahead.

"I'm here," I said, leaning over and putting my face into his line of vision.

There was immediate and utter recognition.

A little moan came from somewhere, and a single tear ran out of the corner of his eye.

"There! You see!" said Nita triumphantly.

I could hardly believe it. My heart leapt in my chest, and I grinned from ear to ear. I could tell he was trying to smile, but the tube and his poor, dry, cracked lips wouldn't allow him. But the look in his eyes spoke volumes.

"You're back!" I said, and felt a little pressure on my hand as Joe tried to communicate.

He slowly withdrew his hand from mine and lifted it to stroke my face with his fingertips. He didn't need words.

I sat with him for most of the day. He was weak, and couldn't talk because of the ventilator. I didn't mind, I would talk for both of us.

"I expect you want to know how Lollipop is?"

Tiny nod of the head.

"Well, she's in Germany again today."

Small questioning frown.

"Thea is looking after her, bless her. Thea talks to her in German all the time, so I think we're going to have a bilingual dog by the time you come out of the hospital."

Tiny twitch of the lips.

"Thea is going to make you one of those delicious German lemon and almond cakes when you come home. Oh, and Reinhard has a book he thinks you'll like. It's all about the First Fleet, you know, the eleven ships carrying convicts from Portsmouth to settle in Australia in 1787."

I prattled on and on. I told him about Emma's kindness and how her dog, Baxter, treated Lola like an annoying little sister. I told him about the antics of the magpies and about the baby plovers on the oval.

I described how things were progressing at home.

"Reg, the tiler, is coming along nicely with the

en suite tiling. Should be finished soon and then the plumber can come in and fit the sink and toilet. And then Reg can start laying the travertine pavers outside. I've met his son, Kurt, by the way."

A minuscule questioning flick of the eyebrows.

"Kurt? He's really just a younger version of his dad. Red-faced, a bit belligerent. He doesn't make eye contact when you speak to him."

I didn't tell Joe that Fred had voiced his misgivings about the father and son duo. That was an issue Fred and I needed to tackle and wasn't Joe's worry.

I drove home in high spirits and sat down to write an email to our friends and family in the UK, who were justifiably anxious for news.

At ten o'clock, I phoned the hospital to be reassured that Joe was still doing well.

"It won't be long before we remove the tube and let him try to breathe by himself," the nurse informed me.

That was very good news.

The next day, Monday 3rd October, was a public holiday and I had no tradesmen in the house to worry about. Looking at my phone, I saw I'd received a text from Fred that I hadn't noticed before.

I'm thinking about you tonite babe

I snorted. It didn't bother me because I was one hundred per cent certain that Fred had sent it to me in error, but I wondered who his 'babe' was. It reminded me I needed to discuss the tilers with him, but that could wait.

I phoned the hospital and was told that Joe had enjoyed a good night. A plan was in place to reduce his sedation still further, then take him off the ventilator later in the morning. Consequently, I waited until later before driving over to see him. I remember singing happily along with Sia as the radio played *Cheap Thrills*.

In the ICU, I was surprised to be met by the senior doctor.

"Hello, Vicky, I hoped I'd see you," said Gordon. "Not great news, I'm afraid."

"Oh no!"

"We reduced the sedation level in order to remove the tube, but Joe suffered a panic attack. His blood pressure sky-rocketed and was putting a dangerous strain on his heart. I'm afraid we had to abandon the attempt and increase the sedation again. So he's still on the ventilator."

"On no!"

"I'm so sorry."

"Is he back in an induced coma?"

"Yes, I'm afraid so."

"Will he know me?"

"No. He's heavily sedated. We'll see how it

goes and maybe try again tomorrow."

I didn't stay long. On the return journey, when Sia came back on the car radio, I switched her off. I wasn't in the mood for singing.

That night, wild weather arrived. The wind howled around our house like an angry monster, throwing branches into our pool, which was already green from neglect. The storm raged all night.

The next day was calm, and I can tell from my journal entries that Joe had turned a bit of a corner. Things were looking more positive.

> 4th October, 2016.
>
> He's now been in the hospital for one week! High winds brought down power cables last night. The radio says the road to hospital is blocked so won't attempt to go in. Phoned. Sedation reduced again, removal of tube successful (HOORAY) although he still can't breathe by himself. Oxygen and BiPAP machine but at least he's no longer on a ventilator. Sedation increased again but coping on BiPAP. Good sign?

In the morning, the staff in the ICU told me that Joe was conscious but still being fed intravenously and unable to communicate because of the oxygen mask.

As usual, I waited to be escorted into the ward and entered in some trepidation. I peeped around the curtain to see Joe propped up almost into a sitting position. A mask was clamped over his nose and mouth, and I saw the many dials and numbers flickering on monitors behind him. His eyes were closed.

"How is he?" I asked his nurse quietly.

"Why don't you ask him yourself?" she said, smiling.

I tiptoed to his bedside.

"Joe?" His eyes sprang open, and his arms reached for me. "How are you?" I whispered.

He tried to speak, but the mask transformed his words into comical grunts.

"Here," said the nurse, passing us a stack of paper and a thick marker pen.

Joe nodded his thanks and accepted them. He clutched the pen and began scribbling. Joe's writing is usually meticulous, but all spelling and punctuation flew out of the window in his need to communicate.

its so god to see you

"Hah! It's so good seeing you sitting up and awake! How are you feeling?"

sor throat

"I'm not surprised. You've had that tube down your throat, and every time they tried to take it out, you panicked, and they had to push it back in again."

i know nurse rebeca said

I looked up at Rebecca, and she smiled.
"He's doing really well, isn't he?" she said, then went back to her paperwork.

how long i ben here

"Well, you've been in hospital for more than a week, but not in the ICU all the time. Can you remember anything?"

resp ward then no more

I explained to him how we'd all expected him to come home after the family had visited, which he remembered. Beyond that, he could recall nothing.

i nearly died yes?

"Yes, I think you did," I said, nodding my

head. "I reckon you were only good for landfill a couple of days ago."

I stayed for three hours. I told him almost everything that was happening at home, keeping it all very light. I still didn't tell him about Fred having a problem with the tilers.

"Guess what? I got another message from Fred. Hang on, I'll find it for you. Ah, here it is: *I'm thinking about you tonight babe.*"

I couldn't help giggling.

babe?

"Haha! I know! Don't worry. I'll never be Fred's babe!"

Now Joe was laughing too, but the mask turned his chuckles into monstrous snorts. This only made us both laugh more, and even Nurse Rebecca was laughing until Joe managed to scribble:

stop hurts to larf

Joe was worn out, and it was my cue to leave. I kissed him goodbye and left, confident that things were finally looking up.

Sometimes it's a good thing we can't see into the future. Our rollercoaster of a journey hadn't come to a halt quite yet.

HONEY-GLAZED SPARE RIBS

Here's a really simple special crowd-pleaser for summer get-togethers. Prepare the night before, then sling them on the barbecue. They also cook beautifully in a slow cooker.

Ingredients

2kg beef spare ribs

2 tablespoons tomato paste

½ cup diced tomatoes

⅓ cup honey

1 tablespoon Worcestershire sauce

2 teaspoons soy sauce

1 tablespoon white vinegar

Method

Trim spare ribs. Make the marinade by combining tomato paste, diced tomatoes, honey, Worcestershire sauce, soy sauce and vinegar.

Mix well and stand for several hours or refrigerate overnight.

Barbecue until tender and golden-brown.

25

MONSTERS BENEATH

Unaware of what was in store for us in the future, I drove home, singing along with Ed Sheeran. I laughed again, remembering Joe's snorts behind his mask.

Sometimes in life, the faintest whiff or scent, or a glimpse of a view will remind us of some past event. Often it's difficult to place the exact time and location of the memory, even though it might be intensely familiar. I *knew* I'd heard those snorts before, behind a mask, and I suddenly remembered the occasion.

It was at our beach in Spain, when Joe walked into the sea, already wearing his mask, snorkel and flippers. As the cool water lapped his sun-warmed skin, he bellowed. Of course, he sounded and looked ridiculous. I imagine a cornered wildebeest might make the same sound. Small wonder that I used to pretend he wasn't with me.

There was another time, many years ago, when Joe heard that same sound, and we often used to chuckle about it. Way back in 2008, before we even dreamed of living in Australia, we had a fantastic holiday driving up the Australian east coast. At Airlie Beach, in Queensland, we took a boat trip and headed for a section of the Great Barrier Reef. Arriving at our destination, the boat was moored, and we were provided with wetsuits, masks, snorkels and flippers, and encouraged to explore the reef.

"You'll have two hours here," said our guide. "There is a lot to see, and you'll be able to identify many species of fish and coral from this chart. This section is not deep but beware of swimming beyond the markers. The ocean suddenly becomes very deep past them."

It is unwise to tell Joe what he must *not* do; it's like a red rag to a bull. I never break laws or disobey rules without making myself extremely uncomfortable, but Joe thrives on risk-taking.

We had a fabulous time watching the fish and admiring the exotic creatures that call the coral home. But that wasn't enough for Joe. He's a much better, stronger swimmer than I am and we soon parted company. I didn't follow him. I stayed quite close to the boat where the water was shallow, and the reef was quite near the surface.

Joe swam much further afield, to the edge of the reef shelf where it suddenly dropped away and became immeasurably deep. He wasn't the only one: there was a little group of Chinese tourists also intent on pushing the boundaries.

I knew nothing of what happened next until he returned to the boat, beetroot with excitement.

"What happened?" I asked.

"Well, I swam to the edge of the shallow part, then past the marker. The reef edge drops like a cliff, and you can actually feel the temperature of the water change. I was watching all these little fish disappear into crevices in the cliff face; it was fascinating. Then I heard this weird noise!"

"Noise?"

"Yes! I bobbed straight up to the surface and looked around. The noise was coming from three Chinese swimmers. They were all hanging onto the buoy for dear life, making these extraordinary noises as they yelled through their snorkels. I could see their faces behind their masks. They were terrified!"

"Why? What was the matter? Had they just discovered they were out of their depth?"

"No! They were all climbing over each other, trying to get out of the water onto this buoy that kept bobbing about, and they were pointing down. I couldn't see anything so I went underwater to take a look."

"Weren't you scared?"

"Yes! Terrified! But I had to see what they were pointing at. I saw it straight away…"

Joe paused and took a deep breath, reliving the moment.

"Well?"

"It was the biggest fish I have ever seen! A *monster* fish!"

"Wow! How big? Not a shark?"

"No, it wasn't a shark; it was the wrong shape. I don't know what it was, but it was *enormous*! Well, my eyes nearly popped out of my head. And all I could hear were these noises coming from our snorkels as we all shouted! Kind of 'Hoo!' 'Hoo!' 'Hoo!' noises! No wonder they were clinging onto the buoy, and I wasn't hanging around either. I swam back onto the shelf as fast as I could."

"And the Asians?"

"They let go of the buoy, one by one, and swam like the clappers back onto the shallow area. They were only small, and I reckon that the monster could have swallowed one in a single bite."

Still breathless with excitement, Joe described the fish to our guide, hoping she could identify it.

"It was *huge*, with a massive mouth!"

"Was it kind of mottled and spotted?"

"Yes!"

"Oh, you must have met George!" she said, smiling. "He's a giant Queensland groper, or grouper. He's harmless, but he would be dead scary if you met him face to face. You'll probably see him again soon because he often comes up to be hand-fed when we leave."

She was right, and I was lucky enough to see George at close quarters, too, later. And what a magnificent fellow he was! However, I think I would have died of fright if I had come across him while snorkelling.

When I got the chance, I researched the giant Queensland groper species.[1] Apparently, they are the biggest reef-dwelling fish in the world and are renowned for their curiosity. They are usually solitary in nature and live to a ripe old age. Giant Queensland gropers are commonly seen in caves on coral reefs and around wrecks. They feed on small sharks, juvenile sea turtles, crustaceans and molluscs, all of which are sucked into that colossal mouth and swallowed whole.

Perhaps those Asian swimmers, being so slight, had a lucky escape.

Reluctantly shaking off thoughts of those happy bygone days, when Joe's breathing was strong and taken for granted, I arrived home. All the tradies had finished for the day and already left. All, that is, except Reg. To my huge surprise, Reg, the tiler, was mowing our front lawn. Or as much as he could reach between the stacks of tiles, bricks, and the rubbish skip.

Had Fred misjudged him? Was there a heart of gold lurking somewhere within that we hadn't seen any sign of yet? I thanked Reg sincerely for his kindness.

"That's okay," he said. "While I've got you, we need some more cash to go to the suppliers tomorrow. We're running short of tile cement and suchlike."

"No problem," I said, and paid him the sum he requested.

It was time to find out from Fred exactly what was concerning him about Reg. I resolved to tackle him about it as soon as possible.

Thursday, 6th October was a good day. Joe was still in the ICU, attached to oxygen via a lightweight tube, the cannula placed in his nostrils, delivering a mixture of air and oxygen. The BiPAP mask was almost dispensed with, and he was inhaling and exhaling without help. Better still, he was encouraged to get up for the first time and spent three-quarters of an hour out of bed. He told me he managed a hearty breakfast, and his spirits were high.

That afternoon, I sat down with Fred, and we quietly discussed the progress of the renovations.

The tiling in the en suite bathroom had been completed in spite of Reg's haphazard attendance. He and his son, Kurt, were now beginning to lay the beautiful travertine pavers outside.

"The tiling looks fantastic," I said, patting Dinkum, who had commandeered Lola's bed again. "So what's the problem with Reg?"

"The tiling in the en suite should have been finished ages ago," said Fred. "It's only a tiny area. And I think I know part of the problem. Booze. I've caught him and his son, Kurt, drinking on the job many a time. Have you noticed they always have a tinny nearby?"

"Yes, but I thought that was just a can of cold drink, I didn't realise it was alcoholic. No wonder they always refuse my offers of tea and biscuits. But their work is good, isn't it?"

"It is now. I've had to tell him to re-do those niches twice, and I'm not sure that he's sloped the floor tiles enough for the shower water to drain away. And there's something else bothering me."

"Oh dear, what?"

"He comes straight to you for more money for materials, doesn't he?"

"Yes…"

"Well, I think he's using some of your materials, like the tile cement, for other jobs. He can't possibly get through the amount he says he uses. I've also noticed that whenever you pay him, the pair of them disappear for a few days. I reckon they're doing another job, or they're going on a bender, and when they run out of money, they come back."

"Oh no!"

"I'm afraid so. Did you pay Reg last night?"

"I did."

"Well, I've not seen them at all today, and I'll wager they won't rock up for a couple of days. I've had my suspicions for a while. I had a quiet word with Seth, the concreter."

"Oh, I wouldn't take *his* word for anything…"

"I know, but he's worked with those two on another job, and it seems they got the sack from that job for the same thing."

"Are you sure?"

"Pretty sure. I'm going to watch them closely from now on. It's your call, but I recommend you terminate them."

"So we'll have to find another tiler?"

"'Fraid so. If I'm right."

I nodded. It couldn't be helped. I desperately wanted the new bedroom and en suite finished before Joe came out of the hospital, so that he could have a clean, comfortable retreat.

"The good news," said Fred, as though reading my mind, "is that the plumber is all set up to come in and put in the vanity, toilet and shower."

"Oh, that's good! I'll carry on painting the bedroom and organise the fitted wardrobe, carpet, bed and bedside tables."

I was making lists as we talked.

By the end of the meeting, I felt pretty overwhelmed by all that needed to be done. But there wasn't time to complain. I had a bedroom to paint. And I had to control an enthusiastic puppy determined to be my assistant.

I finished painting late that night. I washed my brushes and cleared up, then made myself something to eat. As usual, I phoned the ICU and was told that Joe was doing well, and was asleep. It was already past ten o'clock, but I thought I'd eat with a tray on my lap and watch half an hour of TV before going to bed.

I was just finishing up when I heard an unusual noise. Although I'd never heard her do it before, I knew exactly what it was. Lola was growling.

Perfectly aware that her hearing was one hundred times better than mine, I paid attention.

Had she heard something unusual outside? I stood up to investigate.

To my surprise, she was growling at something under the dining table.

"What's the matter, Lola? Why are you growling?"

She didn't even look up. More deep, throaty growls.

I bent down to take a look, and then I saw it.

A spider. A spider (almost) the size of an upturned soup bowl. A *monstrous* spider.

I froze. I'm terrified of spiders even though I have great respect for them. Knowing that some can be aggressive and dangerous, I grabbed Lola's collar. I certainly didn't want her bitten by this crouching monster.

Australians reading this will be scoffing and rolling their eyes by now, but they have always lived alongside snakes and spiders. Me? I was terrified, and my knees were trembling. Was it a harmless huntsman? Or one of those jumping ones?

What to do? It was far too late to call Thea; I knew she and Nixi would be tucked up in bed by now. Emma? She went to bed early, too. I had to deal with the situation myself.

The spider sat there, all eight eyes staring at me.

I had to do something, but what?

Everything is much worse at night. Shadows are deeper, and every tiny sound is augmented. Lola was still growling, setting my nerves on edge.

I needed a plan. I didn't want to kill it, but it certainly wasn't going to leave by itself, however politely I asked.

Then I remembered. There was a can of One-Shot on the windowsill on the other side of the room. This insect killer works like a dream on flies which instantly drop and soon die. I had to trust that it had the same effect on giant arachnids.

"Listen, my friend," I whispered, "I don't want to do this, but you leave me no choice. You weren't invited, and you don't pay rent."

Reluctantly, I prepared myself for the ordeal ahead. Anybody who shares my fear of spiders will understand what I am going to say next.

I had to keep my eye on this intruder at all times.

I had to know where it was. To lose sight of it would mean it was still somewhere in the house and could reappear at any time.

Slowly, smoothly, I backed away, never for one second losing sight of the monster...

I felt behind me, groping blindly until my fingers found the can of insecticide spray. Success. Lola's leash was also within reach. I quickly clipped that on her collar. I couldn't allow her to run free. My eye never lost sight of the spider.

Slowly, smoothly, I approached my quarry again, getting as close as I dared.

---

1. This Youtube clip shows just how big the giant Queensland gropers are: https://www.youtube.com/watch?v=5FaDq_k1ZQM

SLOW COOKER CHOCOLATE FUDGE

Slow and constant heat is all you need to make this delicious chocolate fudge. A great recipe to make with the kids. From kidspot.com.au

Ingredients

2 blocks cooking chocolate (broken into pieces)

1 tin sweetened condensed milk

1 tbs butter

1 packet mini M&Ms for final decoration

Method

Place chocolate, condensed milk and butter into slow cooker on High with the lid off.

Stir with a metal or silicone spoon every 15 minutes until melted.

Turn setting down to Low and continue to stir every 15 mins for up to 2 hours.

Pour into a lined 20cm x 20cm (7" or 8") square cake tin and smooth over the top.

Sprinkle with mini M&M's and place into the fridge to cool for 1 hour.

Cut into squares and serve.

26

BAD STUFF

Lola and I stared at the spider while the digital clock on the wall ticked the seconds away. The spider stared back at us. I clutched Lola's lead tightly.

A car drove past and, just for a moment, I toyed with the idea of running out and flagging it down. Our house was in a cul-de-sac so it must have been a neighbour. But what might a neighbour think, seeing a crazed elderly woman in Disney pyjamas, with a dog on a lead, running from her house in the middle of the night?

And anyway, I couldn't leave the spider. What if it scuttled somewhere and hid, only to come out later at night and join me in bed?

No, I had to fight this battle on my own.

And then something horrible happened.

BAD STUFF

The spider's eyes and mine were locked into a stare when, without warning, the spider lifted one leg and beckoned me.

"Aaagh!" I gasped and jerked back.

My unexpected reaction made Lola jump, and she barked in excitement, first at me, then at nothing in particular, bouncing around as much as the lead would allow.

It took a while for her to calm down but I never took my eyes off the spider. Thank goodness, the commotion didn't seem to disturb it, and it put its leg down again. It remained still, silent. I hoped it wasn't limbering up for a sprint.

"Right, Lola," I said quietly, "I'm going to spray it now."

Perhaps I believed that if I voiced my intent, it would give me the courage to do it.

I did spray it, long and hard, but it just sat there in a cloud of insecticide. It didn't even cough. I tried again, hating myself for punishing a spider for being a spider. It wasn't its fault that it terrified me.

Then it gathered itself up, seemingly unaffected by the spray, and ran out from under the table, across the floor and up the back of the sofa. At the top, it rested, waving two defiant legs at me.

For more than half an hour, it sat there. I was at the other side of the room by now, all lights switched on, the spider always in sight. Lola was asleep at my feet, but I was transfixed. I couldn't allow myself to lose sight of the enemy.

Which way would it run next? Reluctantly, and cautiously, I moved in and sprayed it again. It ran down the other side of the sofa and across the cushions. I sensed it had slowed down, as though the spray was finally affecting it.

It came to a halt on a cream-coloured cushion. The pale background provided a perfect backdrop for it, the contrast showing every hair on every leg in sharp relief.

I watched that spider until it crawled behind a cushion, out of sight. A sensible person would have called it a day and gone to bed, but I couldn't do that. I had to watch the cushion in case the spider emerged.

I waited nearly all night, eyes glued to the cushion, but the spider didn't reappear. I wasn't brave enough to move the cushion and try to find it, but neither did I want to leave it and go to bed.

Eventually, absolutely exhausted, I convinced myself the spray had probably done its job by now, and the spider had died somewhere in the depths of the sofa. I went to bed, taking Lola with me.

But before I could sleep, I stuffed rolled-up towels along the bottom of the door to fill any gap, in case the spider revived and came looking for me.

I didn't sleep well, and the next day dawned much too soon. I phoned the hospital to check on Joe's progress.

"Oh, he's doing really well," said the nurse. "We're going to take the IV line out of his groin today, and the one in his hand. If there's a bed free, he may go back to the general ward later today or tomorrow."

That was *fabulous* news. Joe was on the mend, and he no longer needed to be in the Intensive Care Unit! I looked forward to visiting him, but first I had to deal with the eight-legged midnight intruder.

I emerged from the bedroom. Sunlight flooded through the windows, and I was beginning to feel rather foolish. However, I couldn't pluck up enough courage to move the cushion aside and look for the spider.

When I'd given Lola her breakfast, I checked it wasn't too early, then phoned Thea.

"Thea, can I ask you a favour?" I asked, attempting to sound casual. "Would you mind popping round as soon as you have a moment?"

"I come now."

I loved her Teutonic abruptness. She must have sensed that this was an emergency and was on my doorstep within minutes, not even bothering to don either her white or brown hat. Lola treated her to an over-enthusiastic welcome. She couldn't believe she was seeing one of her best friends so early in the morning.

"*Donnerwetter!*" Thea exclaimed as Lola jumped up, nearly knocking her over.

I grabbed Lola.

"You look tired," remarked Thea. "Are you sick?"

"No, there's a gigantic spider in the depths of my sofa. I sprayed it last night then I saw it crawl behind a cushion and I had to stay up all night to make sure it didn't come out."

"Pardon? You stayed up all night watching your sofa?"

I nodded. "Yes. I think the spider must be dead, but I'm too scared to look. Could you please check?"

"Where did you last see this creature?"

I pointed at the cushion and held Lola back as Thea approached it. She moved it aside.

"Ah, here it is!" she said.

"Is it dead?"

"Oh yes, very dead."

"Can you get rid of it, please?"

"Yes. Perhaps I don't touch it. Do you have a bag and a tweezer?"

I scuttled off to find the items and handed them to her.

"*Donnerwetter*, it's a big one," she said and held the corpse up for me to see, dangling off the tweezers.

Of course, Lola also wanted to see and nearly broke away from my grasp.

"*Donnerwetter*, Lola! No, take your snoot away; this is not for you."

I shuddered. The spider *was* big, but it had looked ten times bigger last night. Now it was scrunched up and stiff, poor thing. I wasn't proud of myself at all.

Thea dropped it into the plastic bag I'd given her and threw it away in the bin. Had she not removed it, I would never have sat on that sofa again. In fact, I may have considered selling the house.

Thea, the Ranger, had saved the day.

It was still quite early in the morning, and there was a lot to do.

In Australia, some days are so perfect that I wish I could preserve them and take them out again to enjoy later. A photograph isn't good enough because it doesn't capture the sounds and scents.

The 7th of October was a day such as this.

I took Lola for a run at the oval, hoping to tire her out before I went to the hospital. The sky was unblemished by even the smallest, puffiest of clouds, and stretched, bluer than an ocean of forget-me-nots. A warm, gentle breeze tickled the leaves on the trees, and a line of pink and grey galahs sat on the high fence glowering down at us.

Galahs weren't the only parrots present that day. A huge flock of screeching white cockatoos flapped overhead, clearly disturbed by something. Shielding my eyes from the sun, I saw the reason for their indignation. High in the sky, an eagle wheeled, wings motionless as it harnessed a column of rising warm air.

The eagle wasn't the only one making use of the thermals. A dozen multi-coloured paragliders soared silently above the distant bush. Conditions would have been perfect at Splinterbone Crag, a favourite spot for paragliding enthusiasts.

Lola romped, and my heart sang. The day couldn't have been more beautiful, and Joe was out of danger and on the mend.

It was just as well that I didn't know what was in store for me just hours later. I still have the email I sent that evening to family members in Britain, outlining the events of the day.

7th October
Dear All,
Today has been a very mixed, somewhat surreal day, which I will try to describe...

BAD STUFF

As you know, Joe was doing great when I phoned this morning, and the plans were to send him back to the general ward. I went in about two hours later, and (after circling the carpark for 20 mins waiting for a space) I finally got to the ICU. You have to phone from a large waiting room to be let in. They said I couldn't come in for a while, because the doctors were having a meeting at his bedside, so I waited.

And waited.

After three-quarters of an hour, I was allowed in. Joe was asleep and had the BiPap mask back on, and the arterial and other line were back in place. He wasn't sedated, but in a very deep sleep, and the mask was breathing for him. This was pretty disappointing as he seemed to have gone backwards again. The consultant said they were puzzled because Joe had appeared so much better, but then he kept falling asleep again. They were going to run more tests, and do a CT scan of his chest.

Joe didn't know I was there. He was totally out of it. I finally left.

The journey from the hospital to our house is about 35/40 minutes. I had reached about halfway when my phone rang. (Here's the surreal bit.) It was Joe, asking why I hadn't come in, and could I go in now? So I turned the car around immediately.

At the ICU, they wouldn't allow me in again. I was shown into the Relatives' Room that I was taken into once before, when Joe was first admitted into the ICU, and asked to wait for the consultant.

He arrived and explained that they'd had no choice but to put him back on the ventilator. Square One. He explained that they were baffled by the test results. He has got over his chest infection, and his chest is relatively clear. But something is making him slip into unconsciousness with no warning. He said it was a good thing that he hadn't made it down to the general ward, or they may not have noticed it happening.

So the next thing is to find out what this "something else" is. He will have an MRI, fully sedated, which is a good thing, and maybe that will throw some light on the matter.

So that is where we are now. I will phone the hospital later tonight and again in the morning, as I always do. One step forward and two back. I am exhausted.

Really hoping I have better news soon,
Vicky x

CREAMY CURRIED SNAGS

These curried snags (sausages) have a mild creamy sauce and a good variety of vegetables. Another great recipe from kidspot.com.au

Ingredients (serves 3)

5 beef sausages (thick)

1 onion (sliced)

1 carrot (diced)

1 tsp sweet paprika

1 tsp turmeric

1 tsp curry powder

freshly cracked pepper

2 zucchini (courgettes), sliced

100g (3½oz) green beans

375 ml (12½floz) light evaporated milk

1 cup water

1 tsp cornflour

1 tbs brown sugar

Method

In a frying pan, cook the sausages until just done, slice and set aside. Discard residual oil from the pan.

In the same pan, add the onion, carrot and cook until the onion is transparent.

Add the paprika, turmeric, pepper, brown sugar and curry powder. Fry this for 2 minutes.

Add the sliced sausages to the pan with the evaporated milk and stir.

Mix the cornflour into the glass of water and add to the pan. Stir continuously until the sauce thickens.

Add the zucchini (courgette) and beans and cook for 3 minutes.

Serve with rice or mashed potatoes.

27

DIFFICULT DAYS

By now I was sure I could have driven to and from the hospital blindfolded. Every day I wasted precious time trying to find a parking space and spent a fortune in parking fees which were charged by the hour.

They were grim, dark days that even the perfect Australian spring weather couldn't dispel.

I neglected Lola because there weren't enough hours in the day. I insisted on taking her for a daily run, but her training went to pot. I was forever grateful to Emma and Thea for looking after her when I was away too long.

While Joe battled for his life in the ICU, Fred was handling the many problems that arose at home.

I happened to be at home the day Fred

confronted father and son, Reg and Kurt. They had turned up to work, for a change, and were laying the travertine pavers around the pool. It was a modestly-sized pool, so the job shouldn't have taken long. However, their frequent absences had slowed work to almost a standstill. The omnipresent tinnies were clearly on view.

I was inside, with the window open, and their raised voices could easily be heard. I couldn't resist peeping around the blind.

"Reg, Kurt, can I have a word?" called Fred.

"What about?" asked Reg, already bridling.

"Eh?" said Kurt. He put down his trowel and walked over.

Both tilers towered above Fred, but he was undaunted.

"I think we have a bit of a problem," he started. "This job is taking far too long."

"Wot you on about? We been working hard," protested Reg.

"Yes, mate, when you're actually here."

I have discovered that in Australia, 'mate' can convey a variety of sentiments which I will attempt to demonstrate, with examples.

It can be used in a friendly way, like, "Hello, mate! How are you?"

Or it can be used to address somebody if you can't remember their name, as in, "Haven't seen you for ages, mate!"

DIFFICULT DAYS

It can be used to express disbelief, "Mate! You *didn't*!"

And it can be used very effectively to threaten or warn somebody, as in, "Watch it, mate!"

Fred was most definitely using the last one.

The father and son tiler team looked at each other, clearly surprised.

"Wot d'you mean, when we're here?" asked Reg, staring Fred down.

"Come on now," said Fred. "Did you think we hadn't noticed you two sneaking off whenever you please and not coming back for days?"

Reg gaped at him and Kurt reached for his tinny. He took a swig, then replaced it on the rock. As always, the can was clothed in a cooler, a foam sleeve designed to insulate it and keep the contents cold. I'm positive the coolers were also used to disguise the contents of the cans.

"And that's another thing," said Fred.

"Wot?"

"You're drinking on the job."

"Just a bloody minute, are you saying we can't have a drink when we're working?"

"Drink, yes, Kurt. Alcohol, no," said Fred, folding his arms.

Kurt's face turned beetroot, his eyes narrowed, and his hands turned to fists. He stepped forward.

"Did you just call me Skirt?"

Fred blinked behind his thick-lensed, horn-rimmed glasses and looked puzzled.

"No, I didn't. I said 'Yes, Kurt…'"

"You just did it again!" bawled Kurt, ready to lunge at Fred.

Reg grabbed his son's arm and pulled him back.

"It's okay, son," he said, "leave it!"

I had to admire Fred. Small in stature, he only reached Kurt's shoulder, but he didn't back down.

"Look," said Fred. "I'm giving you fair warning. I expect you to stay on-site and finish this paving. And no more drinking on the job."

Kurt's face was thunderous, but Reg had a firm hold of his son's arm as Fred turned away, his mission accomplished.

I had to rush away to the hospital, but I made time to first thank Fred. I also thanked him silently for making me smile for the first time in days.

Perhaps I sound as though all our tradesmen were problematic, but that wasn't true. One of our favourites was Bob the Brickie. He was semi-retired and only accepted jobs if he felt like it. Luckily for us, he was happy to build our bathroom wall.

Bob was one of life's gentlemen. His handshake was warm, his smile genuine, and his passion for bricklaying was evident. Bob brought along his battered, cement-splattered radio which was tuned in permanently to a country music station. As he mixed cement and laid bricks, he sang along to Dolly Parton or Tammy Wynette.

Bob was shocked to hear that Joe was so sick and arrived next morning clutching a bottle of Blackmore's echinacea liquid.

"Put a few drops in his coffee," he said to me. "It'll protect him from colds and flu. I take it every day, and I haven't had a cold in sixty years."

In the ICU, Joe was conscious but still unable to breathe by himself. He could, however, write notes so at least we could communicate.

I still have those notes; huge, shaky scrawls across many pages. Rereading them to write this chapter brought everything back. Joe's bewilderment, confusion, love, fear, gratitude, all expressed in malformed, smudgy words, laboriously written with a marker pen on scrap paper.

All the time, the machine breathed for him and the dials, graph lines, and countless lights flickered on and off, displaying numbers.

I tried hard to keep the visit lighthearted and

told him a watered-down version of the 'Skirt' incident which made him laugh.

no larf - hurts!!!

I apologised, and he changed the subject to a far more serious matter. His hand clutched the marker, and he wrote:

dr wants speak w you tomorrow

"Oh, really? Does he want to update me on your progress?"

no

"Oh! Okay, do you know why he wants to see me?"

yes. you know my thoughts

"What do you m..."
Before I could finish, two nurses bustled up to us.
"I'm sorry, we'll have to interrupt," said one. "It's time to prepare your husband for his MRI."
I left Joe in their capable hands. I didn't get the opportunity to quiz him further and returned

DIFFICULT DAYS

home, wondering what the doctor wanted to see me about or was going to say to me.

I collected Lola from Emma, who had kindly taken Lola and Baxter to the oval for a run. Lola gave me her usual exuberant welcome, breaking every rule about jumping up when meeting people.

I inspected the renovation progress. The travertine pavers were looking fabulous, especially on the new patio outside the bedroom door, covering up the ugly pipework leading from the new en suite bathroom to the drain.

Before I went to bed, I called the hospital and was informed that the MRI went well.

"Ah, I have a note here to say that Dr Gordon would like to have a word with you as soon as possible."

"Yes, Joe told me. Do you know what it's about?"

"I'm sorry, I don't."

I spent a restless night worrying about what the doctor would say. It must be very important if it was on Joe's notes, and a nurse couldn't, or wouldn't, simply tell me. Whatever did the senior doctor want to say to me?

As I dozed, I remembered the date. This weekend the *fiesta* would be taking place in our village in Spain, on the other side of the planet.

Had I really been in Australia for more than a year?

Of course, there would be dancing in the village square, noise, games, contests and processions. But had Lola Ufarte and Father Samuel patched up their differences, or had Lola decided that Esteban was more to her taste? And what about Geronimo and Valentina? Had Geronimo agreed to leave the comfort zone of the village and accompany his fiancée on a trip overseas?

I hoped my young penpal would keep me up to date.

And I prayed that Dr Gordon had good news for me tomorrow.

"Would you mind waiting in the Relatives' Room and I'll page Gordon," said the young nurse who had come to collect me from the ICU waiting room.

My heart dropped. The Relatives' Room? *No, not again...*

Dr Gordon arrived, smiling kindly. We greeted each other, and after a short pause, he explained why I had been summoned.

"I've already had a good chat with Joe," he said, "and he was keen for me to talk with you, too."

He told me that they still didn't know why Joe's breathing was failing, as the two viruses seemed to have cleared up.

"Unfortunately," he said, his kind eyes watching me, "the infections have caused his lungs to deteriorate even more. But that doesn't explain why he is struggling to breathe unaided."

"But he'll come off the ventilator, won't he?" I asked, appalled.

"Yes, just as soon as we feel he's strong enough. The reason I called you in for a chat was because you and Joe have options."

"Options?"

And then he spelt it out.

"I need to make you aware that this could happen again with no warning. And if it does, you need to decide."

Long pause. I held my breath and waited, reading the compassion in his eyes.

"Decide?" I whispered.

"Yes, if this happens again, you can make the choice not to put Joe through any more. Unfortunately, the use of ventilators to support breathing can cause further lung injury, particularly in older patients or patients whose lungs are already damaged."

Another long pause. I felt the doctor's eyes on

me, but he said no more. I tried to absorb his words.

"So you are saying..."

"Yes. I'm saying that if it happens again, and he is in a weakened state on a ventilator, you may both decide that it might be better not to resuscitate."

There. He'd said it.

"We can sedate patients and keep them in induced comas, but they may never regain any quality of life. And we must take into consideration that ventilators can keep people breathing, but there are huge risks. The breathing tube can allow bacteria to enter the lungs, which may cause pneumonia."

My mouth was dry. I looked down and saw my hands were balled into fists in my lap.

"And you had this conversation with Joe?"

"I did."

"What did he say?"

"He listened very calmly and didn't hesitate. I'll let you talk to him then you can both be clear about how you feel."

I was numb as I made my way back into the ward. How could things have come to this point so quickly? I didn't know what to say to Joe.

But I didn't need to broach the subject.

Even though he was still on the ventilator, propped up on cushions, attached by lines to drips and machines, he was able to read my mind. He began writing.

u chat w dr?

I didn't want to talk about it. I didn't even want to think about it. Not now. Not when he was getting better again.

But I knew exactly what Joe's reaction would have been and what he would have said to the doctor.

Joe's eyes bored into mine above the breathing tube. He raised his eyebrows in question and pushed the paper at me again, ordering me to answer.

I sighed and reached for his hand.

"Yes, I talked with Dr Gordon. He's such a nice man. What an awful job he has sometimes."

Joe squeezed my hand and raised his eyebrows, urging me to get to the point.

"I know how you feel about it, Joe. And I would feel the same if it was me. Don't leave me on a ventilator with no quality of life. And I also agree with you, donate any of my organs if they are of any use. And use my body for science."

Joe nodded vehemently. We'd discussed organ donation many times.

"But you're improving. You're conscious, and you'll get better every day."

Joe nodded, but I knew we were both thinking the same thing.

It could happen again.

He could catch another virus. He could end up on a life-support machine.

He picked up the marker once more and scribbled three words.

pull the plug

AUSSIE HAM AND CHEESE PULL-APARTS

Perfect for any festive party, or TV supper. Kids will love it and I guarantee it'll be gone in seconds. Ham can be replaced with cooked turkey or chicken for a change. From newideafood.com.au

Ingredients (serves 8)

Cooking oil spray

2 crusty baguettes, about 34cm long (12 inches)

Olive oil cooking spray

125g (4½oz) brie cheese

⅔ cup cranberry sauce

150g (5oz) sliced ham

1½ cups grated mozzarella (200g)

Parsley, to garnish

Method

Spray a 35 cm (12 inch) round pizza tray with a perforated base with oil.

Trim ends from baguettes. Cut into 2 cm (¾ inch) round slices. Place slices side-by-side on prepared tray. Spray with oil.

Cook in a hot oven 200°C (390°F) for about 5 minutes, or until crisp.

Remove. Stand for 5 minutes.

Meanwhile, cut brie into thin wide slices. (It's easier if the brie is chilled.)

Spread cranberry sauce over toasted bread. Top with brie then ham. Sprinkle with mozzarella.

Cook in a hot oven 200°C (390°F) for about 15 minutes, or until golden and cheese is melted.

Serve garnished with parsley.

28

WORMS

Joe's health improved daily. The breathing tube was successfully removed and he was able to breathe by himself. At last he was considered to be out of danger. He was moved out of the ICU and given a bed in the general ward.

He was on the mend.

Two days later, on the 13th October, he was discharged. But first we had to wait several hours in the hospital Transit Lounge. Joe, never patient at the best of times, voiced his displeasure at having to wait to go home to all who would listen. The administration staff ignored him, and the other patients rolled their eyes and looked away. It was good to hear him grumbling again, a sure sign that he was feeling better.

At long last, all the papers were signed, and we were given a pack containing up-to-date medical notes and CD records of his scans. We were very grateful, and Joe apologised for his impatience.

Coming home was a mixed blessing because he was appallingly weak. He couldn't walk or stand long without support, so I purchased a walking frame and a shower seat. During those early days, he didn't have the strength to put toothpaste on his own toothbrush and even eating left him breathless. Thea arrived with a beautiful German cake, which I ended up eating almost entirely myself because Joe couldn't manage it.

Thank goodness for the team of after-care nurses who came out daily to check on Joe's welfare. They must have been shocked by the state of the house, with no kitchen, and a bathroom fit for nothing but demolition. But, to my relief, the new bedroom and en suite were ready to move into.

I had painted the bedroom walls white. I couldn't have been more delighted by the lime-washed bed, bedside cupboards, and the white plantation shutters. The white marble tiles in the en suite gleamed, and the black tapware looked sensational. Now Joe had a retreat. A clean, dust-free zone.

But there was a significant problem.

Although our plumber had finished his job, he had gone overseas. That shouldn't have concerned us because we could easily find another for the main bathroom and kitchen, when the time arose. But in his haste to jump on a plane, our plumber had cut corners and left us with a difficult situation.

When we began using the en suite, it didn't take long for a most unpleasant problem to rear its ugly head. Something was blocking the toilet. It wouldn't flush away, and the water rose up the bowl alarmingly.

I've noticed that domestic emergencies alway occur on public holidays, weekends, or during the night. True to form, this happened on a Sunday. I had a card for an emergency plumber, sporting the slogan: Pipework is our Pleasure. So I rang the number.

Dean arrived with a bag of tools and examined the toilet. The water had slowly drained away by now, so he flushed it again.

"A good flush beats a full house," he said happily.

Joe and I looked at each other. We'd never met such a perky plumber before.

The water rose in the bowl and stayed there.

"Hmm," he said. "You definitely have a blockage. Leave it with me, and I'll see what I can do. We're Number One in the Number Two business."

Five minutes later, Dean delivered his verdict.

"Nope, I can't see what's causing the blockage. Whatever it is must be further down the pipe."

"We've just had a new patio laid," I said. "Those pavers won't need to be lifted, will they?"

"Nope. I suggest I come back tomorrow with my jet spray and camera. We'll send them down, and we'll be able to see what's causing that blockage."

"Oh, that sounds like a good idea."

"In the meantime, don't use the toilet, and I'll see you tomorrow."

With that, he gathered up his tools and left.

Hola tía Vicky y tío Joe,

I hop you are wells. My family is completely wells and I am sad *tío* Joe is not completely wells. I am writing you a letter because my teacher say i must write very good english like my sister. Papa say why i not work very hard like my sister but my sister not love dancing crazy so much like me and Mama. My sister want be a travel shop person. I want to dance flamenco for the television and in weedings and i am not need very good english.

Now we have the *fiesta* and I and Mama and my sister dance flamenco very much then my dancing shoe have hole. My papa make music with the guitar and all the peoples claps hands. When we finish all the peoples shouts and say dance again. Like MacDonalds I am lovin' it.

Also i have now a secret. If you not say to my mama i will say to you in my next letter.

Felicitations, Catalina xx

I finished reading the email to Joe and looked up.

"Well, it's a very nice email," I said. "I wonder what the secret is? But she hasn't given me all the information I was hoping for."

"What information?"

"Don't pretend you're not interested! You know, village stuff."

"You mean gossip, don't you?"

"No! Not really... I mean like, has Valentina persuaded Geronimo to go on a trip overseas with her? And did her aunt, Lola Ufarte, go to the *fiesta*? And poor Father Samuel, where is he? And what about Esteban, has he come back to the village?"

"Gossip," said Joe, shaking his head. "That's definitely gossip. If you're so interested, why don't you ask her?"

"I think I will. Just to help her improve her written English, of course."

"Of course."

Dean, the plumber, arrived with not only his bag of tools but also a carry-case housing his camera setup. He lifted the inspection hatch on the patio.

"Does your hosepipe reach this spot?" he asked.

I scrambled to get it, and by the time I returned, Dean was on all-fours feeding the probe with the camera fixed to the end down the drain.

"Let's have a look what we've got here," he said. "Would you like to see?"

Of course we would!

"Right, watch the monitor as the camera travels along underground. It's got its own little light so you'll see everything."

One might think that seeing the inside of an underground pipe as it makes its way to the main drain at the bottom of the garden would be dull. It wasn't dull at all. It was fascinating.

Having travelled some distance, the probe came to a halt, blocked by an obstruction.

"What's stopping it?" asked Joe.

The camera swivelled a fraction until we could see it clearly. Sodden cardboard pieces.

"Who on earth would put cardboard down a drain?" I asked, aghast.

"Well, judging by the writing I can make out, I'd say it was your tiler trying to save time clearing up. He's torn a box up into little shreds, but it's all gathered together and caused an obstruction."

We had to agree that was likely, judging by the '6 ceramic tiles' legend stamped on one shred.

"How do we shift it?"

"I'll aim the hose down there first. See if that and the camera probe will dislodge it. If not, I'll use the water jet."

I turned on the tap and sprinted back, not wanting to miss seeing it on the screen. I was in time to see a mini tsunami hit the cardboard wall, and with a little extra nudge from the camera, the obstruction broke up and floated away.

We all cheered.

"Try flushing the toilet now," said Dean, the dam buster.

I ran inside and flushed the toilet. To my dismay, once again, the water filled the bowl.

"It's still blocked," I reported.

"Right," said Dean. "That can only mean one thing."

"What?"

"The blockage must be *before* this inspection hatch. It must be somewhere under the floor of the house. Let's push the camera in and find out."

His enthusiasm was infectious, but I wasn't

really sure I wanted to see what was blocking the drain closer to the toilet.

"Right! All cisterns go!" cried Dean, and thrust the camera back down the hole.

Joe chuckled. He loves a good pun and Dean had a stock of them.

The camera nosed its way along until…

"There it is!" Dean sang out, as delighted as though he'd won the lottery. Then his expression changed. "What the…"

He stopped. We all stared at the screen. The camera was showing us a large pile of white, gleaming worms, all intertwined.

"Good grief," said Joe.

"What *is* that?" I squeaked.

"I'm not sure," confessed Dean. "That's just plumb crazy."

"Are they alive?"

"I don't know. I've never seen anything like this before, but I haven't had the camera very long. They look like worms."

He was right. They appeared to be writhing in and out of each other's coils as the camera hovered around the heap.

"Maybe they're tree roots?" volunteered Joe.

We all looked over our shoulders to check, but there were no trees nearby, so that was unlikely.

"Baby snakes?"

"A strange Aussie fungus?"

"Whatever they are, they're causing your toilet to block."

He prodded the squirming mass with the camera. The whole pile seemed stuck together and sprang back when he withdrew the camera.

"I know what it is!" Dean exclaimed. "It's not a pile of worms at all! It's silicone sealant! Your last plumber must have broken the pipe, and instead of replacing it, he tried to mend it with silicone. The silicone's found a hole and squirted through. Mystery solved!"

Joe and I stared at the screen again. Yes, that's precisely what it was.

"It's too solid and rubbery for the camera to dislodge," Dean decided. "I'll blast it with the pressure jet."

And that's exactly what he did. We had the satisfaction of watching the silicone break away and wash harmlessly down the drain.

The toilet flushed beautifully, and all was well.

"Would you like a magnetic business card to put on your fridge?" Dean asked. "Got a leak, I'll take a peek."

We thanked him and took his card, keen to employ him again in the future, although hopefully not in an emergency. Whistling, he marched off with his bag of tools and camera, back to his van.

"And don't forget, you never need to go to bed with a drip!" he called over his shoulder.

That made me laugh, but Joe didn't find it so funny. In fact he sulked for a good hour afterwards.

Joe encouraged me to leave him and take Lola for walks.

"I'll be fine," he said. "I'm getting stronger every day and Lollipop needs a walk. If I have any problems, Fred will be here. Or I'll phone you. Don't worry, go and enjoy yourselves."

Sometimes Lola and I walked by ourselves, or with Thea and Nixi. At other times, we met up with Deb and Molly. As Molly and Lola possessed more than their fair share of energy, we usually chose to walk along the beach where they could romp unrestricted.

It was low tide, and the beach was almost deserted as Deb and I walked over the wet sand, occasionally dodging over-enthusiastic wavelets that threatened to soak our feet. Lola and Molly dashed this way and that, stopping only to sniff a seagull feather, or heap of seaweed, or other fascinating items the waves had carried ashore and dumped on the sand.

When the tide was high, we often passed lone

fishermen casting their lines into the waves. But today there was nobody about apart from a single figure. This man had neither fishing rod nor net, and as we drew closer, his behaviour baffled me. This man stood at the water's edge, dragging something quite heavy, tied to a line, across the wet sand. A bucket stood close by, and in his other hand he held a pair of pliers.

"What is he doing?" I asked Deb, who I always regarded as my personal Aussie reference manual.

"I have no idea."

"Isn't that a *sock* he's dragging around?"

"Certainly looks like it."

Curiosity won over shyness, and I approached the man.

"Excuse me," I said, "can I ask what you are doing, please?"

"Catching beach worms," he said. "I chop 'em up and use 'em for bait."

"Oh! Is that a sock you're dragging?"

"Yep. Called a stink-bag. Stuffed it with rotting fish guts and smelly stuff. Worms love it. Up they pop, drooling at the thought of dinner. Then I grab 'em by the nose with me pliers."

"Oh."

"And then I pull 'em out. Slippery little suckers they are. You have to be fast."

"They're just small, right?"

"Nah."

"Oh, how big are they?"

"More 'n a metre, sometimes."

"Do they just slip out?"

"If yer lucky and yer worm's relaxed, yep. Otherwise I have to drop me stink-bag and dig him out, hanging onto his nose like me life depends on it."

"Gosh! How do you know where to drag your, um, stink-bag?"

"See them holes? That's where the blighters hang out."

We were surrounded by dozens of small holes in the wet sand. Occasionally, a bubble popped out. I'd just thought they were air holes; I hadn't realised a monster worm lurked in each.

I sensed I was outstaying my welcome and the man wanted to continue his worm-hunt. I thanked him and walked back to Deb.

"Thinking about it," said Deb, "I seem to remember there was a Youtube clip about fishing for beach worms. It was in all the local papers because it went quite viral."

I couldn't find that clip, but I found another[1] which shows the art of Aussie beach-worming, with stink-bag and pliers, in glorious detail.

Something was bothering Deb that day. I felt that her mind was elsewhere, and she wasn't her usual bubbly self.

WORMS

"Deb, are you okay? Is something bothering you?"

She took a deep breath and then she told me.

---

1. Youtube clip: Catching beach worms with stink-bag and pliers.
    https://www.youtube.com/watch?v=rMhDMkQkyj0

CHEATING APPLE DUMP DESSERT

Delicious with cream and tastes like a pie. Why 'cheating'? Because you use a packet cake mix. Why 'dump'? Because you dump it all in together.

Ingredients

5 medium apples (peeled, cored and sliced)

1 cup chopped nuts of your choice (lightly toasted)

4 teaspoons cinnamon (divided)

1 teaspoon freshly ground nutmeg

½ cup sugar

1¼ cups apple cider (or apple juice)

1 box yellow cake mix

¾ cup butter (melted)

Method

Preheat oven to 190°C (375°F). Lightly grease a shallow oven-proof dish or pan.

In the dish, add apples and nuts with 2 teaspoons cinnamon, nutmeg, and sugar. Spread evenly and cover with apple cider or juice.

Sprinkle dry cake mix over apple mixture then sprinkle remaining cinnamon.

Drizzle melted butter over top.

Bake for 45 minutes or until golden brown and bubbly.

29

SUMMER DAYS

"I've come to a very reluctant decision," said Deb sadly. "I'm going to consider letting Molly go."

I stopped in horror, allowing her words to sink in. Molly and Lola raced each other over the sand and back to the water's edge. They were in doggy heaven.

"Let Molly go?" I echoed. "No! You can't!"

"I must think about it for both our sakes. We can't carry on like this, with Molly spending several days a week at Doggy Day Care. It's unsettling for her and worrying for me. I have to visit my sister regularly, and there's nothing else I can do."

It was hard to take in. I knew Deb adored Molly as much as I loved Lola. Giving up her dog would be heartbreaking for her.

"I've even had discussions with the vet about it, and we tried medicating her. Nothing works. She's just a severely over-anxious dog, and I hate seeing her distressed."

I listened in silence, not knowing what to say.

"And I'm going to enrol for a course at TAFE which will help me find a job, hopefully. I'll have to put Molly in daycare for those days, too."

I knew TAFE stood for Technical and Further Education in Australia.

"Surely we can come up with something, or somebody, that could help? I know a few people I could ask." I was thinking of my dog walking pals at the oval.

"I think I've tried just about everything. Daycare is costing me a fortune, and I don't think I can afford to do it much longer. And finding somebody to look after her for odd days is probably not the answer. Molly needs stability. She needs to live with somebody who understands her terrible separation anxiety. Somebody who doesn't go out to work and can be with her all the time. She's not a demanding, difficult dog; she just needs human company."

It was hard to take in, but I understood. Deb was putting Molly's welfare above her own.

Joe was still weak, but we felt he was gradually making progress. The after-care nurses stopped visiting him, and we were coping alone. Every day he could walk a little further, and his appetite was good.

Not everything went so well. It was only a question of time before we parted company with our troublesome tilers. Fred caught Reg and his son drinking on the job again and sacked the pair of them on the spot.

Work was delayed while we searched for replacement tilers but the team we found was far more professional. They finished laying the silvery-blue travertine pavers around the pool, and the completed job looked terrific. They then began tiling the new main bathroom.

With the outside paving finished, I asked Fred to remove some of the rusty railings surrounding the pool. Then I booked a company to replace it with glass fencing. A date was set, and we happened to be out on that particular day. We left Fred in charge.

When we returned, I rushed out to inspect the new glass fence.

"Joe! They haven't done it. They didn't turn up! I'm really disappointed..."

"Vicky, put your specs on. It's done!"

I looked again and gasped. The glass was frameless, and I hadn't even seen it at first glance. The garden had been utterly transformed.

The pool and garden was revealed through sheets of gleaming and, seemingly, invisible glass. Poor Lola learned about it the hard way. Thinking she now had free access to all that wonderful water, she flattened her nose against one of the waist-high vertical sheets. Happily, no harm was done but she didn't try it again.

"Poor Lola!" I said, but she was already wagging her tail, the incident forgotten.

"She almost turned into a bulldog," observed Joe, chuckling.

Work inside the house also progressed well. The new main bathroom was looking spectacular, and I was delighted with it. I had chosen oversized white tiles, a freestanding bath, black tapware and a semi-frameless shower cubicle with black trim and a black door handle.

"I'd never choose a black-edged shower panel," said one of the men who had come to install the cubicle, unaware that I could hear.

"Nor me," said his mate. "I'd have chrome or gold trim every time."

They finished the job and stood back.

"Actually, that looks bloody lovely," said the first man, scratching his head.

"I agree! Let's take a photo for the website," said his mate.

I checked their website a couple of weeks later and was amused to see a photo of our bathroom in prime position.

Our new tilers broke the news that they would need to use a jackhammer to remove the tiles throughout the living room area and kitchen. Laying a new floor on the top of the old tiles would bring the level too high.

"It's a really messy job," the foreman told us. "It's loud, and the dust is unbelievable. It will get everywhere. I suggest you seal off the rooms you don't want covered in dust and move out for three days."

Joe's lungs could never have withstood such a dusty environment, so we prepared to leave. The smaller pieces of furniture and TV were moved into the bedrooms and sealed off. The bigger items, like the couch, armchairs, sideboard, and dining room table, were carried outside and placed under the pergola.

"We're going to be homeless while they work on the floor," I told Karly.

"Come and stay with us," she suggested.

"Are you sure?"

"Absolutely! We can take advantage of live-in babysitters."

So for three days we stayed with Karly and Cam. It was a pleasure to spend time with them and the girls, and I tried to be useful by helping out with the laundry and cleaning chores.

Indy loved pretending to make phone calls. One day she was sitting in her child-seat in the back of Bruce. She and I were driving to the shops to pick up a few things for her mum. Indy held her toy phone to her ear.

"Ring-ring!" she called. "Ring-ring!"

That was my signal to pick up an imaginary phone and answer. I took one hand off the steering wheel and cupped my ear.

"Hello? Nanny speaking. Who's that calling?"

"It's me, Indy!"

"Oh, hello Indy, how are you today?"

"Good. I want to know what is your favourite animal."

"Hmm… Excellent question. What is *your* favourite animal?"

"Guinea pig."

"Oh, really? And why is that?"

I don't think I ever heard her answer because I suddenly felt extremely uncomfortable. We had stopped at traffic lights and the car alongside us was a police car. Both uniformed occupants had swivelled their heads in my direction and were staring at me with expressionless faces. Our eyes met.

It suddenly dawned on me that they thought I was making a real phone call. The use of a mobile phone while driving is highly illegal in New South Wales. My window was half open, so they had probably heard me talking, and had seen my hand over my ear.

I dropped my hand and opened it, palm out, fingers outstretched to show them I didn't have a phone.

"Silly Nanny!" cried Indy from the back seat. "You dropped your phone."

"No, I didn't! I don't have a phone!" I protested loudly.

The policeman's eyes bored into me.

"Yes, you have, Nanny!" crowed Indy.

The policeman's eyes narrowed.

"Nanny! Pick it up!"

"Indy, show the policeman your phone!" I commanded.

Indy obediently waved her toy phone at them, but I don't think they saw her. The lights had changed and we all drove off but not before I caught the expression in the nearest policeman's eyes. He clearly thought I was behaving very oddly.

After that, I made sure both my hands were on the steering wheel all the way to the shops.

During our stay, Bandsaw made herself scarce. This wasn't unusual. Bandsaw was probably tired of being hauled around like a sack of potatoes by a toddler. Karly was convinced the cat had adopted another family and was dividing her time between two homes.

"She's like a furry barrel on legs," said Karly. "She can't have put on that much weight with the food we give her. She must be being fed somewhere else as well."

LJ wasn't at all impressed with Lola's presence and made it quite clear she wasn't welcome. Karly took both of them for a long walk, on neutral territory, which helped a little, but LJ remained very territorial. It wasn't an ideal situation.

After three days, I phoned the tiler.

"Is it okay for us to come home?" I asked.

"No, we won't finish lifting the old tiles until tomorrow. And then it's going to be another three days to lay the new ones."

Shocked, I relayed the news to Joe. We both agreed we didn't want to outstay our welcome, so I found a local dog-friendly motel and booked us in.

"You don't have to do that, you can stay as long as you like," said Karly and Cam, but our minds were made up.

The motel accommodation was a trifle cosy for the three of us, but we coped. We went for walks, watched the TV, and read, and tried to stop Lola barking at passers-by.

Another three days crawled by. We had time

on our hands and plenty of opportunities to discuss important topics.

"You know what to do, don't you?" Joe often said, even a couple of times in front of Karly and Cam. "If I'm taken to the hospital again and put on a life support machine…"

"I know…"

"Pull the plug. I mean it."

"Well, judging by that huge dinner you've just polished off, I doubt that's going to happen any time soon!" I said.

But his words had struck home. They stayed in my head, and I couldn't dispel a sense of foreboding, a fearful apprehension as though something terrible was waiting around the next corner.

"They must have finished the tiling by now!" Joe complained, changing the subject.

"I doubt it. Don't forget we've just had a weekend. I doubt they worked on Saturday or Sunday."

I was right, unfortunately. When I rang again, I was told the job would take a further three days.

In total, we stayed at the motel for a week.

During that time, the weather suddenly changed, and black storm clouds rolled in across the lake. Strong winds bent the trees and driving rain sent everybody scuttling indoors.

In our motel room, the TV news informed us that the rain would continue for days.

"At least we're warm and snug here," I remarked.

"Have you forgotten all our furniture is outside?" asked Joe. "The sofa, dining room table, everything."

I had forgotten, but there wasn't anything we could do about it.

Eventually, the storm moved on. Deb and I met up and took Lola and Molly for a walk beside the lake. I was almost afraid to ask whether she had thought any more about re-homing Molly.

We stopped for a coffee at a very nice cafe with a slightly alternative menu.

"Do you fancy something to eat?" asked Deb. "How about one of those lemon myrtle slices?"

"Lemon myrtle?"

"Oh, it's bush tucker. No calories."

Deb could always make me smile, and actually, the lemon myrtle cake was delicious.

"I've been asking around," said Deb, reading my mind. "I'm not going to come to a decision quickly, but my sister isn't getting any better, and I know I need to find Molly a new home. I just have to be one hundred per cent sure that it's the right one."

I wholeheartedly agreed. But did a perfect home exist for such an anxious little dog?

"I'm a member of a lot of doggy Facebook groups," Deb went on. "I'm just putting out feelers, but I haven't done anything yet. How's Joe?"

"Oh, getting a little better every day, thank you. I know he'll never be cured, but he managed to beat those viruses, I think. We just have to hope he doesn't pick up another one."

That cold feeling of dread came back as I spoke.

At long last, we were told that the tiling was finished and that we could return home. I couldn't pack our cases fast enough. But all the inconvenience and the long wait were worth it. I didn't even care about our dripping wet sofa and dining room table outside. The floor looked stunning.

"Look, Joe! It looks amazing. It's funny how you forget all the pain, isn't it? Like childbirth."

"I wouldn't know. But the floor does look great."

Our soaked furniture gradually dried out and

wasn't much damaged. We still didn't have a kitchen, but we were definitely making huge progress. We had three working bedrooms, two beautiful bathrooms, and a garden to die for. Summer had arrived, and we swam in the pool every afternoon.

"Can Molly swim?" I asked Deb once. Molly and Lola often paddled in the sea, but they didn't actually swim, probably nervous of the waves.

"No, she's never tried as far as I know."

"Instead of a walk, why not bring her with you to our house next week. Let's see what she thinks of the pool."

Deb arrived bearing cupcakes for us and treats for Lola. Joe excused himself, saying he needed a nap.

"I'll leave you ladies together," he said, and disappeared into the house.

Lola adored jumping into the pool, and I threw a toy into the water. Lola leapt in and retrieved it, swimming back with it in her mouth. Molly was very interested and watched her carefully. She stood in the shallow end, the water lapping her belly.

Deb threw a toy for Molly, and she was desperate to get it.

"Molly! Go and get it!" we urged.

She paddled the water with one paw, then the other. Suddenly she launched forward, now out of her depth. For a split second, she looked terrified, and then it dawned on her that she was swimming. She *loved* it.

"Yay! Well done, Molly!"

"Hurrah! Molly's swimming!"

From that moment, both Molly and Lola were in and out of the pool like twin furry seals.

They were happy days, drenched in sunshine and laughter.

It was easy to forget how sick Joe was. And how Molly's days with Deb were numbered.

LEMON MYRTLE CAKE

Lemon Myrtle is a beautiful, native Australian shrub. It grows up to three metres high, and clusters of cream fragrant, feathery flowers occur in autumn.

Ingredients

125g (4½oz) butter, chopped

¾ cup caster sugar

1 teaspoon vanilla essence

2 eggs

2 cups self-raising flour, sifted

⅔ cup milk

1 tablespoon Lemon Myrtle powdered spice

Method

Preheat oven to 180°C (350°F).

Lightly grease a deep, 20cm (7 inch) round cake pan. Line base with baking paper.

Beat butter, sugar and vanilla together in a large bowl using an electric mixer, until pale and creamy.

Add eggs one at a time, beating well after each addition, scraping down sides of the bowl.

Lightly fold flour into creamed mixture alternately with milk, beginning and ending with flour.

Add lemon myrtle in with cake mixture.

Spoon mixture into prepared pan.

Bake for 40-45 mins, or until cooked.

To make the vanilla icing:

Sift icing sugar into a bowl.

Add butter, water and vanilla. Add a little lemon myrtle. Beat well with a wooden spoon until a smooth spreadable consistency.

Spread over cooled cake.

From bindibindidreaming.com.au, a website celebrating aboriginal culture. (bindi bindi means 'butterfly')

30

OXYGEN

Some weekends, Karly, Cam and the children came to stay. Being summer, it didn't matter a bit that we had no finished kitchen yet, because we cooked on the barbecue, as all Aussies do.

Lola adored having the family around. She played with Indy, stole the kids' socks and toys, and never complained when baby Winter yanked her eyebrows. Like most dogs, she soon learned that it was a worthwhile exercise to hang around under the dinner table, vacuuming the scraps that regularly hit the floor.

It was a fundamental rule of mine that Lola must keep off the furniture. Whenever she jumped onto the sofa, I had only to look at her and she would immediately jump off, looking guilty. I was pleased that my training had worked. Or, I should say, I thought it had.

One morning, Cam said, "I got up in the night and guess who I saw fast asleep on the sofa?"

"Not Lola. She knows she's not allowed on the sofa," I said, shaking my head.

"Well, she was!"

"I don't believe you."

Later that day, he tricked me. While I was outside, he sat on the sofa.

"Lola was on the sofa again," he said, when I came in.

"Cam, I don't believe you, she wouldn't do that."

"Honestly! She heard you coming and jumped off quickly. If you don't believe me, feel the sofa here," he said, pointing at the area where he had been sitting. "It's still warm where she was."

Only when he started laughing did I realise he was telling fibs. I was certain that well-trained Lola would never dream of sleeping on the sofa. Unfortunately, at a later date, Cam got up in the night again and produced photographic evidence of Lola blatantly flouting the rules.

It reminded me of my Facebook friend, Elle, telling me about her dogs. They were never allowed onto the sofas. But she and her partner were well aware that when they'd gone to bed, and the coast was clear, the dogs would be on the sofa in a trice. It got to the point where the first person to get up in the morning would cough loudly as he, or she, came down the stairs, giving the dogs time to relocate and look innocent.

I don't know how it happened, but Lola gradually managed to bend the rules. It wasn't long before she was not only allowed on the sofa, but on our laps too, despite her size.

A Facebook friend once showed me a tea towel. It was decorated with cartoons and the following captions, which made me laugh. Dog owners will understand.

DOG RULES
• The dog is not allowed in the house.
• Okay, the dog is allowed in the house, but only in certain rooms.
• The dog is allowed in all rooms but must stay off the furniture.
• The dog can get up on the old sofa only.
• Fine! The dog is allowed on all the furniture but is not allowed upstairs.
• Okay, the dog is allowed upstairs but not on the bed with humans.
• Fine! The dog can sleep on the bed but only by invitation.
• Okay, the dog can sleep at the end of the bed but only on a blanket.

- The dog can sleep between us and share the pillows.
- Humans must ask permission to sleep on the bed with the dog.

One evening, as we were sitting watching TV, my phone lit up, showing an incoming message. It was yet another saucy message from Fred, clearly sent to me by mistake.

I need you to keep me warm.

"Joe, another message from Fred," I said, giggling. "I wonder who that one was meant for?"

I showed him the message, but he didn't reply. I'd noticed he seemed overly sleepy that evening, dozing off in front of the television, which wasn't normal for him.

Suddenly, I remembered the doctor's words. If Joe kept 'drifting off' it could be a sign of high levels of carbon dioxide in his blood and not enough oxygen. He could be losing consciousness.

"Joe? How do you feel?"

"Sleepy. I'm okay, honestly." He stared vacantly at the TV.

The TV show kept playing, but I could see that Joe wasn't concentrating. His eyelids were closing again.

"Joe? I'm worried about you."

He opened his eyes halfway. "No, I'll be okay."

I wasn't so sure as I studied his face. He didn't seem to have much colour. In fact, his lips looked a little bluish, as did his fingernails. Next time I looked, he was asleep again, and now I was seriously concerned.

"Joe? Wake up!"

I sensed he was trying to open his eyelids a crack, but the effort was too much. I grabbed his shoulders.

"Joe!" My heart raced. "Joe! Wake up! I'm going to call for help."

"Yes, call..." he whispered, and his voice faded away. I grabbed the phone and dialled triple zero.

"Which service do you require, Police, Fire or Ambulance?"

"Ambulance, I think my husband is slipping into unconsciousness."

"What is the exact address of your emergency?"

I gave them all the information, then turned my attention back to Joe. He was barely conscious.

"Joe, wake up! An ambulance is coming, and they'll sort you out." I chafed his lifeless hands. "Stay with me, just hold on."

Every second felt like a lifetime. I willed him to breathe. I willed the ambulance to hurry. No! It hadn't come to this! Not now!

But all the time, as I waited for the ambulance to arrive, his words replayed in my head.

"You know what to do, don't you? If I'm taken to the hospital again and put on a life support machine..."

"I know..."

"Pull the plug. I mean it."

My heart thumped so loudly, I could hear it. *Pull the plug, pull the plug,* it drummed.

It seemed like hours, but within ten minutes, blue flashing lights pierced the night outside our home. I leapt up.

"Joe! They're here. Just hold on, everything's going to be okay now."

I threw open the front door and ran outside.

"Quick! He's hardly breathing!"

The ambulance staff hurried into the house where Joe was motionless, slumped back on the sofa, his skin grey. The two men were wonderful. They were calm, exuding an air of confidence as they began work immediately, checking and measuring Joe's vital signs.

One nipped back to the ambulance for more equipment and came back with an oxygen tank. They placed a mask over Joe's face and gave him something from a phial and then oxygen. Slowly but surely some colour returned to his face, and his chest moved up and down as he breathed more easily. His eyes opened.

OXYGEN

"You're pretty crook," said the driver. "You should've called us earlier, mate."

Joe spent many days in the ICU. Thank goodness his breathing was gradually stabilised without the need of a ventilator, and I never had to say those three terrible words. However, he needed oxygen twenty-four hours a day and slept with the aid of a BiPap machine in case he stopped breathing in the night.

At first, his skin was almost as white as the hospital sheets, but gradually he took on a healthier hue.

He was encouraged to sit up as soon as possible, but he was pitifully weak. Physiotherapists arrived to teach him how to breathe correctly, and help him walk a few steps. When I thought about the games of squash he had played, the marathons he had run, and the heavy work he had carried out renovating our home in Spain, it seemed incomprehensible to me. It was hard to believe that this frail creature, struggling to breathe or take a few steps, was the same person.

But Joe never gave up. With the help of the hospital staff, he grew a tiny bit stronger every day.

I tried my best, but sometimes it was difficult to stay cheerful with the harrowing sounds of the ICU around us. Curtains surrounded each bed, but they didn't shut out the suffering. Sometimes we heard patients crying out in pain, or relatives weeping. So many tragic stories. Such sadness.

Yet, if I looked out of the ICU window, I could see blue sky stretching for ever, and flocks of cockatoos flying over. Sometimes a single eagle hung in the air, or a group of pelicans in V-shaped formation passed, their silhouettes like prehistoric pterodactyls.

Finally, the day came when Joe could walk to the bathroom by himself, with the oxygen tank in tow.

"They're just waiting for a bed to become available in the respiratory ward," he told me. "Then they'll move me down."

We were delighted when that happened because it was a sign that he was improving. However, the respiratory ward was crammed full, and the nurses were rushed off their feet. The side wards were also full. Every bed contained a very sick person fighting to breathe, whether from lung cancer, COPD, or some other terrible breathing affliction.

I often thought how I'd always taken the act of breathing for granted. Not now. Now I often breathe deeply, sucking in the sweet, fresh air, *just because I can*.

I visited Joe every day, leaving Lola with Emma and Baxter, or taking her to Germany. Lola's tummy grew rounder as I walked her less, and she enjoyed the many treats Thea gave her.

In the evenings, I made myself useful by painting walls. Joe couldn't have coped with the paint fumes, so I rushed to get it finished. As Lola snored, I painted walls, doors and skirting boards, until I dropped into bed, exhausted.

Joe grew stronger, and I was able to wheel him onto the balcony for some fresh air. He was still connected to his oxygen cylinder, and all that paraphernalia had to accompany us. It was a challenge getting through the big swing doors that opened onto the balcony, but worth the battle.

Outside was another world far removed from the hospital ward. That balcony became our escape, our refuge, our favourite place.

I tried to entertain Joe with small events, snippets of what was going on at home. Fred had brought in his son to help him, a big strapping, capable young man who towered over his father. Together they knocked down a wall and rebuilt another. The kitchen began to take shape.

I told Joe which countertops I'd chosen for the kitchen, and which blinds for the windows. I told him how the men arrived to fit the plantation shutters and how Lola had 'helped' them by putting her toys in their toolbox. I told him how she had learned, on the first day, to open the shutters with one paw so she that she could keep a lookout for cats.

"Have you seen Deb and Molly?"

"No, she's been really busy visiting her sister and job hunting. She says she has some news, though. I'm sure she will tell me the next time I see her."

"Does Lollipop still love her walks on the oval?"

"Of course, and the cockatoos are keeping her exercised. She catches sight of a flock grazing on one side of the field, and chases them. Meanwhile, another flock lands on the other side of the field, so she gallops after those. Meanwhile, the first flock has landed again and needs chasing, so she swings around and pelts after them."

It was good to make him smile and see his strength slowly return.

And one welcome thing came out of that hospital stay.

Joe has never been keen on ice cream, but I love it. As his appetite came back, he was served ice cream and discovered he did like it after all. In future, I could add ice cream to our menu.

Joe was eventually able to walk short distances and shower by himself. The overcrowded respiratory ward was probably anxious to free a bed, and the doctors decided Joe was ready to go home.

But first, a technician arrived at his bedside.

"We're going to give you a BiPap machine to take home with you," he explained. "I'm going to set it all up for you and show you how to maintain it. It has a computer chip inside which will record all your sleep patterns. When you come back to the hospital for out-patient check-ups, the doctors will be able to download all the information and see how you're doing."

"How long will I need to use the BiPap machine for?"

"Probably for life. The act of breathing is hard work, but the machine will do it for you. You'll love it, and you'll sleep like a baby, I promise you!"

Joe was sceptical, but the man was right. Joe got used to wearing a mask at night and enjoyed restful sleep. We would never need to worry again about his breathing during the dark hours.

"We're also going to lend you a couple of portable oxygen tanks, which you'll need for a while. I'll give you the number of a local company that the hospital recommends. They'll keep you supplied with oxygen. They'll take the empty tanks away and bring new ones."

"Will I always need oxygen?"

"Not necessarily. Some patients do, but many regain their strength and don't need the extra oxygen after a while."

Joe and I looked at each other. I could read his mind. I knew how stubborn he was. And I knew he would be utterly determined to get well enough to dispense with that oxygen tank.

I squeezed his hand and smiled at him.

There was so much that we hadn't yet done. So many places and beaches we hadn't yet explored. So much wildlife we hadn't seen. We needed to settle into our lovely new home and enjoy the changing seasons and watching Indy and baby Winter grow.

"Do you know," said Joe, reading my mind as usual. "We've been so busy; we haven't even made it to Splinterbone Crag yet, to watch the humpback whales swim past."

"You're right! And it's only five minutes away from home. That's definitely something we must do!"

Joe had battled viruses that had nearly stolen his breath for ever. But he had won.

At last, it was time to thank the staff and leave the hospital that had saved Joe's life three times.

I pushed his wheelchair and the oxygen tank across the car park to Bruce. We were free to go home and build the rest of our lives together. Future adventures were beckoning.

VEGEMITE PASTA

For the final recipe, I had to include something really Aussie, and what could be more Aussie than Vegemite? From notquitenigella.com

Ingredients

375g (14oz) dried spaghetti

50g (2oz) unsalted butter

1 teaspoon Vegemite (or Marmite)

Freshly grated parmesan cheese, halved cherry tomatoes and baby spinach leaves to serve (optional)

Method

Cook the spaghetti in a large pot of salted boiling water according to directions. Drain and rinse under water keeping a cup of the pasta water.

In the same pan, put on the heat and evaporate the water and then melt the butter and add the Vegemite and a tablespoon of the pasta water and mix to dissolve.

Add the cooked pasta and more pasta water to combine if necessary.

Garnish with grated parmesan cheese if you like, and baby spinach leaves and halved cherry tomatoes.

EPILOGUE

Lola was beside herself with delight when Joe came home. Somehow she knew that the oxygen line was not a toy and never touched it, which was remarkable considering she played with everything else.

Thea made a beautiful German cake to welcome Joe home. It didn't last long, it was far too delicious, and Joe was regaining his appetite fast.

We had one final email from our young 'penpall', Catalina, in Spain.

Hola tía Vicky y tío Joe,

I hop you are well. My family is completely wells and I am content *tío* Joe is very better.

I have many news for you. Geronimo and

Valentina they went to London for vacation after the *fiesta*. They have very good times and soon there will be a weeding and my sister and me we can dance flamenco. Valentina she say Geronimo has eyes like a fish he stare at all things in London. Geronimo he say he like London but he like El Hoyo very better. He say the colour of London is very grey and if he want grey he can look at his donkey.

Valentina she say to my mother that they has a big surprise in London. ¡¡¡¡¡They see *tía* Lola!!!!! She is with her friend Esteban and they have vacation in London also. Mama she say we not talk about it and it is not the business of children. Then she say to papa poor father Samuel and Lola has not change her skin.

I am sad *tía* Lola and father Samuel not have a weeding but i can dance flamenco at the weeding of Valentina and Geronimo and perhaps a man from television see me.

I not be your penpall no more because I must dance and i have a boyfriend also. My boyfriend is Manolo the grandson of Marcia at the shop of El Hoyo. Before it is a secret but now it is not a secret because my little brother Pollito he see me and Manolo he tell mama but mama say it is OK. Manolo say me he think father Samuel will go to the country of africa and be a *misionero*. One day perhaps there will be a weeding

EPILOGUE

with *tía* Lola and Esteban and I can dance flamenco. But perhaps then i will be flamenco dancer *famosa* and you will see me on the television.

My sister not have a boyfriend.

Felicitations, Catalina and Manolo xx

"Well!"

"That answers all your questions, doesn't it, Miss Nosy Parker?"

"I guess it does… Do you know what that story of seeing Lola Ufarte and Esteban in London reminds me of?"

"Reykjavík!"

"Yes!"

We both laughed, recalling the memory. It took place in the nineties, when the flashiest plane in the sky was Concorde, long before the tragic crash that grounded Concorde planes forever.

One of our close friends, Al, booked a flight on Concorde, as a surprise for his father, who was celebrating his 80th birthday. It was an expensive, luxurious day trip and the flight would go supersonic, breaking the sound barrier, before landing in Iceland. There, the passengers would disembark and explore the city of Reykjavík before boarding Concorde in the evening and returning to London.

Al and his dad had a wonderful day. They

enjoyed an authentic lunch in a restaurant, then strolled through the streets, admiring the Icelandic architecture and exotic sights.

Imagine everybody's utter astonishment when they bumped into a familiar couple from their small home town back in Sussex.

Al and his father knew the couple well, but the chance meeting was not a happy one. Why? Because the couple walking with arms entwined, were married.

But not to each other.

The unfortunate lovers had probably chosen a trip to Iceland because, not in their wildest dreams, could they imagine they'd be seen by anyone who knew them.

But they were. Coincidences do happen.

Likewise, Lola Ufarte and Esteban must have thought that nobody they knew would ever see them in London.

But they were spotted.

Al and his dad were very discreet and never told us who the couple in Reykjavík were. Even now, years later, I still wonder who it was.

Joe's healing would be slow, and it was unlikely he would be able to join Lola and me on long, brisk walks in the near future. I carried on

EPILOGUE

meeting with Deb and Molly and was keen to hear Deb's news.

"I think I've found the perfect home for Molly," she said, and I could see conflicting emotions in her eyes.

"Where?" I asked, trying hard to sound enthusiastic. "Who with?" It was the worst news, and the best news.

"You remember I put feelers out in some of the Facebook groups I belong to?"

"I remember."

"Well, I never actually posted anything about re-homing Molly, but I did chat privately with a few people. One of them suggested a lady she knew who was looking for a dog, not a puppy, for her grown-up daughter."

"Really?"

"Yes, and she put us in touch with each other, me and the lady with the daughter. It turned out that we actually have friends in common from the time when I used to live in Sydney."

"Gosh, what a coincidence!"

"I know! Anyway, we got talking, and I was very honest about Molly's issues. Whoever takes her on must understand that she has problems. I doubt she'll ever be cured of her anxiety and her new owner must be aware of that."

"Did the mother take all that onboard?"

"She absolutely did. The more we talked, the

more we both thought Molly might be the ideal companion for her daughter."

"Why, exactly?"

"That's the extraordinary part! Her daughter, Ruth, suffers from severe social anxiety. She lives alone and is capable of looking after herself, but her mother pops in every day. Ruth's anxiety is extreme. She can't work, except for cutting friends' hair in her own home, and she rarely has the confidence to go out alone."

"Oh my goodness!"

"Ruth's mother believes that being responsible for Molly and having her as a companion will help her daughter in so many ways."

My eyes strayed to Molly and Lola who were chasing seagulls across the sand. My heart was heavy. I would miss these sun-drenched days, watching the pair of them race, side by side, while the sea sang its song and washed their paw prints away.

"So, what happens next?"

Deb sighed. "I can hardly bear to think about it," she said, "but it does seem like a match made in heaven. I've arranged to meet them, to see if Ruth and Molly like each other. Then we'll go from there."

Ruth and Molly did like each other. A lot. A play-date was arranged, and Deb left Molly with Ruth for a few hours. It went well.

EPILOGUE

Next, Deb and Ruth's mother set up a sleepover date.

"It was so hard leaving her there," said Deb. "Ruth was planning to take Molly out for a walk, and they would visit Ruth's mum round the corner. They were going to have dinner there and introduce Molly to the rest of the family."

"How did that go?"

"Really well. Everybody made a fuss of Molly and she loved it. She sat on everybody's laps and had a great time. I didn't ask where Molly slept, but I imagine she shared Ruth's bed, like she does mine."

Debs smiled but her voice sounded hollow. I couldn't even begin to imagine how she was feeling. Had I been forced to give Lola away, it would break my heart.

A month later, Deb bravely gathered up Molly's bed, toys and leads and drove to Ruth's house in Sydney.

"Please take these," she said, handing over Molly's bag of belongings to Ruth's mother while Molly jumped into Ruth's arms and covered her face with kisses.

"Just one thing," Deb said to Ruth and her mother. "If, for whatever reason, it doesn't work out, please tell me, and I'll take her back."

Both Ruth and her mother promised and

insisted that Deb could visit whenever she liked. Deb hugged Molly for the last time.

The deed was done, and Deb turned away to lick her wounds and try to fill the void that Molly had left in her life.

Ruth's mother and Deb did keep in touch.

"Ruth walks Molly every day," Deb told me. "Her mother says the pair of them are inseparable, and that Ruth has become so much more confident and self-sufficient. Ruth's mum and dad have even booked an overseas holiday, which they haven't been able to do for years. Before Molly came, Ruth couldn't cope without them."

"That's wonderful!"

"I know! It's so good to know that not only is Molly happy, but she's brought happiness to somebody else and is helping to heal a troubled soul."

It was the best of all possible outcomes.

Sometimes, after a swim, Lola wears the hooded, yellow *Surf Dog Australia* towel that used to belong to Molly. Immediately my mind is cast back to Molly and Lola pounding along the wet sand, barking at seagulls, and digging holes, simply for the sheer joy of it. And all the while, the rhythm of the sea sent frothy waves to lap at their toes and fill in their newly-dug excavations.

EPILOGUE

Time has passed. At first, Joe couldn't walk far, but now he can manage a good hundred metres before stopping to rest.

Doctors are keeping a close watch on the tumour in his pituitary gland. It's been pronounced benign and non-aggressive. It has been decided not to meddle with it unless it changes.

In addition, his prostate cancer has been successfully kept at bay.

Work on our house was finally finished, and we are delighted with the result. It's not a big house, but it's easy to maintain, light and airy. I doubt the former owners would recognise it.

Fred, the builder, has since completed other odd jobs for us. Sadly, Dinkum passed away, but Hulk is thriving and, thankfully, has stopped growing. Fred no longer sends me saucy texts.

Baby Winter's first word was "Lola", and Indy prepared to start school.

Sometimes I think of our life in Spain and the folk who enriched it. Will Lola Ufarte ever behave? Will Catalina become a famous flamenco dancer, or will she settle down with Manolo and produce lots of beautiful children just as her mother has done? And what about our lovely neighbours, Paco and Carmen? And Geronimo and Valentina? Did Father Samuel really become a missionary in Africa?

Moving to Australia was a tough decision, but absolutely the right one. We adore everything about Australia. We love the open spaces, the unexplored bush, the endless beaches, the colours, and the Australian wildlife. We love the informality, the friendliness and the humour of Australians.

We are so lucky to spend our twilight years here, where we can watch Indy and Winter grow. Australia is the perfect place for children (and puppies) to be raised, a land of opportunity and adventure.

And I'm convinced that Joe would have died, had we still lived in the tiny, remote village of El Hoyo.

Sometimes I suffer from night terrors. I hear soft voices in my ear.

"*Pull the plug,*" they whisper. "*Pull the plug.*"

Joe may not be as strong as he was, but we have plans. Wonderful, exciting plans. We haven't finished having adventures, and I haven't finished writing about them.

We're not ready to pull any plugs.

A REQUEST...

We authors absolutely rely on our readers' reviews. We love them even more than a glass of chilled wine on a summer's night beneath the stars.

Even more than chocolate.

If you enjoyed this book, I'd be so grateful if you left a review, even if it's simply one sentence.

THANK YOU!

SO WHAT HAPPENED NEXT?

To find out, please join us in the next Old Fools adventure, *Two Old Fools Fair Dinkum*, currently a work in progress, due out 2023.

If you'd like to keep up with our lives, and be notified when the next book comes out, please join me on Facebook where I hang out at http://www.facebook.com/victoriatwead

And if you are not subscribed already, or have fallen off our mailing list, do subscribe to our newsletter on my website. I send one out every few months and it typically contains news, stories, competitions, photos, free books, book recommendations and a recipe.

Victoria Twead, 2022

P.S. I've been a little delayed with producing the next *Old Fools* book for a very good reason. I was asked to publish *another* book and it is such an extraordinary true story that I couldn't concentrate on anything else for months.

The book is "Dear Fran, Love Dulcie: Life and death in the hills and hollows of bygone Australia" and is a rollercoaster read. If you are anything like me, it will inform you, surprise you, reduce you to tears and haunt you forever. I've never been quite the same since Dulcie's life touched mine.

I do hope that you agree that "Dear Fran, Love Dulcie" is as astonishing as I do. I cannot praise it enough and I'm deeply humbled to have been been able to put it together for the world to enjoy.

Each book purchased will help support Careflight, an Australian aero-medical charity that attends emergencies, however remote.

"Shocking, yet heart-warming. Overwhelmingly

gripping." Beth Haslam, author of the Fat Dogs and French Estates series.

"Wow! Goosebumps." Elizabeth Moore, author of the Someday Travels series and Top 1000 Amazon reviewer.

"A truly remarkable young woman and a unique record of Australian life." Valerie Poore, author of Watery Ways.

"Once read, never forgotten." Victoria Twead, New York Times bestselling author of the Old Fools series.

"There are no words that can do this book justice." Julie Haigh, Top 1000 Amazon reviewer.

THE OLD FOOLS SERIES

SEVEN OLD FOOLS BOOKS, PLUS TWO YOUNG FOOL PREQUELS, A COOKBOOK AND STILL COUNTING!

Book #1 **Chickens, Mules and Two Old Fools**
If Joe and Vicky had known what relocating to a tiny Spanish mountain village would REALLY be like, they might have hesitated...

Book #2 **Two Old Fools - Olé!**
Vicky and Joe have finished fixing up their house and look forward to peaceful days enjoying their retirement. Then the fish van arrives, and instead

of delivering fresh fish, disgorges the Ufarte family.

Book #3 Two Old Fools on a Camel
Reluctantly, Vicky and Joe leave Spain to work for a year in the Middle East. Incredibly, the Arab revolution erupted, throwing them into violent events that made world headlines.
New York Times bestseller three times

Book #4 Two Old Fools in Spain Again
Life refuses to stand still in tiny El Hoyo. Lola Ufarte's behaviour surprises nobody, but when a millionaire becomes a neighbour, the village turns into a battleground.

Book #5 Two Old Fools in Turmoil

When dark, sinister clouds loom, Victoria and Joe find themselves facing life-changing decisions. Happily, silver linings also abound. A fresh new face joins the cast of well-known characters but the return of a bad penny may be more than some can handle.

Book #6 **Two Old Fools Down Under**

When Vicky and Joe wave goodbye to their beloved Spanish village, they face their future in Australia with some trepidation. Now they must build a new life amongst strangers, snakes and spiders the size of saucers. Accompanied by their enthusiastic new puppy, Lola, adventures abound, both heartwarming and terrifying.

Book #7 **Two Old Fools Fair Dinkum (coming)**

Subscribe to the Old Fools Updates for advance news, free books and recipes. https://www.victoriatwead.com/free-stuff/

Two Old Fools in the Kitchen, Part 1 (Cookbook)

The *Old Fools' Kitchen* cookbooks were created in response to frequent requests from readers of the *Old Fools series* asking to see all the recipes collected together in one place.

One Young Fool in Dorset (Prequel)
This light and charming story is the delightful prequel to Victoria Twead's Old Fools series. Her childhood memories are vividly portrayed, leaving the reader chuckling and enjoying a warm sense of comfortable nostalgia.

One Young Fool in South Africa (Prequel)
Who is Joe Twead? What happened before Joe met Victoria and they moved to a crazy Spanish mountain village? Joe vividly paints his childhood memories despite constant heckling from Victoria at his elbow.

THE SIXPENNY CROSS SERIES
SHORT FICTION, INSPIRED BY LIFE

A is for Abigail

Abigail Martin has everything: beauty, money, a loving husband, and a fabulous house in the village of Sixpenny Cross. But Abigail is denied the one thing she craves... A baby.

B is for Bella

When two babies are born within weeks of each other in the village of Sixpenny Cross, one would expect the pair to become friends as they grow up. But nothing could be further from the truth.

C is for the Captain

Everyone knows ageing bachelors, the Captain and Sixpence, are inseparable. But when new barmaid, Babs, begins work at the Dew Drop Inn, will she enhance their twilight years, or will the consequences be catastrophic?

D is for Dexter (coming soon)

Subscribe to the Old Fools Updates for advance news, free books and recipes. https://www.victoriatwead.com/free-stuff/

MORE BOOKS BY VICTORIA TWEAD...

Dear Fran, Love Dulcie (letters collated by Victoria Twead)

An unforgettable glimpse of life and death in the hills and hollows of bygone Australia through the letters of two newly-weds.

How to Write a Bestselling Memoir

How does one write, publish and promote a memoir? How does one become a bestselling author?

Morgan and the Martians - A COMEDY PLAY FOR KIDS

Morgan is a bad boy. A VERY bad boy. When a bunch of Martians gives him a Shimmer Suit that makes him invisible, he wastes no time in wearing it to school and creating havoc. Well, wouldn't you?

Two Old Fools in the Kitchen, Part 1 (Cookbook)

The *Old Fools' Kitchen* cookbooks were created in response to frequent requests from readers of the *Old Fools series* asking to see all the recipes collected together in one place.

ABOUT THE AUTHOR

Victoria Twead is the New York Times bestselling author of *Chickens, Mules and Two Old Fools* and the subsequent books in the Old Fools series.

After living in a remote mountain village in Spain for eleven years, and owning probably the most dangerous cockerel in Europe, Victoria and Joe retired to Australia.

Another joyous life-chapter has begun.

For photographs and additional unpublished material to accompany this book, download the **Free Photo Book** from
www.victoriatwead.com/free-stuff

CONTACTS AND LINKS
CONNECT WITH VICTORIA

Email: TopHen@VictoriaTwead.com (emails welcome)

Website: www.VictoriaTwead.com

Old Fools' Updates Signup: www.VictoriaTwead.com

This includes the latest Old Fools' news, free books, book recommendations, and recipe. Guaranteed spam-free and sent out every few months.

Free Stuff: http://www.victoriatwead.com/Free-Stuff/

Facebook: https://www.facebook.com/VictoriaTwead (friend requests welcome)

Instagram: @victoria.twead

Twitter: @VictoriaTwead

Publish with Ant Press: www.antpress.org

We Love Memoirs

Join me and other memoir authors and readers in the We Love Memoirs Facebook group, the friendliest group on Facebook.

www.facebook.com/groups/welovememoirs/

ACKNOWLEDGEMENTS

Thanks as always to **Nick Saltmer** who painted the fabulous cover picture. I've lost count how many covers you have designed for me, Nick, and I love them all.

Thanks also to **Julie Haigh**, **Pat Ellis** and **Pauline Armstrong** for your friendship and beta-reading talents. Skills like yours are essential for knocking any book into shape.

Big thanks and hugs to you, **Joe**, for your input and editing skills, and heartfelt thanks to my family for allowing me to write about you. **Joe, Karly, Cam, Indy, Winter**, my books would be so much duller without you.

Thank you Spain and El Hoyo for putting up with us for eleven years. To say you will always be in our hearts is a huge understatement.

Sincere thanks to all the wonderful **Facebook friends** I have made since I wrote my first book. Your loyalty and support often take my breath away. Particular thanks to the members of the We Love Memoirs Facebook group. You are totes stonking amazebobs…

MORE ANT PRESS BOOKS
AWESOME AUTHORS ~ AWESOME BOOKS

If you enjoyed this book, you may also enjoy these other Ant Press memoir authors. All titles are available in ebook, paperback, hardback and large print editions from **Amazon**.

These two booksellers offer FREE delivery worldwide.
Blackwells.co.uk and **Wordery.com**

More Stores
Waterstones (Europe delivery), **Booktopia** (Australia), **Barnes & Noble** (USA), and all good bookstores.

VICTORIA TWEAD
New York Times bestselling author
The Old Fools series

1. Chickens, Mules and Two Old Fools
2. Two Old Fools ~ Olé!
3. Two Old Fools on a Camel

4. Two Old Fools in Spain Again
5. Two Old Fools in Turmoil
6. Two Old Fools Down Under
7. Two Old Fools Fair Dinkum
8. One Young Fool in Dorset (Prequel)
9. One Young Fool in South Africa (Prequel)

Dear Fran, Love Dulcie: Life and Death in the Hills and Hollows of Bygone Australia

PETER BARBER
Award-winning bestselling author
The Parthenon series

1. A Parthenon on our Roof
2. A Parthenon in Pefki
3. A Parthenon on our Roof Rack

Musings from a Greek Village

BETH HASLAM
The Fat Dogs series

Fat Dogs and French Estates ~ Part I
Fat Dogs and French Estates ~ Part II
Fat Dogs and French Estates ~ Part III
Fat Dogs and French Estates ~ Part IV
Fat Dogs and French Estates ~ Part V

Fat Dogs and Welsh Estates ~ The Prequel

DIANE ELLIOTT
Lady Goatherder series

Butting Heads in Spain: Lady Goatherder 1
El Maestro: Lady Goatherder 2 (to follow)

EJ BAUER
The Someday Travels series

1. From Moulin Rouge to Gaudi's City
2. From Gaudi's City to Granada's Red Palace
3. From an Umbrian Farmhouse to Como's Quiet Shores

NICK ALBERT
Fresh Eggs and Dog Beds series

Fresh Eggs and Dog Beds: Living the Dream in Rural Ireland
Fresh Eggs and Dog Beds 2: Still Living the Dream in Rural Ireland
Fresh Eggs and Dog Beds 3: More Living the Dream in Rural Ireland
Fresh Eggs and Dog Beds 4: More Living the Dream in Rural Ireland

For more information about stockists, Ant Press titles or how to publish with Ant Press, please visit our website or contact us by email.

WEBSITE: www.antpress.org

EMAIL: admin@antpress.org

FACEBOOK: https://www.facebook.com/AntPress/

INSTAGRAM: https://instagram.com/publishwithantpress

PUBLISH WITH ANT PRESS
AWESOME AUTHORS - AWESOME BOOKS

This book was formatted, produced and published by Ant Press.

Can we help you publish your book?

Website: www.antpress.org
Email: admin@antpress.com

Facebook: www.facebook.com/AntPress
Instagram: www.instagram.com/publishwithantpress
Twitter: www.twitter.com/Ant_Press

We publish beautiful, bestselling books.

www.ingramcontent.com/pod-product-compliance
Lightning Source LLC
Chambersburg PA
CBHW021137080526
44588CB00008B/93